3592

D0253418

MISSION TRENDS No. 2

PHOENIX FIRST PASTORS COLLEGE
13613 N. Cave Creek Rd.
Phoenix, AZ 85022
Library

Oakland S.U.M.

Mission Trends No. 2

Evangelization

Edited by
Gerald H. Anderson
and
Thomas F. Stransky, C.S.P.

PAULIST PRESS
New York/Paramus/Toronto
AND
WM. B. EERDMANS PUBLISHING CO.
Grand Rapids

The Editors

Gerald H. Anderson, associate director of the Overseas Ministries Study Center in Ventnor, New Jersey, was formerly professor of church history and ecumenics, and academic dean of Union Theological Seminary, Manila, Philippines; and president of Scarritt College for Christian Workers, Nashville, Tennessee.

Thomas F. Stransky, president of the Paulist Fathers—the first missionary society of priests founded in the United States—was a staff member of the Vatican Secretariat for Promoting Christian Unity from 1960 to 1970. He is a member of the United States Catholic Mission Council and a consultant to both the Commission on World Mission and Evangelism of the World Council of Churches and the Vatican Christian Unity Secretariat.

Copyright ©1975 by
Paulist Fathers, Inc.
and Wm. B. Eerdmans Publishing Co.

All rights reserved. No part of this book may be reproduced or transmitted in any form or by any means, electronic or mechanical, including photocopying, recording or by any information storage and retrieval system, without permission in writing from the Publishers.

Library of Congress
Catalog Card Number: 75-29836

Published by
Paulist Press
Editorial Office: 1865 Broadway, N.Y., N.Y. 10023
Business Office: 400 Sette Drive, Paramus, N.J. 07652

ISBN: 0-8091-1900-5

and
Wm. B. Eerdmans Publishing Co.
255 Jefferson, S.E., Grand Rapids, Mich. 49502

ISBN: 8028-1624-X

Printed and bound in the
United States of America   *Reprinted, October 1978*

Contents

Foreword

The favorable reception of our initial collection of wide-ranging, representative essays on Christian mission—*Mission Trends No. 1*—has encouraged the co-authors and co-publishers to launch another self-contained edition. This second volume focuses on "Evangelization."

The theme has suddenly become popular, and the old-fashioned word has been revived ("evangelization" is now used in all Christian traditions, while "evangelism" seems largely confined to the Protestant). The attempted descriptions and definitions show bewildering variety, yet throughout there is the urgent concern to understand and effect those ways by which the Gospel is proclaimed and explained and living faith is awakened in those who bear the name of other world faiths, or in those unchurched or unaffiliated who are in some way searching for a saving community of faith and life. This Christian effort, lest we be simplistic, considers evangelization in relation to authentic, living dialogue with every person, to the ecumenical task of a fragmented Christian family, and to the total mission of the Church in and to six continents.

Several consultants have recommended articles, but ours alone is the final responsibility for the selection of essays by twenty-one authors, as well as of conclusions from recent major assemblies. We are grateful to these advisor friends, the authors and, particularly, the editors and publishers who have permitted us to reprint their material. Reactions to our efforts will, of course, be appreciated as we prepare *Mission Trends No. 3* dealing with "Third World Theologies."

Gerald H. Anderson

Thomas F. Stransky, C.S.P.

I: Mandate and Meaning of Evangelization

The Biblical Basis
of Evangelism

John R.W. Stott

How is evangelism to be defined biblically, and how does it
relate to mission, dialogue, salvation and conversion? In his
address at the International Congress on World Evangelization
at Lausanne, Switzerland, in July 1974, where he defines these
terms, John R. W. Stott says that mission is "everything the
church is sent into the world to do," while evangelism—an essential part of mission—is specifically the spreading of the Good
News of Jesus. "The challenge of the Incarnation," he says, is
"to renounce evangelism by inflexible slogans and instead to involve ourselves in the real dilemmas of other men," which "is
surely one of our most characteristic evangelical failures." Yet
Stott—who is rector of All Souls Church, London—also maintains that humanization, development, wholeness, liberation and
justice, while "included in 'the mission of God,' " nevertheless
"do not constitute the 'salvation' which God is offering the world
in and through Christ." He cogently urges evangelical Christians
to view dialogue with non-Christians as an indispensable aspect
of true evangelism "in which we are prepared to listen as well as
speak." Stott's much-discussed address is reprinted from the official reference volume of the Lausanne Congress, *Let the Earth
Hear His Voice*, edited by J. D. Douglas (Minneapolis: World
Wide Publications, 1975).

Introduction

The task assigned to me is to take a cluster of related words
in the forefront of recent debate—mission, evangelism, dialogue,

4

salvation and conversion—and attempt to define them biblically.

Please do not misunderstand my purpose. I do not propose to put up a few ecumenical skittles in order to knock them down with well-aimed evangelical balls, so that we can all applaud our easy victory! We all know that during the last few years, especially between Uppsala and Bangkok, ecumenical-evangelical relations hardened into something like a confrontation. I have no wish to worsen this situation. Mind you, I believe some ecumenical thinking is mistaken. But then, frankly, I believe some of our evangelical formulations are mistaken also. Many ecumenical Christians seem hardly to have begun to learn to live under the authority of Scripture. We evangelicals think we have—and there is no doubt we sincerely want to—but at times we are very selective in our submission, and the traditions for the evangelical elders sometimes owe more to culture than to Scripture.

So I hope in my paper to strike a note of evangelical repentance. Both our profession and our performance are far from perfect. We have some important lessons to learn from our ecumenical critics. Some of their rejection of our position is not a repudiation of biblical truth, but rather of our evangelical caricatures of it.

Because I have been invited to speak on "the nature of biblical evangelism," I shall try to define it according to Scripture and so bring both ecumenical and evangelical thinking to the same independent and objective test.

1. Mission

The first word is "mission," for it is here that we have to begin.

In the past—at least until the IMC[1] conference at Willingen in 1952—it was taken for granted that mission and evangelism, missions and evangelistic programs, missionaries and evangelists were more or less synonymous. "The place of missions in the life of the church," said Archbishop Randall Davidson on the first night of the Edinburgh conference, "must be the central place, and none other." I do not think he was using the word "missions" in any special or technical sense, any more than when the Division of World Mission and Evangelism was brought into being the expressions "world mission" and "evangelism" were neatly distinguished from one another.

Recently, however, the word "mission" has come to be used in a wider and more general sense to include evangelism but not to be identical with it, and I see no reason why we should resist this development. "Mission" is an activity of God arising out of the very nature of God. The living God of the Bible is a sending God, which is what "mission" means. He sent the prophets to Israel. He sent his Son into the world. His Son sent out the apostles, and the seventy, and the Church. He also sent the Spirit to the Church and sends him into our hearts today.

So the mission of the Church arises from the mission of God and is to be modeled on it. "As the Father has sent me," Jesus said, "even so I send you" (John 20:21 cf. 17:18). If, then, we are to understand the nature of the Church's mission, we have to understand the nature of the Son's! Not, of course, that his Church can copy him in all things, for he came to die for the sins of the world. Nevertheless, in at least two major respects, he sends us as he was himself sent.

First, he sends us *into the world*. For he was sent into the world, and enter the world he did. He did not touch down like a visitor from outer space or arrive like an alien bringing his own alien culture with him. No. He took to himself our humanity, our flesh and blood. He actually became one of us and experienced our frailty, our suffering, our temptations. He even bore our sin and died our death.

And now he sends us "into the world," to identify with others as he identified with us, to become vulnerable as he did. It is surely one of our most characteristic evangelical failures that we have seldom taken seriously this principle of the Incarnation. "As our Lord took on our flesh," runs the report from Mexico City in 1963, "so he calls his Church to take on the secular world. This is easy to say and sacrificial to do." But it comes more natural to us to shout the Gospel at people from a distance than to involve ourselves deeply in their lives, to think ourselves into their problems and to feel with them in their pains.

Second, Christ sends us into the world to *serve*. For he came to serve. Not just to seek and to save, nor just to preach, but more generally to serve. He said so. His contemporaries were familiar with Daniel's picture of the Son of man receiving dominion and being served by all (7:14). But Jesus knew he had to serve before he would be served and to endure suffering before he could receive dominion. So he fused two apparently incompatible Old Testament images, Daniel's Son of man and Isaiah's suffering servant, and said, "The Son of man . . . . came not to be served but to serve, and to give his life a ransom for many" (Mark 10:45). What is unique is that he came to "give his life," to die. But this supreme atoning sacrifice was the climax of a life of service. In his public ministry he proclaimed the Kingdom of God and taught its implications, he fed hungry mouths and washed dirty feet, he healed the sick, comforted the sad, and raised the dead. He gave himself in selfless service for others.

Now he tells us that as the Father sent him into the world, so he sends us. Our mission, like his, is to be one of service. He emptied himself of status and took the form of a servant (Phil. 2:7). So must we. He supplies us with the perfect model of service and sends his Church into the world to be a servant Church. Is it not important for us to recover this biblical emphasis? In many of our attitudes and enterprises, we (especially those of us who come from Europe and North America) have tended to be more bosses than servants. Yet is it not in a servant role that we can find the right synthesis of evangelism and social action? For both should be authentic expressions of the service we are sent into the world to give. How, then, we may ask, are we to reconcile this concept of mission as service with the Great Commission of the risen Lord? Often, perhaps because it is the last instruction Jesus gave before returning to the Father, I venture to say that we give it too prominent a place in our Christian thinking. I beg you not to misunderstand me. I believe the whole Church is under obligation to obey its Lord's commission to take the Gospel to all nations. But I am also concerned that we should not regard it as the only instruction Jesus left us. He also quoted Lev. 19:18, "You shall love your neighbor as yourself," called it "the second and great commandment" (second in importance only to the supreme command to love God with all our being), and elaborated it in the Sermon on the Mount. He insisted that in God's vocabulary our neighbor includes our enemy and that to love is to "do good," and to give ourselves to serve his welfare.

Here, then, are two instructions, "love your neighbor" and "go and make disciples." What is the relation between the two? Some of us behave as if we thought them identical, so that if we have shared the Gospel we consider we have completed our responsibility to love him. But no. The Great Commission neither explains nor exhausts nor supersedes the Great Commandment. What it does is to add to the command of neighbor-love and neighbor-service a new and urgent Christian dimension. If we truly love our neighbor we shall without doubt tell him the Good News of Jesus. But, equally, if we truly love our neighbor we shall not stop there.

So we are sent into the world, like Jesus, to serve. For this will be the natural expression of our love for our neighbor. We love. We go. We serve. And in this we have (or should have) no ulterior motive. True, the Gospel lacks credibility if we who preach it are interested only in souls and have no concern about the welfare of people's bodies, situations and community. Yet the reason for an acceptance of social responsibility is not in order to give the Gospel a credibility it would otherwise lack but simple uncomplicated compassion. Love does not need to justify itself. It expresses itself in service wherever it sees need.

"Mission," then, is not a word for everything the Church does (including, for example, worship). "The Church is mission" sounds fine, but it's an overstatement. Nor does "mission" cover everything God does in the world. For God is the Creator and is constantly active in the world in providence and in common grace, quite apart from the purposes for which he sent his Son, his Spirit, his apostles, and his Church into the world. "Mission" rather describes everything the Church is sent into the world to do. "Mission" embraces the Church's double vocation to be "the salt of the earth" and "the light of the world." For Christ *sends* the Church into the earth to be its salt, and *sends* the Church into the world to be its light.

There are important lessons for us evangelicals to learn from those two controversial ecumenical reports on the missionary structure of the congregation published in 1968 under the title *The Church for Others*. A good deal in it we would not be able to accept, but much is stimulating and challenging. In particular, relating to our present theme of "mission," there is the call to the Church to live "ex-centredly," to find its center not in itself but outside itself, "to turn itself outwards to the world" and to be truly a "church for others." Such an inside-out revolution would lead to a radical change in our church structures. The book is right to brand many of them "heretical structures" because they deny the Gospel and impede the mission of God. Too often we are "waiting churches" into which the people are expected to come. We must replace our "come-structures" by "go-structures." All this is implicit in "mission."

2. Evangelism

Evangelism is an essential part of the Church's mission. What is it?

Euangelizomai is to bring or to announce the *euangelion*, the good news. Once or twice in the New Testament it is used of secular news items, as when Timothy brought Paul the good news of the Thessalonians' faith and love (1 Thess. 3:6) and when the angel Gabriel told Zechariah the good news that his wife Elizabeth was to have a son (Luke 1:19). But the regular use of the verb relates to the Christian Good News. It is the spread of this that constitutes evangelism. This fact has important consequences.

First, evangelism must not be defined in terms of its *results*, for this is not how the word is used in the New Testament. Normally the verb is in the middle voice. Occasionally it is used absolutely, for example, "there they evangelized," meaning "there they preached the Gospel" (Acts 14:7, cf. Rom. 15:20). Usually, however, something is added: either the message preached (e.g., they "went about evangelizing the word," Acts 8:4), or the people to whom or places in which the Gospel is preached (e.g., the apostles "evangelized many villages of the Samaritans" and Philip "evangelized all the towns" along the coast, Acts 8:25, 40). There is no mention whether the word that was "evangelized" was believed, or whether the inhabitants of the towns and villages "evangelized" were converted. To "evangelize" in biblical usage does not mean to win converts (as it usually does when we use the word) but simply to announce the Good News, irrespective of the results.

You may recall that the famous call of the Student Volunteer Movement, "the evangelization of the world in this generation," was criticized for this reason. Professor Gustav Warneck attacked it at the ninth Continental Missions Conference at Bremen in May, 1897 on the ground that it was a naively optimistic and rather man-confident forecast that the world would be won for Christ in that generation. But John Mott rallied to the defense. He maintained that "the evangelization of the world" meant neither its conversion nor its Christianization, that it did not encourage superficial preaching and that it was not to be regarded as a prophecy. As William Richey Hogg writes, it was "a call to obligation, not a prophecy of fact!"

In a somewhat similar way J. I. Packer in his *Evangelism and the Sovereignty of God* has justly criticized the famous definition of evangelism first formulated in England in 1919 by the Archbishops' "Committee of Enquiry into the Evangelistic Work of the Church." It begins: "To evangelize is so to present Christ Jesus in the power of the Holy Spirit that men shall come to put their trust in God through him. . . ." Dr. Packer draws attention to the form of the sentence "*so* to present Christ Jesus . . . that men *shall* . . ." This is to define evangelism in terms of success. But to evangelize is not to preach so that something happens. Of course the objective is that something will happen, namely that people will respond and believe. Nevertheless, biblically speaking, to evangelize is to proclaim the Gospel, whether anything happens or not.

Second, evangelism must not be defined in terms of *methods*. To evangelize is to announce the Good News, however the announcement is made, or to bring good news, by whatever means it is brought. We can evangelize by word of mouth (whether to individuals, groups, or crowds); by print, picture and screen; by drama (whether what is dramatized is fact or fiction); by good works of love; by a Christ-centered home; by a transformed life and even by a speechless excitement about Jesus.

Third, evangelism may and must be defined only in terms of the *message*. Therefore, biblical evangelism makes the biblical evangel indispensable. Nothing hinders evangelism today more than the widespread loss of confidence in the truth, relevance and power of the Gospel. When this ceases to be Good News from God and becomes instead "rumors of God," we can hardly expect the Church to exhibit much evangelistic enthusiasm!

If we agree that the Gospel is God's Good News and that, despite all the rich diversity of its formulation in the New Testament, this was only one basic apostolic tradition of the Gospel (as Paul claims, I Cor. 15:11), we should be able to reconstruct it. Indeed, many have done so. All concur that, in a single word, God's Good News is Jesus. He is the heart and soul of the Gospel. Thus, what Philip told the Ethiopian was simply "the Good News of Jesus" (Acts 8:35), and Paul began his great manifesto of the Gospel—his letter to the Romans—by describing himself as "set apart for the Gospel of God . . . concerning his Son . . . Jesus Christ our Lord" (Rom. 1:1-4).

But how did the apostles present Jesus? If we compare the early sermons recorded in the Acts with each other and with Paul's statement of the Gospel at the beginning of I Corinthians 15, it becomes clear that the Good News contained at least the following four elements.

First, there were *the Gospel events*, primarily the death and resurrection of Jesus. Sometimes the apostles began with a reference to the life and ministry of the man Jesus and usually they went on to his enthronement as Lord and his return as Judge. But their message focused on his death and resurrection. Nor did they proclaim these (as some say) as nontheological history, just "you killed him, but God raised him." Already they had a doctrine of both. His death was "according to the definite plan and foreknowledge of God" (Acts 2:23), and the Cross on which it took place they deliberately called a "tree" to indicate the divine curse under which he died (Acts 5:30, 10:39, 13:29; Deut. 21:22, 23; Gal. 3:10, 13; I Pet. 2:24), while the resurrection was a divine vindication, snatching him from the place of a curse to the place of honor and authority at God's right hand (Acts 2:32, 33).

Second, there were *the Gospel witnesses*. That is, the apostles proclaimed the death and resurrection of Jesus both "according to the Scriptures" (Acts 2:25ff, 3:18, 24; cf. I Cor. 15:3, 4) and according to the evidence of their own eyes. "We are witnesses of these things," they kept saying (Acts 2:32, 5:32). So we today have no liberty to preach Christ crucified and risen according to our own fancy or even according to our own experience. The only Christ there is to preach is the biblical Christ, the objective historical Jesus attested by the joint witness of the prophets of the Old Testament and the apostles of the New (Acts 10:39-43). Our witness is always secondary to theirs.

Third, there were *the Gospel promises*. The apostles did not proclaim the death and resurrection of Jesus merely as events even when enriched by doctrinal significance and biblical witness. For the Good News concerns not just the historic but the contemporary Christ, not just what he once did but what he now offers on the basis of what he did. What is this? In Peter's Pentecost address, the first Christian sermon ever preached, he was able to promise with complete assurance that they could receive both "the forgiveness of sins" and "the gift of the Holy Spirit" (Acts 2:38). Salvation is more than this but it is certainly not less. It includes the remission of past guilt and the gift of an entirely new life through the regenerating and indwelling Holy Spirit.

Fourth, there were *the Gospel demands*, namely repentance and faith. "Repent," Peter said (Acts 2:38, 3:19), but also declared that "everyone who believes in him [Jesus] receives forgiveness of sins through his name" (Acts 10:43 cf. 13:38, 39). In addition he commanded, "Be baptized every one of you in the name of Jesus Christ." The apostles certainly never held a mechanical view of baptism, for they always set it in its context of repentance and faith. On the day of Pentecost those Jews were being required to submit to baptism in the name of the very Jesus whom they had previously repudiated. Whatever else baptism may signify it certainly was, and is, a public token of repentance and faith in Jesus.

It is true of course that salvation is by grace alone through faith alone, and we must be careful never to define faith in such a way as to ascribe to it any merit. The whole value of faith lies in its object (Jesus Christ), not in itself. Nevertheless faith is a total, penitent and submissive commitment to Christ, and it would have been inconceivable to the apostles that anybody could believe in Jesus as Savior without submitting to him as

Lord. We cannot chop Jesus Christ into bits and then respond to only one of the pieces. The object of saving faith is the whole and undivided person of our Lord and Savior, Jesus Christ.

Evangelism then is sharing this Gospel with others. The Good News is Jesus, and the Good News about Jesus which we announce is that he died for our sins and was raised from death by the Father according to the Scriptures of the Old and New Testaments and that on the basis of his death and resurrection he offers forgiveness of sins and the gift of the Spirit to all those who repent, believe, and are baptized.

3. Dialogue

The next question about evangelism brings us to our third word. Is there any room in the proclamation of the Good News for "dialogue"? It is well known that during the past decade or two the concept of "dialogue with persons of other faiths" has become the ecumenical fashion, and that we evangelicals have tended to react rather sharply against it. Is our negative reaction justified?

We could begin our answer by realizing that the word "dialogue" is derived from the Greek verb *dialegomai*, to "discuss" or "argue," which Luke used some nine times in the Acts to describe Paul's preaching: "For three weeks he argued with them from the Scriptures, explaining and proving that it was necessary for the Christ to suffer and to rise from the dead . . ." (Acts 17:2, 3, 17, 18:4, 19, 19:8, 9, 20:7, 9, 24:25). This at least shows that Paul was not afraid in his evangelistic preaching to use the massive reasoning powers that God had given him. He did not only "proclaim," Luke says, he also "reasoned," "persuaded" and "proved." At the same time, this is not the sort of dialogue that people envisage today, for Paul's dialogue was part of his Christ-centered proclamation.

James A. Scherer, in his contribution to *Protestant Cross-currents in Mission* (1968), traces the popularity of dialogue back to the 1928 IMC conference at Jerusalem. "Jerusalem had seen a momentary flirtation with religious sophistry," he writes, but ten years later at the Tambaram conference "Christ became once again the Word made flesh in whom God had acted for men's salvation." One of the most influential figures at Tambaram was Hendrik Kraemer. He called the Church to repossess its faith "in all its uniqueness and adequacy and power," and added, "We are bold enough to call men out from them [other religions] to the feet of Christ. We do so because we believe that in him alone is the full salvation that man needs."

It is precisely this emphasis on the uniqueness and finality of Christ that tends to be muted by those who are calling the Church to dialogue. Evangelism gives way to syncretism, and the proclamation of the truth is replaced by a common search for truth. The most extreme ecumenical statement I have read comes from J. G. Davies, who insists on openness as a prerequisite of the dialogue. "Complete openness means that every time we enter into dialogue our faith is at stake. If I engage in dialogue with a Buddhist and do so with openness I must recognize that the outcome cannot be predetermined either for him or for me. The Buddhist may come to accept Jesus as Lord, but I may come to accept the authority of the Buddha, or even both of us may end as agnostics. Unless these are *real* possibilities, neither of us is being fully open to the other. . . . To live dialogically is to live dangerously."

No evangelical Christian could accept this kind of uncommitted openness. On the contrary, if we enter into dialogue with a non-Christian, whether a person of some other faith or of no faith, we enter it as committed men, men unashamedly committed to Christ. The section on dialogue in the Uppsala report expressed this point well: "A Christian's dialogue with another implies neither a denial of the uniqueness of Christ, nor any loss of his own commitment to Christ."

Why then should Christians engage in dialogue with non-Christians? Here are some words from the report of the CWME[2] conference in Mexico City in 1963: "True dialogue with a man of another faith requires a concern both for the Gospel and for the other man. Without the first, dialogue becomes a pleasant conversation. Without the second, it becomes irrelevant, unconvincing or arrogant." Or, as Uppsala put it, "A genuinely Christian approach to others must be human, personal, relevant and humble." It is these qualities that are sometimes missing in our evangelical evangelism. We often give the impression of being glib and brash and our critics accuse us of a wide variety of horrid attitudes like "paternalism," "imperialism" and "triumphalism."

If dialogue is a serious conversation in which we are prepared to listen as well as to speak, is it not an indispensable aspect of true evangelism? Although the Gospel is invariable in its substance, the way we approach people and explain things to them is bound to vary, unless we are totally lacking in sensitivity. Dialogue, writes Canon Max Warren, "is in its very essence an attempt at mutual listening, listening in order to understand. Understanding is its reward."

So dialogue becomes a token of Christian humility and love because it indicates our resolve to rid our minds of the prejudices and caricatures we may entertain about the other man, to struggle to listen through his ears and see through his eyes so as to grasp what prevents him from hearing the Gospel and seeing Christ; to sympathize with him in all his doubts and fears and "hang-ups." No one has expressed this better than Archbishop Michael Ramsey who tells us that we are to "go out and put ourselves with loving sympathy inside the doubts of the doubting, the questions of the questioners, and the loneliness of those who have lost their way." It is once more the challenge of the Incarnation to renounce evangelism by inflexible slogans and instead to involve ourselves in the real dilemmas of other men.

4. Salvation

Having talked about "mission" and "evangelism," it is natural to take the word "salvation" next. For the Gospel is "the power of God for salvation to every one who has faith" and it is through the *kerygma* that God chooses "to save those who believe" (Rom. 1:16; I Cor. 1:21).

But many people are embarrassed by salvation terminology while others reject it as a meaningless inheritance from the traditional religion of the past. So there are not wanting those who are seeking to translate the word "salvation" into a more modern idiom. This is fine and necessary, provided that they remain loyal to the biblical revelation. For a translation is one thing (the old message in new words); a fresh composition is something quite different.

First, some say that "salvation" means psycho-physical health or "wholeness." They point out that Jesus said to the woman with the issue of blood, to blind Bartimaeus, and to a leprosy sufferer, "Your faith has saved you," which in each case the Authorized Version renders "your faith has made you whole" (Mark 5:34, 10:52; Luke 17:19), while we are also told that as many as touched Christ's garment "were made well," which in the Greek is *esozonto*, "were saved" (Mark 6:56). But Jesus spoke to the fallen woman the same words, "Your faith has saved you" (Luke 7:48-50), and "salvation" words are also used of deliverance from drowning and from death (Matt. 8:25; Mark 15:30, 31). Are we then to argue from these uses of the verb "to save" that the salvation Christ offers is a composite, rescue from physical ills of every kind, including disease, drowning and death? It would be impossible to reconstruct the biblical doctrine of salvation in these terms. Salvation by faith in Christ crucified and risen is moral not material, a deliverance from *sin*, not from *harm*, and the reason Jesus said "your faith has saved you" to both categories is that his works of physical rescue (from disease, drowning and death) were intentional "signs" of his salvation and were understood by the early Church to be such.

In saying this I do not deny that disease and death are alien intrusions into God's good world; nor that God heals both through natural means and sometimes supernaturally, for all healing is divine healing; nor that our new life in Christ can bring a new physical and emotional well-being as psychosomatic conditions due to stress, resentment and anxiety are cured; nor that at the consummation when we are given new bodies and enter a new society we shall be rid of disease and death forever. What I am saying is that the salvation offered in and through Jesus Christ today is not a complete psycho-physical wholeness; to maintain that it is to anticipate the Resurrection.

Second, others are saying that "salvation" means, or at least includes, socio-political liberation. It is not now health, but justice for the community.

The Mexico City Conference in 1963 had asked, "What is

the form and content of the salvation that Christ offers men in the secular world?" but left their question unanswered.

At Uppsala in 1968 "the goal of mission" was defined in terms of "humanization." The influence of the report *The Church For Others* was strong. It had affirmed that "wherever men and women are led to restored relationships in love of neighbor, in service and suffering for the sake of greater justice and freedom," these things must be recognized as "signs of the fullness of humanity" that Christ is providing. After Uppsala, at the ecumenical "Consultation on Development" at Montreux (1970), it was said that "God's salvation of mankind in Christ encompasses the development of all of man's faith, institutions and structures. . . . True development is the battle for the wholeness of man, both individual and corporate." The reference to man's wholeness is again significant, although it was conceived now more in social than in physical terms. It was taken up again at Bangkok. Here there was certainly the recognition that "salvation is Jesus Christ's liberation of individuals from sin and all its consequences," but the assembly concentrated on a different kind of liberation, "The salvation that Christ brought, and in which we participate, offers a comprehensive wholeness in this divided life . . . God's liberating power changes both persons and structures . . . Therefore we see the struggles for economic justice, political freedom and cultural renewal as elements in the total liberation of the world through the mission of God."

Humanization, development, wholeness, liberation, justice: let me say at once that all these are not only desirable goals, but that Christians should be actively involved in pursuing them, and that we evangelicals have often been guilty of opting out of such social and political responsibilities. We are to blame for this neglect. We should repent of it and not be afraid to challenge ourselves and each other that God may be calling many more of us than hear his call to immerse ourselves in the secular world of politics, economics, sociology, race relations, preventive medicine, development and a host of other such spheres for Christ.

But these things do not constitute the "salvation" that God is offering the world in and through Christ. They could be included in "the mission of God," insofar as Christians are giving themselves to serve in these fields. But to call socio-political liberation "salvation" is to be guilty of a gross theological confusion. It is to mix what Scripture keeps distinct—God the Creator and God the Redeemer, justice and justification, common grace and saving grace, the reformation of society and the regeneration of man. It is significant that the main biblical argument with which Bangkok tried to buttress its position was the liberation of Israel from the oppression of Egypt, which is not only an embarrassing topic for residents in the Middle East, but a misuse of Scripture. The Exodus was the redemption of God's people. It is used in Scripture as a foreshadowing of redemption from sin through Christ. It offers no conceivable justification or pattern of national liberation movements today.

Third, if biblical salvation is neither psycho-physical wholeness nor socio-political liberation, it is a personal freedom from sin and its consequences, that brings many wholesome consequences in terms both of health and of social responsibility. In many ways "liberation" (personal, not economic or political) is a good modern word for salvation because it not only alludes to the rescue we sinners need but also hints at the liberty into which the liberated are brought.

Freedom is as popular a word today as salvation is unpopular. But unfortunately too many people think and talk of freedom in purely negative terms. One of the Christian's best contributions to the debate about freedom is to insist that we think of it *positively*, in terms not only of what we are set free *from* but of what we are set free *for*. This is what Scriptures does, as I would like now to demonstrate while touching briefly on the familiar three phases or "tenses" of salvation.

First, we have been saved from the wrath of God, from his just judgment upon our sins. It is not merely that we had guilt feelings and a guilty conscience, and found relief from these in Christ. It is that we were actually objectively guilty before God, and that Christ bore our guilt and was condemned in our place in order that we might be justified. The argument of Romans 1-8 is so familiar to us that I do not need to elaborate it. The point I emphasize is that salvation does not stop with justification and must not therefore be equated with it. For with justification comes adoption. We were "slaves" under the curse of the law, but now we are "sons," enjoying free and happy access to our heavenly Father. And the Holy Spirit constantly witnesses with our Spirit that we are indeed his children (Rom. 8:14-17; Gal. 4:4-7). Now we are to live as free men.   ṣanḳḷf̣c̣ạṭọṇ?.

Second, we are being saved. Salvation in the New Testament is as much a present process as a gift or possession received in the past. If you ask me if I am saved, and if I think biblically before I answer, I could just as well reply "no" as "yes." I have been saved by the grace of God, yes, from his wrath, from my guilt and condemnation. But no, I am not yet saved, for sin still dwells within me and my body is not yet redeemed. It is the common tension in the New Testament between the "now" and the "not yet." Nevertheless, during this present time, gradually but surely, the indwelling Spirit of Christ is subduing the flesh within me and is transforming me into the image of Christ, "from one degree of glory to another" (II Cor. 3:18; Gal. 5:16-26).

In this present salvation too we should emphasize the positive. We are being set free from the bondage of our own self-centeredness. Why? In order to give ourselves in service to God and man. We exchange one slavery for another. We are no longer the slaves of sin and self, but we are the willing slaves of God, yes, and you are slaves too for Jesus' sake (Rom. 6:22; II Cor. 4:5). I wonder if it is our evangelical concentration on the negative aspect of salvation which has often brought our doctrine into disrepute? Should we not emphasize far more than we usually do that we cannot claim to be saved from self if we do not go on to abandon our liberated self in selfless service?

Third, our final salvation lies in the future. It is the object of our hope, for Christian hope is precisely "the hope of salvation" (I Thess. 5:8; cf. Rom. 8:24). It is not only that we shall be delivered from "the wrath of God," but also from the whole process of decay in creation and from evil whether in ourselves or in our society. For we are to have new bodies, and there is to be a new heaven and a new earth (Rom. 8:18-25; II Pet. 3:13). Then we shall experience, and the whole creation will experience with us, what Paul calls "the liberty of the glory of the children of God" (Rom. 8:21).

Thus in each phase of our salvation Scripture lays its emphasis not on our rescue (from wrath, from self, from decay) but

on the freedom that this rescue will bring—freedom to approach
God as our Father, freedom to give ourselves in service and finally the "freedom of glory" when, rid of all the limitations of
our flesh-and-blood existence, we can devote ourselves without
reserve to God and to each other. Are we saved? Yes, and "we
rejoice" (Rom. 5:2, 3, 11). Are we saved? No, and in this body
and with the whole creation "we groan inwardly" as we wait for
the consummation. We rejoice and we groan: this is the paradox-
ical experience of Christians who have been saved and are being
saved and at the same time are not yet saved.

5. Conversion

The fifth word we have to consider is "conversion." It indicates that the announcement of the good news of salvation
requires a response. We must reject as hopelessly unbiblical the
notion that all men have been saved by Christ and that the only
function of "evangelism" is to acquaint the ignorant of this
Good News. It is true that "God . . . through Christ reconciled
us to himself," but this does not mean that all men are reconciled to God. For now he commits to us the ministry and the
message of reconciliation and bids us beg people on behalf of
Christ to be reconciled to God. What validity would such an appeal have if those who hear it are already reconciled to God but
simply do not know it? (II Cor. 5:18-20). No. God was indeed
"in Christ" reconciling the world to himself, but now we must be
"in Christ" ourselves if we are to receive the reconciliation and
to become a new creation (II Cor. 5:19, 21, 17).

Solemnly we have to affirm that those to whom we announce the Gospel and address our appeal are still "perishing."
We proclaim to them the Good News of Christ not because they
are saved already but in order that they may be saved. It is impossible to be a biblical Christian and a universalist simultaneously. We may (and I think should) preserve a certain humble
and reverent agnosticism about the precise nature of hell as well
as the precise nature of heaven. We must be clear and dogmatic
that hell is an awful, eternal reality. It is not dogmatism that is
unbecoming in speaking about the fact of hell; it is glibness and

frivolity. How can we even think about hell without tears?

If then a response to the Gospel is necessary, this response is called "conversion." *Epistrepho*, though usually in the middle or passive voice and therefore commonly translated to "be converted," really has an active sense, to "turn." When used in secular contexts in the New Testament it means either to "turn around" (as when Jesus turned around to see who had touched him, Mark 5:30) or to "return" (as when an unwanted greeting of peace returns to its giver, Matt. 10:13. Note that the usual word for "return" is *hapostrepho*, Luke 2:20, 43). And when the word is used theologically it also means to turn from one direction to another, or return from one place to another. Thus, Christians can be described as having "turned to God from idols" (I Thess. 1:9) and, after "straying like sheep," as having "now returned to the Shepherd and Guardian of your souls" (1 Pet. 2:25). Since the turn from idols and sin is usually called "repentance," and the turn to God and Christ "faith," we reach the interesting biblical equation that "repentance + faith = conversion."

As we consider the call to conversion in the contemporary world, it may be appropriate to issue three warnings.

First, conversion is not a work that man can do by himself. True, men are described as "turning to the Lord" (Acts 9:35, 11:21), and conversion is something we do in contrast to regeneration that is something God does, a new birth "from above." True also, evangelists are sometimes described in the New Testament as themselves "converting" people, like John the Baptist who would "turn many . . . to the Lord their God" (Luke 1:16, 17) and like the brother who "brings back a sinner from the error of his way" (Jas. 5:19, 20). Nevertheless, neither could the sinner turn nor could the evangelist turn him but for the work of the Holy Spirit (Acts 26:18). So repentance and faith are plainly declared in the New Testament to be both the duty of men (Acts 2:38, 16:31, 17:30) and the gift of God (Acts 11:18; Eph. 2:8; Phil. 1:29). And however perplexing this antinomy may be, it is necessary in our man-centered, self-confident age to assert it, so that we may humble ourselves before God.

Second, conversion is not the renunciation of all our inherited culture. Conversion involves repentance, and repentance is renunciation. But what needs to be renounced? Too often we expect conversion to take place in a vacuum, without helping the convert to grasp in concrete terms what he is having to turn from. Or, worse still, we expect the convert to step right out of his former culture into a Christian subculture that is totally distinctive. Sometimes we seem to call him to withdraw from the real world altogether. It is probably in reaction to this kind of "conversion" that the CWME study "Conversion in a Secular Age" said, "Conversion . . . is not, in the first place, either saving one's own soul or joining a society." The pre-Uppsala booklet, *All Things New*, added that, though it is both these things secondarily, yet "fundamentally conversion means commitment, in penitence and faith, to what God himself is doing in human history." Candidly, this is overstated, for conversion is turning to God and not to anything God is doing. Nevertheless, the emphasis is understandable. Conversion must not take the convert out of the world but send him back into it, the same person in the same world and yet a new person with new convictions and new standards. Christ says, "Come," but then immediately adds, "Go"—that is, go back into the world for me.

In both West and East it is vital for us to distinguish between Scripture and culture, and between those things in culture that are inherently evil and must be renounced for Christ's sake, and those things that are good or indifferent and may be retained, even perhaps transformed and enriched. In the West, according to the authors of *God's Lively People* (1971), we seem to expect new converts to abandon their contemporary behavior and adopt a new life-style that turns out to be not new but old. "The new Christian has to learn the old hymns and appreciate them. He has to learn the language of the pulpit. He has to share in some conservative political opinions. He has to dress a bit old-fashioned. In brief, he has to step back two generations and undergo what one may call a painful cultural circumcision" (p. 206). In the East too and wherever a non-Christian religion dominates a country's culture, we need great wisdom to discern between what can be retained and what must be renounced. We cannot agree with Dr. M. M. Thomas' call for "a Christ-centered fellowship of faith and ethics in the Hindu religious community." Bishop Lesslie Newbigin is right to call this proposal "quite unrealistic" and to insist that "a man who is religiously, culturally and socially part of the Hindu community is a Hindu." But I think we can agree with Bishop Kenneth Cragg who, against a Muslim rather than a Hindu background, writes that "baptism . . . does not, properly understood, deculturalize the new believer; it enchurches him . . . conversion is not 'migration'; it is the personal discovery of the meaning of the universal Christ within the old framework of race, language and tradition."

Third, conversion is not the end. On the contrary, it is a new beginning. It is to be followed by the life of discipleship, by a growth into Christian maturity, by membership in the church (Acts 2:40, 47) and by involvement in the world.

Such is the nature of biblical evangelism. It is part of God's mission through God's church in God's world. It is the spreading by any and every means of the Good News of Jesus crucified, risen and reigning. It includes the kind of dialogue in which we listen humbly and sensitively in order to understand the other person and to learn how to present Christ to him meaningfully. It is the offer, on the ground of the work of Christ, of a salvation which is both present possession and future prospect, both liberation from self and liberation for God and man. And it invites a total response of repentance and faith that is called "conversion," the beginning of an altogether new life in Christ, in the Church and in the world.

NOTES

1. International Missionary Council.
2. Commission on World Mission and Evangelism of the World Council of Churches.

The Biblical Concept of Conversion

Paul Löffler

After reviewing the testimony of Scripture, Paul Löffler concludes that " 'fellowship' minus the passion for conversion leads to ghettoism; 'service' minus the call to conversion is a gesture without hope; Christian education minus conversion is religiosity without decision; and 'dialogue' without challenge to conversion remains sterile talk." Löffler's special concerns are "to gain a clearer understanding of the significance of conversion today in relation to its biblical basis . . . for what conversion means in a secular context . . . and the strategy of mission in modern society." Written in consultation with a number of missiologists and biblical scholars, this study document was prepared by Dr. Löffler while he was a staff member of the Division of World Mission and Evangelism in the World Council of Churches, for the *Work Book* of the Uppsala Assembly of the Council in 1968. From 1969 to 1974 he was professor of ecumenics and mission at the Near East School of Theology in Beirut, Lebanon. He now serves as theological consultant to the Office for Mission and Ecumenical Relations of the Protestant Church of Hessen and Nassau, Germany, with offices in Frankfurt.

Introduction

Christian faith of any persuasion involves some form of "conversion." It belongs to its very nature that it calls for response to God's presence in history, for personal commitment and human participation. The new reality given in Christ must

24

find its expression in a change from an old to a new existence. Ever since the calling of the first disciples by the Lake of Galilee we find that throughout Christian history the reality of "conversion" is creating and recreating the Church, underlying its life and mission. Sometimes it erupts into famous instances: the "conversion" of St. Paul, St. Justin, St. Augustine, St. Francis of Assisi, Luther, Wesley. Always it is there as a force of renewal in both the Church and society.

The verbal expression of that reality has differed and varies from tradition to tradition. To the Orthodox Churches the term "salvation" is more familiar than "conversion." The latter has been frequently used by the Protestant missionary movement. Hence it carries certain undertones that can lead to confusion. We have nevertheless continued to use the term "conversion" in this paper as a shorthand expression for a biblical concept that is universally acknowledged. It represents the Old Testament notion of "turn" and "return" (*shubh*), Christ's call to repentance and discipleship, and relates to the divine promise "to make all things new."

Starting from the biblical evidence we can say that the accepted meaning of "conversion" is personal reorientation. While "evangelism" is concerned with the representation of God's acts in history, "conversion" is about the human response. Both deal with human participation in the *missio dei*. The form of the response does not follow, and never has followed, one universal pattern or model. It must vary with those who have been "born into the Church" and those who belong to a different religion or do not hold any religious views. We know of "mass conversion" and individual response. In short it is difficult to give a more precise definition of "conversion" that would be widely acceptable.

In dealing with conversion we are convinced that we must begin with a restudy of the biblical concept *in toto*. The Bible naturally cannot be studied in isolation from contemporary issues. We realize too that there are questions concerning the meaning of conversion today that will not be raised through a biblical analysis. Yet we need a starting point that will provide us with criteria by which we can examine the use and misuse of the concept of conversion throughout Christian history and its current interpretation in the various church traditions as well as in relation to modern psychology and sociology.

The biblical study of conversion is complicated by the fact that there is no one word in the Old and New Testaments that covers the whole concept. Instead we find a variety of terms and of associated strands of thinking, from which a selective choice has to be made in a paper of such brevity. We have tried to minimize the risks thus taken by asking for corrective comments from a number of biblical scholars and by studying some of the recent publications on this subject. Further confusion could arise from the fact that the use of the term "conversion" in the English language varies a great deal. But the point of this study is precisely to break through the crust of traditional use of conversion to its original biblical meaning.

Every Bible study is influenced by the questions that the particular student brings to it. In this case it has been the concern for what conversion means in a secular context that gave a certain slant. Its origin lies in discussions on church and society and on the strategy of mission in modern society. At best, the paper can only be an "opening statement" that will not do full justice to all the different situations in which the Gospel meets people in our world, nor to the wealth of biblical material on conversion. It remains open-ended and requires partnership in its further development. For that reason we offer this paper, seeking comments from differing situations, as well as from various groups.

The situations of which we are thinking reflect the complexity and fragmentation of human society today. We find persons who still live in a primal (primitive) socio-religious setting. We experience the meeting of the Gospel with different faiths, such as renascent non-Christian religions, the new ideological systems, or the secularized modern sects and movements. What are the consequences of conversion in a situation in which the Christian Church is but a tiny minority? What does conversion mean in relation to persons of Jewish faith or in relation to the humanist. What is its significance for those in a complex urban society or for those who live in the world of industry?

In a second way we also want to address the paper to different groups that must offer their insights into the meaning of conversion, if we are to gain a fuller ecumenical understanding of it. There one would think immediately of those Christians who hold a very firm and sincere belief in the necessity of a clear personal experience of conversion: in what way does the biblical material speak to them? Also we think of groups in the Orthodox tradition that has evidently not given a great weight to the question of conversion, yet know the same concept in different contexts. Then we have in mind those Christians who find it difficult to relate the concept of conversion to the scientific evidence concerning evolution and the psychological interpretation of personality. Would they completely discard the possibility of conversion? What meaning has commitment and decision for them? Finally there are the groups that are responsible for missionary strategy, the sending and training of missionaries and so on: what implications do they draw from a study of conversion? We expect through such studies to gain a clearer understanding of the significance of conversion today in relation to its biblical basis.

The call to return in the Old Testament[1]

It is the fairly unanimous opinion of scholars that the deeper roots of the biblical concept of conversion are in the Old Testament, more particularly in one group of words deriving from the Hebrew root *shubh*. This word is used both transitively and intransitively and its main meaning is to "return" or turn back.[2] Theologically the all-important fact is that *shubh* belongs to the covenant context. *Shubh* does not mean to turn to something new but to return to the already given covenant, to the relationship with God into which he has himself drawn Israel. In consequence *shubh* is hardly ever applied to people outside Israel. It is the people of God who are called to return, not the heathen! All the main connections in which *shubh* is used are the great occasions in the history of God's covenant with Israel. *Shubh* is given various interpretations in different parts of the Old Testament and the content of conversion accordingly varies; it can be understood as return to the law statutes of God (Mal. 3:7ff.) or be expressed in cultic forms (as part of the liturgy of the "day of repentance"). Its predominant use is found in the deuteronomistic and prophetic material, and here the emphasis

clearly lies on the historic obedience of the people as the affirmation of a given relationship in which God and his people are
bound together in one common history. The call to "return" is
being heard again and again, because this relationship is nothing
static, but rather the ever new response to God's presence among
human beings.

Some of the classical occasions of this use of *shubh* are
recorded in the historical books. I Samuel 7 reports the decisive
moment when Samuel addresses the people in an hour of national emergency. "If you are returning.to the Lord with all your
heart . . . he will deliver you out of the hand of the Philistines"
(v. 3 RSV).[3] I Kings 18 tells of the dramatic encounter between
Elijah and the priests of Baal that reaches its climax in Elijah's
outcry, "Answer me, O Lord, answer me, that this people may
know that Thou, O Lord art God and that Thou has turned their
hearts back" (v. 37). Here and on other occasions (for instance, I
Kings 8:48, II Chron. 30:6) the common characteristic is that
each passage represents an historic moment in the life of Israel
every time its very existence is threatened, be it by enemy action
from outside or by complete alienation from its destiny through
apostasy within its own ranks. What is at stake is not a particular act of degradation but *the* sin in the history of Israel, its
repetitive rejection of the Sinai covenant. *Shubh* is not concerned
with acts of individual wrong but with what the Bible calls sin,
Israel's disobedience against God. "They have sinned against
Thee" (I Kings 8:33). The issue is therefore to return to God as
an act of complete surrender: "If they repent with all their mind
and with all their heart" (I Kings 8:48). This can only be initiated by God. He must reveal himself again ("that this people may
know that Thou, O Lord, art God" (I Kings 18:37). He himself
must recreate the covenant.

Another context in which *shubh* is used refers primarily to a
particular person and his relationship to God. We find this usage
in the Psalms, notably in Psalm 51, but also in 2 Kings 23:25
related to King Josiah. Yet in both cases the reference is not intended to indicate a moment of private remorse. Character-
istically the term *shubh* appears in the summary of King Josiah's
reign giving a typical evaluation of his kingship. In this case
shubh is used to characterize his right relationship "to the Lord"
that was expected of him within the given covenant. Similarly we

find in Psalm 51 the expression of a typical act of repentance that has been applied and is being applied by different persons to different situations. The unchanging stance is again that of the covenant relationship with the whole people, "Do good to Zion in thy good pleasure, rebuild the walls of Jerusalem, then wilt thou delight in right sacrifices" (Psalm 51:18).

The most expressive use of *shubh* is however found in the prophetic writings. In a striking way we discover two interwoven themes. Hosea emphasizes the need for obedience now in this world. The procession of pious repenters who call out, "Come let us return to the Lord" (Hos. 6:1) is told: "For I desire steadfast love and not sacrifice, the knowledge of God rather than burnt offerings" (Hos. 6:6). Conversion is identified with "love" and "justice" (Hos. 12:6). It means above all the recognition of God's action in history and the response in concrete obedience here and now (Hos. 6:7ff.). This theme is not limited to Hosea. It is also represented in the call to social justice through the earlier prophecies of Amos. In each case the argument is primarily about what the people of God have done or not done in history. *Shubh* is therefore closely related to the announcement that Jahweh will come to judge his people. It is only after this judgment that a return can become reality.

With Ezekiel and especially Jeremiah the prophetic call to return becomes intensified through the insistence on a "new heart and a new spirit" (Ez. 18:31), with the promise of a "new covenant" (Jer. 31:33, Ez. 36:24). Here in the book of Jeremiah where the use of *shubh* is most frequent we find the second theme in the foreground: "return" stands for a choice of loyalty: God or the idols (Jer. 2-4). The call is for a renewed relationship with Jahweh with emphasis on the preposition return "to" the Lord (Jer. 3:7, 10, 5:3, Hos. 5:4, 7:10). The promise of a "new covenant" in Jeremiah introduces a dimension of fulfillment to *shubh* which lies in the future. It is paralleled by Isaiah's reference to the holy remnant (Isaiah 10:21), and taken up with particular emphasis during the period of exile: "The ransomed of the Lord shall return, and come to Zion with singing" (Isaiah 35:10). Deutero-Isaiah demands the break away from idols to become free to tackle the future. The return to God becomes interrelated with an expectation of a return to Jerusalem in a geographical sense. But the hope goes beyond that and is connected with the fate of the other nations: "Turn to me and be saved, all the ends of the earth" (Isaiah 15:21). The crowning vision is that of all the nations turning to Mount Zion (Isaiah 2) or of all "the foreigners who join themselves to the Lord . . . these I will bring to my holy mountain" (Isaiah 56:6f.).

In summary: the use of *shubh* in the different strands points to a number of consistent characteristics that describe the concept of conversion in the Old Testament:

1. Conversion is participation in a historic movement. *Shubh* refers as much to a given event in the past, to a turning point in history that the people must reaffirm again and again as it refers to the goals of God's action in history. The frequent use of the "way" metaphor is characteristic. Israel has been called to be a people of the way, constantly challenged to return to its servant role among the nations moving on behind its Lord.

2. The crucial point about the prophets' call to "return" is that it is based on the coming of Jahweh and on his action (which can be an action in the past that is becoming a reality again). Conversion is not a response to the needs of the hour but the ever new response to God's mighty acts among men. It is not a human attempt at appeasement but God's offer of a new beginning after His judgment.

3. As part of the covenant, Old Testament conversion has primarily a collective connotation. Not that this would completely exclude a personal use of *shubh*. In the Psalms we find personal confession and repentance. But even there we know that the "I" of the Psalmist is that of a "typical" person, who stands for the whole of the covenant people. On the other hand, the call to return addressed to Israel clearly concerns each of its members personally.

4. Finally, conversion always involves a horizontal response. It does not primarily refer to an affirmation of metaphysical beliefs but to concrete obedience and a renewed relationship in history. What is expected of Israel is to follow a risky political course in the midst of threats from mighty nations, the renunciation of military power, the giving up of idols that promise security and stability. The reality of conversion to God is tested by service to neighbors.

"Turning" in the New Testament[4]

In the New Testament *shubh* is taken up directly by two terms: *epistrephein* (and its cognates) and *metanoein* occasionally used side by side.[5] The first often literally describes the physical turning of a person. In the nonliteral sense the active use prevails, making the person concerned the subject of the turning. "And all the residents of Lydda and Sharon saw him, and they turned to the Lord" (Acts 9:35). *Metanoein*, which is often translated by "repent," more precisely means "to change one's mind or being."

However both *epistrephein* and *metanoein* do not occur very often in the New Testament. The first term is mainly found in the Acts of the Apostles where it refers to "mass conversion" rather than conversion of individuals. Equally *metanoein* or *metanoia* are not very prominent either. Their complete absence in the Johannine literature and almost complete absence in the Pauline writings is conspicuous. Certainly there is not enough evidence to allow the construction of a New Testament model. A "turning" can reoccur after years of discipleship, as with St. Peter (Luke 22:32) who is called back from an act of apostasy, or is used for the act of forgiveness between a disciple and his brother (Luke 17:4). *Epistrephein* appears as part of an exhortation to Christians in James 5:19. The one dominant impression is on the contrary how little interest we find in the Synoptic Gospels in describing actual conversion stories.

Yet for two reasons it would be quite wrong to draw the conclusion that the concept of conversion is unimportant.

a) On the few occasions when *metanoein* is used in the Synoptic Gospels, it appears in extremely significant connections. Mark 1:15 and parallels ("The time is fulfilled, and the kingdom of God is at hand; repent [*metanoeite*], and believe in the gospel"), give part of the summary that describes the purposes of the entire preaching and presence of Christ. Christ's ministry is accompanied by a constant call to repent and by decision for or against him.[6] *Metanoein* occurs again in the crucial phase after the resurrection (Luke 24:47), and the call to conversion is an essential part of the pentecostal event and in the mission of the church beginning at Jerusalem. After Pentecost, conversion, baptism and receiving of the Holy Spirit are inseparably linked together (Acts 2:38), as they already were in the preaching of John the Baptist (Mark 1:4ff.).

b) The second point is that in the New Testament the emphasis lies on the concept of conversion and not on any particular term. Besides the occasional use of the two words there are many other passages that indirectly report of Christ's call to personal response (Mark 2:17). *Krinein* and *krisis* are used frequently. The character of the coming of Christ is also expressed in other ways as in the well known logion that he has "not come to bring peace, but a sword" (Matthew 10:34). Above all one would have to consider Christ's calling of disciples and the various discourses on discipleship. All this makes it sufficiently clear that a mere semantic or terminological approach will not suffice if we are concerned with the total biblical concept of conversion.

This conclusion is even more obvious in relation to the Pauline and Johannine writings. Here one would have to draw on such wider terms as that of "faith," "justification" and "election." The close interrelation of *metanoein* and "baptism" provides a particular link with the Pauline writings. For here conversion is absorbed into St. Paul's understanding of "baptism" as the expression of being taken into Christ's death and resurrection (Rom. 6:1ff.). Baptism as renewal through death signifies the same concern as conversion in the Synoptic Gospels (compare also the Adam-Christ parallel in Rom. 5). One other reason why the actual terms *metanoein* and *epistrephein* are only marginally used seems to lie in the fact that the Pauline epistles are of a homiletic character, addressed to Christian congregations. This also applies to the Johannine writings, where again we have to look at different context such as that of "birth-rebirth" and *krisis*! But there can be no doubt that the revelation of truth in the person of Christ, the coming of the light into the darkness, causes a process of decision, as it does indeed in any other part of the New Testament.

Another strand of material stresses the interrelation of conversion and sanctification. A passage like I Peter 1 is characteristic in this connection. Using the expression "born anew" (v. 3) it underlines first the givenness through the resurrection of Jesus Christ of "the inheritance which is imperishable" (v. 4) and then goes on to draw out the immediate implications of it for a Christian life now: "therefore gird up your minds . . . be holy yourselves in all your conduct" (vs. 13, 15). The rest of the epistle is devoted to this subject of sanctification that must be the immediate consequence of conversion. The congregation is exhorted to realize the new life that has already been given to it. A strong link between conversion and the fruits that follow from it is equally established in the Book of Revelation (2:5, 21f.; 9:20f.). Thus conversion becomes only the beginning of a process of renewal that aims at the making new of all things (Rev. 21:5).

This sketch reveals the wealth of New Testament material. While it is clearly not possible to survey in breadth the whole spectrum of terms relevant to the concept of conversion, an attempt is made to study in depth some of its main aspects in the major strands of New Testament tradition. The passages and references used in that connection have been selected as characteristic illustrations that however must be seen within the total framework of a biblical theology.[7]

The Synoptic Gospels. The connection between the Old Testament concept represented by *shubh* and the New Testament is particularly close in the Synoptic Gospels. John the Baptist in a special way sums up the prophetic call to conversion and relates it to the coming of Christ (Mark 1:1-8 parallels).

John, like the prophets of old, is a particular person called to a particular place at a particular moment in history; Luke's editorial comment in 3:1 is quite precise: "In the fifteenth year of the reign of Tiberius Caesar." The preaching of repentance is not divorced from time; it attains its meaning, its *krisis* character, in and through history, both "secular" and "sacred." The reference to Tiberius Caesar is a "secular" reference. Without it the Baptist's call hangs in the air, just as the year fifteen of Tiberius Caesar is meaningless without the preaching of John. Behind the lone figure of the Baptist unfolds the whole history of God's dealing with his people and the world. This makes John's preaching meaningful as an event in both *Heils-* and *Weltgeschichte.*

The content of repentance is again a call to concrete obedience: "Bear fruits that befit repentance" (Matthew 3:8). There is no dichotomy between John's preaching and his ethical teaching. The one leads into the other; "He who has two coats, let him share with him who has none," and so on (Luke 3:10ff.). Repentance can on occasion be spelled out in terms of social action and response in everyday life. A renewed relationship with God implies a new relationship with one's neighbors. A change of one's heart cannot be real apart from a change of one's relationships. Conversion to God and neighbor thus occur in one and the same act (cf. also Luke 7:18ff.; Matthew 5:23ff. etc.).

The decisive new context of conversion in the Synoptic Gospels, however, is that of the "kingdom." The coming of the *basileia* is the one and only reason given for the urgency of repentance. "The time is fulfilled and the Kingdom of God is at hand: repent and believe in the Gospel" (Mark 1:15 and parallels). The one-verse description of Christ's ministry in that place is meant as a heading for the whole of the Gospel. Without the givenness of the Kingdom, the self-revealing presence of God in the world, repentance does not make any sense. The "kingdom" takes the place of the covenant as the framework within which the turning takes place. As a given reality it precedes conversion. But the person only begins to participate in the Kingdom through the act of commitment by conversion (Matthew 23:13). Conversion is an essentially joyful event, about which there is jubilation in heaven (Luke 15:7-10).

A clear distinction between the Kingdom and the Old Testament covenant is that it represents a different mode of the presence of God in history. It is the difference between John the Baptist and Christ. In the Gospel according to St. Matthew exactly the same formulation is used to describe both the preaching of John and Jesus: "Repent, for the Kingdom of heaven is at hand" (Matthew 3:2 and 4:17). The significant difference lies in the event reported in between, the baptism of Jesus, with its crowning pronouncement: "This is my beloved Son" (Matthew 3:17). The sonship of Christ does not give an authority to his ethical teaching such as the prophets could not have. But it also leads through the calling of disciples to the Church, to which conversion inevitably relates. The tension between the calling of few into discipleship and the final recreation of all things constitutes the dynamic nature of the Kingdom that opens it towards the future and expresses its foreward moving character.

The Acts of the Apostles. *Epistrephein* and *metanoein* are more frequently used in the Gospel according to Luke. This trend continues in the Acts of the Apostles. Here both terms are closely interrelated (Acts 3:19, 26:20) and it is hardly possible to discover a different emphasis. *Epistrephein* is mainly used in the active mood and "aorist" tense, which indicates a more sharply identifiable moment of action of which the person concerned is the subject. On the whole, it is clear that both terms represent the core of missionary preaching on very important occasions such as Pentecost (Acts 2:38) or in Peter's sermon at the temple (Acts 3:19). Similarly, Paul's missionary activity centers on the call to conversion (Acts 26:18f.). In addition we find five reports in the Acts of the Apostles that have been commonly regarded as "conversion stories." In Acts 8 we hear of the baptism of the eunuch from Ethiopia, in Acts 9 Paul's sudden conversion near Damascus is reported, in Acts 10 there is an extensive account of how the Roman centurion, Cornelius, became a Christian, in Acts 16 we are told of the baptism of Lydia and in the same chapter we hear of the conversion and baptism of the jailor in the Philippian prison.

However in none of these five stories does either the term *metanoein* or *epistrephein* occur. The stories too are clearly of different character. In particular, the so-called conversion of Paul represents an event *sui generis.* According to I Corinthians 15:3ff. it must be regarded as the last appearance of the risen Christ through which he calls Paul into apostleship rather than as a conversion account. Among the rest the length and detail of description varies considerably. The immediate causes for conversion differ between, for instance, preaching (eunuch, Lydia) a vision (Cornelius) and a miracle (jailor). Yet there are a number of common points. Conversion is closely related to, and sometimes even identified with baptism, which means for Luke the visible entry into the Church. Conversion is in each case essentially commitment to Christ, or more precisely to the Lord (*kyrios*). While the role of a human agent remains marginal (he can be an interpreter of Scriptures or preacher and herald of the Gospel, but the act of conversion is in most cases not initiated by him), the author of the act of conversion is clearly, as in the Old Testament, God himself.

In neither case, however, is it possible to construct a model of conversion (though Luke implies a certain *ordo salutis* in which faith is followed by baptism). This is not only so because we lack sufficient common detail between the different stories and references to conversion, but even more so because the writer of the Acts does not look at those reports primarily as conversion stories of individuals. He reports them for one reason only. Each story marks a decisive moment in the history of the spread of the Church from Jerusalem to Rome. For instance for Luke the main turning point for the mission of the early Church arrives when it passes from the Jews to the Gentiles. This is why he reports so extensively the conversion of Cornelius in Acts 10. In that story he is not primarily interested in how and even why this particular man Cornelius is converted but what this event means to the apostles, the Church in Jerusalem and the Christian mission as a whole. Similar points can be made about any other of the accounts. What they are about is the purpose of God within his Church into which the personal experience is fully integrated.

The Pauline and Johannine Writings. In the Pauline Epistles we have to turn, as we have seen before, to other terms. *Pisteuein* in particular, means here to believe *de novo* and thus takes in large part the place of conversion.[8] *Pistis* is for St. Paul exclusively dependent on the reality of the Christ event and its proclamation (cf. Rom. 10:17, Gal. 3:5, etc.). Exactly like repentance in the Synoptic Gospels it is a response to the givenness of God's presence and action in Christ. Though faith is a reaction to God's doings, it is entirely wrought by him. The righteousness of God is the only basis of faith (cf. Rom. 1:17; 3:21; 5:1). Yet faith does not exclude definite personal commitment and works but rather must result in them (cf. Gal. 5:6). Through faith we are participants in the works of Christ. Thus *pistis* has a decision character that effects the total being but that also relates to the cosmic relevance of Christ. On the one hand we find therefore the long exhortations, so characteristic of St. Paul's writings, which call for the realization of the turning to God in every sphere of Christian personal and corporate life. On the other hand conversion is seen vis-a-vis the dethronement of the powers and forces of which Ephesians and Colossians speak. Here reappears the insistence of the Old Testament prophets that "turning" means to reject the false idols and securities while becoming a servant of the living God.

In II Corinthians 5 this is stated from a different angle when St. Paul asserts: "If anyone is in Christ, he is a new creation" (v. 17). The connection lies in the reality of the Christ event that marks the beginning of the Kingdom (I Cor. 15:24ff.; Col. 1:12ff.). In Christ the purpose of the whole universe is unfolded, in him the meaning of history unfolds (Eph. 1:9f.). The body of Christ, the Church, is part of that meaning. The individual enters into it through baptism in the Spirit (I Cor. 12:13). However, with the focus on the Church, the lines are this time drawn out towards the missionary ministry. "All this is from God who through Christ reconciled us to himself, and gave us the ministry of reconciliation" (II Cor. 5:18)—reconciliation with Christ and one's fellow beings, in fact, with the whole world, is one and the same; therefore, it must lead not only to a new life but to commitment of the whole Church to mission: "God was in Christ reconciling the word to himself . . . so we are ambassadors for Christ, God making his appeal through us: we beseech you on behalf of Christ, be reconciled to God" (vs. 19f.). The role of the Christian Church is that of becoming the first fruit of all creation (cf. Rom. 8:23, also James 1:18). Conversion is an examplaric act of response on behalf of and for all humanity.

In the Johannine writings, too, faith means response in concrete obedience (cf. John 3:36, 14:12, I John 3:23). Particular stress is laid on the interrelation of "belief" and "knowledge of God" reflecting an Old Testament tradition (cf. John 6:69, 7:17, 8:31f.). God reveals himself and only then is conversion possible. The Father draws to the Son (cf. John 6:44f., 10:26, 12:39). It is only through the coming of the light that the darkness becomes dark. This is precisely why Christ's coming necessarily results in a decision for or against him. The frequent use of the terms *krisis* and *krinein* is significant. John 3:19—"And this is the judgment, that the light has come into the world, and men loved darkness rather than light because their deeds were evil." The decision concerns the total world, not just a few individuals (cf. John 12:31, 16:8). It belongs to the special authority of Christ that he can bring about *krisis* (John 5:22), which however becomes only fully visible on the Cross and is only fully endorsed through his resurrection. Nicodemus (John 3) thus only understands the full significance of conversion after the crucifixion and the disciples only discover its full meaning when the risen Christ breathes on them and they receive the Holy Spirit.

But the peculiar characteristic of the Johannine material lies in the use of terms such as birth/rebirth (John 3:5ff.), born of God (I John 5:4), children of God (John 1:12f.). Phrases like "passing from death to life" (John 5:24) belong to the same context. They obviously do not want to exclude the necessity of personal decision as I John 5:1 proves. Rather they emphasize the continous "being in Christ" (as the Father is in him) in contrast to an act or instant of decision (cf. John 10:38, 17:21, 23, 26). This reminds us of the predominance of a strand of statements in the Pauline writings that refer in a similar way to "being in Christ" as the essence of a Christian existence, and use the term of adoption into the sonship (cf. Gal. 4:5; Eph. 1:5; Rom. 8:15). Consequently the reference to conversion as a particular point of turning is less accentuated.

Summary. There can be no doubt that conversion, as the Bible sees it, is a theologically valid and viable concept in both the Old and New Testament. To that extent the concern for conversion shown in many epochs of Christianity and more recently by the Protestant missionary movement has been confirmed. Yet, at the same time, we have found a much greater diversity in the biblical understanding of conversion, a much more open-ended use of the theme than the common English connotation of the term suggests.[9] Never is conversion understood as a mere individual spiritual experience. Rather it relates to the total meaning of history revealed in Christ. It centers on the Kingdom and not on the individual or the Church. The following points can be further drawn out:

1. Conversion is a personal reorientation towards God. We can undoubtedly observe that in both Old and New Testaments there are throughout personal and social sides to the process of turning to God. The disciples are called by name. God's action in history demands concrete response by historic persons. Yet this must not be misunderstood individualistically. Christ does not happen to have met a number of individuals who get converted and accidentally add up to twelve. It is the other way round: he calls twelve men because they have been designated to become the new Israel, the nucleus of a new humanity. In accordance

there is no dichtomy in the New Testament between the conversion of single persons and the corporate conversion of groups of people.

2. Conversion and sanctification cannot be separated. Yet the biblical evidence points to a distinction between them. As far as *metanoein* and *epistrephein* carry any precise meaning, it always relates to the beginning, not to the whole of the process of becoming a Christian. In other words, whereas sanctification refers to an ongoing movement, conversion literally means a particular "turning." Such "turning" is not necessarily a once-and-for-ever event in the Bible, though we can observe a tendency to regard conversion as a nonrepeatable experience (Heb. 6:12). It must be likened to the turnings of a way, not to the process of movement on it, which might be compared with sanctification. Or to put it differently: the Christian life of service and witness is in need of both conversion and sanctification. One without the other is void.

3. As in the Old Testament, conversion is in the first instance commitment *to* and participation *in* a movement forward. But in a second (not secondary) way it means at the same time liberation *from* the past and from the forces and powers of evil. In the Old Testament the prophetic call to conversion always includes an emphatic no to idolatry. In the New Testament conversion sets free to a new life in Christ. It is obedience of faith based on acceptance of forgiveness. Such liberation has not only to do with sins, the moral wrong and evil deeds of men, it equally concerns the forces of society and the cosmic powers of the universe. Neither the scope nor the significance of conversion can be confined to the narrow personal sphere.

4. In any case, the need for and urgency of conversion does not derive from the peculiar psychological setup of human personality nor from the individual's requirement to make a particular decision or to go through a particular experience. The only New Testament basis of conversion is the Christological one. Most definitely in the Pauline theology conversion/baptism are tightly interlocked with the death and resurrection of Christ. The reference to God as the one to whom persons must turn is gradually and without any break substituted by the reference to Christ (rather parallel to the use of the name of Christ in bap-

tism). Through the coming of Jesus Christ the reorientation to God attains a new meaning and historicity. It simply means now to follow him, to enter into his discipleship in the power of the Holy Spirit.

5. The beginning of the Kingdom through Christ's entry into history is the main context of conversion in the New Testament. From it three decisive criteria derive for conversion: *(a)* it reinforces that the triune God is the author of every aspect of conversion. The givenness of the Kingdom means that its reality is there before persons acknowledge it by conversion and that all human beings live within that reality; *(b)* the universal significance of the Kingdom means that the call to conversion is now explicitly linked with the commission to preach "to all nations" (Luke 24:47; Acts 2:38). Just as the prophets expound Israel's destiny within that of the nations, so conversion is concerned with the destiny of all human beings. In the New Testament the universal dimension of conversion is fully drawn out. It must lead to mission. *(c)* The Kingdom represents a reality which is moving towards the future and the end of time. It leads to the restoration of the whole cosmos, to the renewal of all things. With it conversion shares that eschatological character. It is not an end in itself but the beginning of a re-creation that must ultimately comprise *ta panta.*

Challenging Consequences

The biblical study of the concept of conversion has an immediate bearing on a number of current issues:

Conversion and Social Transformation. In the New and Old Testaments there is absolutely no gap between turning to God and its realization in the personal and social spheres. The consistent teaching of the prophets that is carried further in the New Testament insists that a new relationship with God and service to humanity belong inseparably together. It is repeatedly said that society at large can only recognize conversion by the "fruits" that it produces. There is a clear recognition that "service to humanity" is not only part of Christ's ministry in its own right but is in itself an expression of a reorientation to God. Yet there is on the other hand the danger of merely identifying turning to

God with personal and social action. This would lead to legalism and activism that are clearly rejected by the biblical writers. As much as the epistles demand a realization in action of the new life given through turning to God they maintain that such doing of works of righteousness must flow from a being in Christ that is the source of all action. Conversion means much more than the sum total of good deeds.

Another conclusion from the close interrelation of conversion to God and humanity can be drawn in the words of the World Missionary Conference at Jerusalem in 1928: "The New Testament does not recognize the antithesis frequently emphasized by later ages between individual and social regeneration" (The Council's Statement, volume V, p. 143). From that must follow that the call to conversion deals as much with personal reorientation as with the structures of society, economic processes and political forces. The fallacy of some traditional understanding of conversion is precisely that it mistakes the means of personal commitment as an end in itself. Those who are called are singled out for the sake of the world. They are called into the ministry of reconciliation, and reconciliation is an indivisible whole that concerns both the whole person and total society. The quality of the new life must therefore find expression in both personal and social justice. In Christian belief the change of persons and of structures depend on each other.

Conversion, Baptism and the Church. The immediate interdependence between conversion and baptism has been visible at several points of the New Testament survey and in fact exists from the very beginning (Mark 1:4ff.). This subject would obviously require a separate study in its own right and there is by no means unanimity on the New Testament understanding of baptism among scholars. But, following John Baillie, "there are one or two things that may surely be said without fear of contradiction. The first is that in the New Testament baptism always marks the incorporation of the individual within the Body of Christ (I Cor. 12:13) . . . Further it seems clear that, as marking incorporation into the Body of Christ, baptism is inseparably connected with regeneration or being born again."[10]

Whatever may be the precise nature of that connection, the fact itself cannot be challenged. The argument as to whether baptism or conversion marks the beginning of Christian life states a false alternative. Both terms correspond to each other and an absolute order of priority cannot be established. They both together are the work of the Holy Spirit.

If baptism is sometimes given a greater prominence in the New Testament then it is for that reason that it refers to the incorporation of the individual into the body of Christ. Conversion has by contrast occasionally been understood as an isolated experience of the individual with no further reference to the Church. But in the Synoptic Gospels, Christ's call to repentance is immediately followed by his calling the disciples. The coming of the Kingdom finds a visible manifestation in the creation of a new first-fruit community. Conversion in consequence cannot be separated from the Church that is the beginning of the realization of God's plan for his creation.[11] Conversion to Christ without the Church decapitates the head from the body. The reality of the Kingdom became manifest in new relationships.

Conversion and Mission. However the New Testament Church is not a juridically defined ecclesiastical body. The boundaries between the disciples close to Christ and the multitudes are always open (Matt. 5:1). We hear of a constant coming and going, of changing commitments. Most important, conversion and baptism, while linked with the entry into the Church, do not serve its interests but the larger purpose of God for the whole creation. The Church itself exists as a *pars pro toto*. It lives for the mission of God: "fellowship" minus the passion for conversion leads to ghettoism; "service" minus the call to conversion is a gesture without hope; Christian education minus conversion is religiosity without decision; and "dialogue" without challenge to conversion remains sterile talk. Conversion points to the possibility for man of ultimate disaster and judgment as well as renewal and final recreation. If our study made it clear that there is no conversion without the Church it has also affirmed the centrality of mission for the Church.

But the biblical concept of conversion also corrects some traditional understanding of mission. The eschatological character of conversion excludes a numerical misinterpretation of the goal of world mission. Too often missionary zeal falls into two traps. Either it concerns itself only with the few who are to be saved from the wickedness of the world, or it aims at numerical church extension, as if the kingdom will come about through an accumulative process within world history, by which an increasing number of people become Christian until finally all nations kneel at the feet of Jesus. Instead, the biblical concept of conversion relates to a representative number. From the days of Abraham through the Sinai Covenant to the calling of the twelve disciples and Paul's reference to the first fruits, conversion has resulted in the representative response of the few for the sake of all. Conversion has to do with the "salt" character of the Church, with its role to be the part for the whole.[12] The temptation has often been to short-circuit the eschatological tension either by reserving conversion for the responsive individual or by letting it be submerged in a universalism that does not recognize any definite commitment. The criterion for the necessity of conversion is the need to re-present Christ through discipleship.

Finally, we must come back to the fact that there is no single model for conversion in the New Testament. Neither do we find a comprehensive strategy for the preaching of conversion. The first converts to the New Testament Church after Pentecost were not won through planned action. The spread of the Church from Jerusalem started with the unexpected scattering of its members through persecution, and the news was not received without surprise that some of the Gentiles had "turned to the Lord" (Acts 11:21). The well-known slogan, "beginning from Jerusalem," which suggests some strategy of advance for the Gospel, bears little resemblance to the reality. True the Acts of the Apostles show us a pattern for the spreading of the Gospel from Jerusalem to Rome. But this becomes visible only in retrospect. On the contrary, the commission to preach "repentance" in Jerusalem and in all Judea and Samaria and to the end of the earth (Luke 24:47 and Acts 1:8) is remarkable for its gaps: What strategy is to be followed between Samaria and the end of the world? From that there does not follow a rejection of missionary methods in the New Testament. According to the Acts of the Apostles, St. Paul employs a quite persistent missionary approach.[13] But such missionary methods never harden into a preconceived strategy. Rather they remain completely open to the constant guidance of the Holy Spirit.

If method and planning in mission are flexible, the central

content of the biblical concept of conversion as a whole is quite consistent and can be summed up in these words of Lesslie Newbigin: "Conversion in this context is a turning round in order to participate by faith in a new reality that is the true future of the whole creation. It is not *in the first place* either saving one's own soul or joining a society. It is these things only secondarily because the new reality is one in which every soul is precious, and because there is a society that is the first fruit and sign of the new reality. If either of these things is put at the center, distortion follows. Biblically understood, conversion means being so turned round that one's face is towards that 'summing up of all things in Christ' that is promised, and of which the resurrection of Jesus is the sign and first fruit. It means being caught up into the activity of God that is directed to that end."

NOTES

1. Cf. *Theologisches Wörterbuch zum Neuen Testament*, Vol. IV, p. 972ff.; W. L. Holladay, *The Root Shubh in the Old Testament*, Leiden, 1958; H.W. Wolff, "Das Thema Umkehr in der alt testamentlichen Prophetie" und "Das Kerygma des deuteronomistischen Geschichtswerks," both in *Gesammelte Studien*, München, 1964.

2. Holladay defines: The verb *shubh* in the qal, means: "having moved in a particular direction, to move thereupon in the opposite direction, the implication being (unless there is evidence to the contrary) that one will arrive again at the initial point of departure." (p. 53).

3. All biblical quotations are from the Revised Standard Version.

4. Cf. *Theologisches Wörterbuch zum Neuen Testament*, Vols. IV, p. 972ff. and VII, p. 722ff. Also S. S. Smalley and others as given in Appendix II. For definition, see E. F. Thompson, *"Metanoeo" and "Metamelei" in Greek literature until 100 A.D.* University of Chicago Press, 1908.

5. Though the two terms are not completely synonymous it is hardly possible to draw theological consequences from their different use.

6. The quotations from Isaiah 6, "Lest they should turn again and be forgiven" (Mark 4:12 para. also Acts 28:26ff.) would require special analysis and evaluation that cannot be undertaken here.

7. In addition to the terms mentioned already one would have to consider "skandalon," "judgement," "reconciliation," "obedience," "knowledge," as well as verbs like "receive," "enter," "save," "seek," "be given," in order to get a full picture.

8. The *aorist* form of *pisteuein* is especially used in a missionary sense, meaning to begin to believe, to become a believer.

9. See the definition of conversion below.

10. John Baillie, *Baptism and Conversion*, Oxford, 1964, pp. 16f.

11. Cf. V. Borovoi in *Study Encounter*. Vol. 1/2, WCC, 1966, pp. 90f.

12. Cf. H.-R. Weber, "God's Arithmetic," *Frontier*, Vol. 6, 1963, pp. 298ff. [Reprinted in this volume of *Mission Trends*.]

13. There is obviously some theological significance in the fact that St. Paul began his missionary activity among his own people in the synagogue.

Evangelization
and the World

René Padilla

"A gospel that leaves untouched our life in the world . . . is not
the Christian Gospel, but culture Christianity, adjusted to the
mood of the day." Speaking at the International Congress on
World Evangelization in Lausanne, Switzerland in July, 1974,
René Padilla refers especially to the form of Christianity that
churches in the United States have often exported to the Third
World. He warns: "This kind of gospel has no teeth. . . . It
demands nothing." For Padilla "the greatest need of the Church
today is the recovery of the full Gospel of our Lord Jesus Christ
—the whole Gospel for the whole person for the whole world."
This means that "reconciliation with God cannot be separated
from social justice," that "there is an internal connection between the life of the Church and its prophetic ministry, and between the prophetic ministry of the Church and its evangelization." Dr. Padilla, an Ecuadorian Baptist, is Associate General
Secretary for Latin America of the International Fellowship of
Evangelical Students, with headquarters in Buenos Aires. This
excerpt from his address first appeared in *engage/social action*
for November, 1974, published by the United Methodist Board
of Church and Society in Washington, D.C. The full text appears
in *Let the Earth Hear His Voice*, the official reference volume
for the Lausanne Congress, edited by J. D. Douglas and published in 1975 by World Wide Publications, Minneapolis.

According to scriptures the Gospel is addressed not to people as isolated beings called to respond to God with no reference
to their life context, but rather to people in relation to the world.
The Gospel always comes to people in relation to the world of

creation, the world that was made through Jesus Christ and that is to be recreated through him. It comes to individuals within the present order of existence, immersed in the transient world of material possesions. It comes to people as members of humanity —the world for which Christ died but, at the same time, the world hostile to God and enslaved to the powers of darkness.

The aim of evangelization is therefore to lead people not merely to subjective experiences of the future salvation of the soul but to a radical reorientation of their lives, including deliverance from slavery to the world and its powers on the one hand, and integration into God's purpose of placing all things under the rule of Christ on the other hand. The Gospel is not addressed to human beings in a vacuum. It has to do with the movement from the old humanity in Adam, which belongs to this age that is passing away, into the new humanity in Christ, which belongs to the age to come.

Because Jesus has been made Lord and King over all things through his death and resurrection, here and now, in anticipation of the deliverance of the whole creation from its bondage to decay, those who believe in him are delivered from slavery to the world and its powers.

Salvation is not exclusively forgiveness of sins but also tranference from the dominion of darkness to a realm where Jesus is recognized as *Kyrios* of all the universe—the kingdom of God's beloved son (Col. 1:13).

American Culture-Christianity

I do not wish to imply that American Christians are the only ones who may fall into the trap of confusing Scriptures and culture. The fact however is that, because of the role that the United States has had to play in world affairs, as well as in the spread of the Gospel, this particular form of Christianity, as no other today, has a powerful influence far beyond the borders of that nation. Behind my condemnation of this variety of cultural-Christianity lies a principle for any kind of culture-Christianity, namely, that the Church must be delivered from anything and everything in its culture that would prevent it from being faithful to the Lord in the fulfillment of its mission within and beyond its own culture. The big question that we Christians always have to ask ourselves with regard to our culture is which elements of it should be retained and utilized and which ones should go for the sake of the Gospel.

When the Church lets itself be squeezed into the mold of the world it loses the capacity to see and even more to denounce the social evils in its own situation. Like the color-blind person who is able to distinguish certain colors, but no others, the worldly Church recognizes the personal vices traditionally condemned within its ranks, but is unable to see the evil features of its surrounding culture.

This is the only way one can explain how it is possible for American culture-Christianity to integrate racial and class segregation into its strategy for world evangelization. The idea is that people *like* to be with those of their own race and class and we must therefore plant segregated churches, which will undoubtedly grow faster. We are told that race prejudice "can be understood and should be made an aid to Christianization." No amount of exegetical maneuvering can ever bring this approach in line with the explicit teaching of the New Testament regarding the unity of men in the body of Christ: "Here there cannot be Greek and Jews, circumcised and uncircumcised, barbarian, Scythian, slave, free man, but Christ is all, and in all" (Col. 3:11). "There is neither Jew nor Greek, there is neither slave nor free, there is neither male nor female; for you are all one in Christ Jesus" (Gal. 3:23).

How can a church that for the sake of numerical expansion deliberately opts for segregation, speak to a divided world? By what authority can it preach man's reconciliation with God through the death of Christ, which is one aspect of the Gospel, while in fact it has denied man's reconciliation with man through the same death, which is another aspect of the Gospel? As Samuel Moffett put it at the Berlin Congress, "When racial discrimination enters the churches, it is something more than a crime against humanity, it is an act of defiance against God himself."

The Prophetic Ministry

It is perhaps in this context that I should say a word on the prophetic ministry today. For it is only in the measure to which the Church itself is the incarnation of God's purpose to put all things under the lordship of Christ that it can denounce the evils in society that are a denial of God's original purpose. There is an internal connection between the life of the Church and its prophetic ministry and between the prophetic ministry of the Church and its evangelization.

The Church is called to be here and now what God intends the whole of society to be. By its prophetic ministry it lays open the evils that frustrate the purpose of God in society; in its evangelization it seeks to integrate people into that purpose of God whose full realization is to take place in the Kingdom to come. Consequently wherever the church fails as a prophet it also fails as an evangelist.

A church that is not faithful to the Gospel in all its dimensions inevitably becomes an instrument of the status quo. The Gospel is meant to place the totality of life under the universal lordship of Jesus Christ, not to produce cultic sects; it is an open break with the status quo of the world. Therefore a gospel that leaves untouched our life in the world—in relationship to the world of humanity as well as in relationship to the world of creation—is not the Christian Gospel, but culture Christianity, adjusted to the mood of the day.

This kind of gospel has no teeth—it is a gospel that the "free consumers" of religion will want to receive because it is cheap and it demands nothing of them. The Gospel in the first century was, according to Michael Green, "politically suspect, socially disruptive." The Gospel of culture-Christianity today is a message of conformism, a message that, if not accepted, can at least be easily tolerated because it doesn't disturb anybody. The racist can continue to be a racist, the exploiter can continue to be an exploiter. Christianity will be something that runs along life but will not cut through it.

A truncated gospel is utterly insufficient as a basis for churches to generate their own Calvins, Wesleys, Wilberforces, and Martin Luther Kings. It can only be the basis for unfaithful churches, for strongholds of racial and class discrimination, for religious clubs with a message that has no relevance to practical life in the social, the economic and the political spheres.

A Technological Problem

Culture-Christianity not only has turned the Gospel into a cheap product, but has also turned the strategy for the evangelization of the world into a problem of technology. One of my critics describes my reservations with regard to this approach to world evangelization as "a Latin American hangup." This is an *ad hominem* argument. Latin Americans have not made any particular contribution to the definition of the limitations of technology. In fact, it is to a Frenchman, Jacques Ellul, that I appeal when I refer to the "technological mentality" that conditions American cultural-Christianity. It is the mentality according to which efficiency is an absolute criterion on the basis of which one should seek the systematization of methods and resources to obtain pre-established results in all areas of human life. It is to the absoluteness of efficiency, at the expense of the integrity of the Gospel, that I object.

Technology has its place in evangelization; it would be foolish for me to deny that. The problem comes when technology is made a substitute for Scripture under the assumption that what we need is a better strategy, not a more biblical Gospel and a more faithful Church. The picture of the Church that one derives from the New Testament is certainly not that of a powerful organization that has achieved success in its conquest of the world by the masterly use of human devices and techniques. It is rather the picture of a community experiencing a new (supernatural) reality—the kingdom of God—to which "the Lord called day by day those who were being saved."

As Michael Green has put it, "In the early Church the maximum impact was made by the changed lives and quality of community among the Christians." "Changed lives and quality of community"—that is, faithfulness to the Gospel in practical life—do not come through technology, but through the word and the spirit of God. Technology will never make up for our failure to let the Gospel mold our lives.

Furthermore, if the strategy for world evangelization is tied to technology, then obviously the ones who have the final word on the strategy for the Church in the future are those who have the technical know-how as well as the resources to make the necessary investigations. The Church in the Third World has nothing to say on the matter. Isn't this again to identify the Gospel with wordly power, a way to perpetuate the domination/dependence patterns that have often characterized missionary work for the last hundred years? What becomes of the universal character and the unity of the Church of Christ? But perhaps these things don't matter. If, after all, the real problem is to produce the greatest number of Christians at the least possible cost in the shortest possible time!

If I have dealt with American culture-Christianity it is not because I am unaware of the fact that in other situations Christians may fall into the trap of accommodating the Gospel to their own culture. It is rather because of the wide influence of *this* variety of culture-Christianity in evangelical circles around the world. The question, raised by an American who acknowledges the problem of culture-Christianity in his own situation, is: "How can I overcome culture-Christianity, when I cannot get out of my own culture?"

In the first place, let us recognize the conditioning that the world and "the things that are in the world" exercise over us even in relation to our service to God. All too often we are ready to condemn the distortions that others have openly allowed to come into their theology through the front door, but remain impervious of the distortions that have come into our evangelization through the back door. The orthodoxy of our creed is no guarantee of our own faithfulness to the Gospel in either our life or service. The key word here is *humility*.

In the second place, let us be aware of the need to place our lives and activities continually under the judgment of the Word of God. We cannot simply assume that we have the truth and that everything else, including our evangelization and our ethics, will just fall in line with that truth. The purpose of theology is not merely to reaffirm what previous generations have said in the past, but to bring the whole life and mission of the Church into line with God's revelation. All our assumptions and methods must therefore be examined in the light of Scripture. The Gospel itself, not success, is the criterion to evaluate our work. The key word here is *theological renewal*.

In the third place, let us take seriously the unity of the body of Christ throughout the world. If the Church is really one, then there is no place for the assumption that one section of the

Church has the monopoly on the interpretation of the Gospel and the definition of the Christian mission. Those of us who live in the Third World cannot and should not be satisfied with the rote repetition of doctrinal formulas or the indiscriminate application of canned methods of evangelization imported from the West.

I am not advocating here a relativistic approach to theology. I am calling for the recognition of a problem and a change of attitude with regard to the making of theology and the planning of world evangelization. The problem is that one version of culture-Christianity, with an inadequate theological foundation and conditioned by "fierce pragmatism"—the kind of pragmatism that in the political sphere produced Watergate—should be regarded as the official evangelical position and the measure of orthodoxy around the world. The change of attitude is the renunciation of ethnocentrism and the promotion of theological cross-fertilization among different cultures. Under the spirit of God, each culture has something to contribute in connection with the understanding of the Gospel and its implications for the life and mission of the Church. American culture-Christianity should not be allowed to deprive us of the possibility that we all—whatever our race, nationality, language or culture—as equal members in the one body of Christ, "attain the unity of the faith and of the knowledge of the Son of God, to mature manhood, to the measure of the stature of the fullness of Christ" (Eph. 4:13). The key word here is *cross-fertilization*.

Evangelism and Other Worldliness

There are two extreme positions with regard to the present world. The one conceives of salvation as something that fits within the limits of the present age, in terms of social, economic and political liberation. The personal dimensions of salvation are eliminated or minimized. The individual is lost in society. There is little or no place for forgiveness from guilt and sins, for the resurrection of the body and immortality. This world is all there is and the fundamental mission of the church must therefore be conceived in terms of the transformation of this world through politics.

At the other end of the scale is the view according to which salvation is reduced to the future salvation of the soul and the present world is nothing more than a preparatory stage for life in the hereafter. The social dimensions of salvation are thus completely or almost completely disregarded and the Church becomes a redeemed ghetto charged with the mission of rescuing souls from the present evil world. Didn't Jesus say, "My kingdom is not of this world"? Why should the Church be concerned for the poor and the needy? Didn't he say, "The poor you always have with you"? The only responsibility that the Church has toward the world is, then, the preaching of the Gospel and the planting of churches: "There are many goods the Church *may* do, of course; but they do not belong to its essential mission."

I maintain that both of these views are incomplete gospels and that the greatest need of the Church today is the recovery of the full Gospel of our Lord Jesus Christ—the whole Gospel for the whole person for the whole world.

On the one hand, the Gospel cannot be reduced to social, economic and political categories nor the Church to an agency for human improvement. Even less can the Gospel be confused with a political ideology or the Church with a political party. As Christians we are called to witness to the transcendental, otherworldly Christ through whose work we have received forgiveness of sins and reconciliation to God.

We believe in man's need of a new birth through a personal encounter with God in Jesus Christ, by the action of the Holy Spirit, through the proclamation of the Word of God. And we maintain that nothing can take the place of spiritual regeneration in the making of new persons. This is biblical soteriology and as evangelicals we are fully committed to it. We cannot accept the equation of salvation with the satisfaction of bodily needs, social amelioration or political liberation.

On the other hand there is no biblical warrant for viewing the church as an other-worldly community dedicated to the salvation of souls or to limit its mission to the preaching of man's reconciliation to God through Jesus Christ. As Elton Trueblood has put it, "A genuine gospel will always be concerned with human justice rather than with the mere cultivation of a warm inner glow" (quoted by D. Bloesch in *The Evangelical Renaissance*, p. 22).

How involved should we be in justice and economics?" The
fact is that whether we like it or not we are already involved.
Politics and economics are unavoidable—they are a part of the
reality that surrounds us while we are in the world. The real
question therefore is: "Because we are in fact involved, how can
we make sure that our involvement is faithful to the Gospel of
our lord Jesus Christ?" Even though we may try not to take any
notice of politics and economics, *they* always take notice of us.

*Is change in the structure of society a part of the evange-
listic mandate?* Here I can only insist that "the imperative of the
evangelical ethic forms an indissoluable whole with the indicative
of the Gospel."

Another way to say it would be that the two tables of the
law belong together, or that concern for human reconciliation
with God cannot be separated from concern for social justice, or
that the evangelistic mandate has to be fulfilled in the context of
obedience to the cultural mandate, or that the Kingdom of God
manifests itself in the midst of the kingdoms of men, or simply
that the mission of the church is indivisible from its life.

No Wedge Between Tasks in the Church

I refuse therefore to drive a wedge between a primary task,
namely the proclamation of the Gospel, and a secondary (at
best) or even optional (at worst) task of the Church. In order to
be obedient to its Lord the Church should never do anything that
is not essential; therefore, nothing that the Church does in obedience to its Lord is unessential. Why? Because love to God is in-
separable from love to people; because faith without works is
dead; because hope includes the restoration of all things to the
Kingdom of God.

I am not confusing the two kingdoms—I do not expect the
ultimate salvation of individuals or society through good works
or political action. I am merely asking that we take seriously the
relevance of the Gospel to the totality of human life in the world.
The only other possible alternative is to say that God is interested in our calling him "Lord, Lord"—but not in our obedience to
his will in relation to such crucial issues as social injustice and
oppression, famine, war, racism, illiteracy and the like.

Is it legitimate to say that Jesus was a political king? When I say that in describing Jesus as the Christ we are in fact describing him in political terms I do not mean that he involved himself in what we today consider political action in a narrow sense, but that *Messiah* (King) is a political description. He did not come in order to create a religion but to accomplish God's purpose of placing all things under his government. Those who acknowledge him as Lord are not only reconciled to God but are also given in him a model for human life, life in the *polis*. Here and now in this world his disciples are called to bring their personal and corporate life into line with the will of God expressed in the ethics of the Kingdom, whose central principle is love.

In emphasizing the ethical, how do we avoid moralism and legalism in our teaching? We do this by teaching the true nature of Christian morality, that morality is not outward subjection to rules and norms but heart obedience in response to God and that the essence of Christian morality is gratitude. The way to avoid the danger of falling into moralism and legalism is not to eliminate the ethical demands of the Gospel, but to see that obedience is an essential aspect of faith's response to the Gospel and is always obedience by the power of God who works in us through the spirit.

What can the Church do when the problems are so staggering? The Church has not been called to solve all the problems but to be faithful to God with what it has. The greatest contribution that the Church can make to the world is to be all that it is supposed to be. Among other things: (a) a community of reconciliation. In the midst of a fragmented world, here is a community where all barriers that divide disappear, where persons learn to welcome one another as Christ has welcomed them, for the glory of God. (b) A community of personal authenticity. In the midst of a world in which each person has fitted into the mold imposed by society, here is a community where each one is accepted to develop fully as human beings made in the image of God. (c) A community of serving and giving. In the midst of a world where people live to be served and to receive, here is a community where they live to serve and to give.

"Strictness" and Church Membership

Thomas R. McFaul

In his book *Why Conservative Churches Are Growing*, Dean Kelley argued that conservative churches are growing because of their "strictness" in religious commitment, while mainline denominational churches are declining because of leniency. To the contrary, says Thomas R. McFaul, the mainline churches grew in the 1940s and 50s precisely because "no real commitment was called for" and "becoming a church member was the thing to do." It was only after "many of the leaders and members became increasingly active in social causes" in the 1960s—especially in civil rights and the Vietnam war—and "began to call for 'strictness' on the part of the Church as a whole . . . to translate its lofty idealism into vigorous programs for justice and social change" that the decline in membership began with the alienation of those "half-committed Christians whose understanding of the faith went little beyond American ethnocentrism," according to McFaul. The conservative churches, "where orthodoxy and social conservatism are highly correlated," benefited and grew. Thus McFaul "completely reverses Kelley's formula," insisting that "membership decline is at least in part the consequence of a return to, rather than a *falling away from*, strictness—if strictness means taking the faith seriously in terms of its implications for prophetic social action." Thomas R. McFaul has his Ph.D from Boston University and is assistant professor of sociology in the School of Human Sciences and Humanities at the University of Houston at Clear Lake, Texas. His article is reprinted from the March 13, 1974, issue of *The Christian Century* (Chicago).

It is common knowledge that for the past several years the mainline Protestant denominations have been declining in membership and the conservative churches growing. As its title implies, a major book—*Why Conservative Churches Are Growing* (Harper & Row, 1972), by Dean Kelley—deals exclusively with this phenomenon. But so far there has been no serious attempt at systematic criticism of Kelley's thesis. Let me therefore try to fill the vacuum.

Kelley maintains that the mainline denominations are experiencing a membership decline because of a weakening of that religious commitment which is itself a function of organizational growth and strength. ". . . social strength and leniency do not go together," he says. This is the essence of what he calls "Wesley's Law of the Decay of Pure Religion" (pp. 83, 105).

This position is really an extension of Ernst Troeltsch's famous church-sect hypothesis. Sectarian churches are driven by the socialization process, hence are formalized, professionalized and institutionalized. But the socialization process inevitably weakens evangelistic fervor and waters down commitment; thus membership drops. Kelley's prescription for the recovery of the mainline churches is simple: a return to "strictness." For "strictness," he says, "is the only way to conserve social strength, whether in *ecclesia* or *ecclesiolae*" (p. 120). Yet he fears that decay is already so far advanced that only a holding action may be possible at best. In any case, Wesley's Law operates: "Strictness is not congenial to the prosperous, and so it ebbs away, and with it social strength" (p. 178).

Church Membership and External Factors

Two basic weaknesses characterize Kelley's book. First, his time perspective is very narrow. Second, the full weight of his position rests on an analysis of the internal dynamics of organizational growth. He scarcely even considers the relationship of church membership to external environmental or social factors.

Denominationalism has been a feature of the American scene for two centuries and more. The mainline churches in particular have long been identified with the more successful classes of society. Also, people of the middle class tend to be more frequent participants in religious activities than those of the working or lower classes. In general the correlation between social class and voluntary organizational participation is consistently positive, and this relationship carries over into church life as well. In addition up to now sectarianism and conservative theology have been predominantly correlated with the lower classes (though change is under way).

However, Kelley's own data confirm that the downturn in membership did not show up significantly until the mid- or late 1960s. Why did the relationship between leniency, institutional success and concomitant decline in social strength not manifest itself earlier, especially in light of the fact that the mainline churches have long been identified with the prosperous?

I offer an alternative hypothesis. *The continous growth in membership among the mainline churches up to the mid-1960s was not a function of strictness, as Kelley suggests, but rather a function of leniency; and the decline in membership is not a reflection of leniency, but of strictness.* This completely reverses Kelley's formula. Where he argues on the basis of the internal dynamics of the Church as an organization, I proceed from an analysis of changes in the social environment and their effect on the Church.

With Leniency, Membership Grows

Throughout the 1940s and '50s the increase in church membership was the result of leniency. Just about anybody could join the mainline churches. Only a minimum understanding of the traditions and tenets of the faith was required, and no real commitment was called for. The culture supported and encouraged church membership; becoming a church member was the thing to do. It was precisely because of this leniency, this pattern of cultural acceptance, and this decline of authentic commitment that Will Herberg could suggest—in his classic 1955 volume *Protestant, Catholic, Jew*—that American religion was little more than a mirror image of the American way of life. The difference between church culture and American culture was all too frequently indiscernible.

In those years the Church provided for the "belonging" and "comfort" needs of most of its members, but its prophetic function waned into nonexistence. After all America did live through the Depression and recovered from it. In the 1940s it successfully fought the fascists, and in the 1950s it carried on the cold war against the Russians. By and large church leaders and members stood solidly behind these efforts. Neither they nor nonchurch Americans saw any reason for national self-criticism. No wonder Herberg concluded that the churches merely reflected the American Way of Life.

Changes in the situation began in the late 1950s and continued throughout the '60s. Civil rights and black power campaigns, urban riots and student demonstrations, the Vietnam war and the ecological crisis unsettled American society. An ever-increasing number of clergymen adopted the prophetic role and, focusing on race, the Vietnam war and the environment, championed the cause of justice. At the same time a barrage of criticism came from all sides, blasting the Church for its "suburban captivity" and its "comfortable pew." Accusations of lack of aggressive action in race relations proliferated as white Protestants turned their backs on the central city and its mounting dilemmas and led the exodus to suburbia.

The *consensus universalis* that exists in the Church began to break apart. Many of the leaders and members became increasingly active in social causes. Presently they began to call for "strictness" on the part of the Church as a whole and challenged it to resume its prophetic function and to translate its lofty idealism into vigorous programs for justice and social change.

Grant that the churches were filled with half-committed Christians whose understanding of the faith went little beyond American ethnocentrism; then the more prophetic the Church became (so far as it did become prophetic), the more it alienated this sector of its membership. After all these people had joined the Church in the first place only because they had internalized the cultural role expectations or because they looked to it to satisfy pastoral or family needs. And the conservative churches, where orthodoxy and social conservatism are highly correlated, benefited from the increasing politicization within and the social change outside the mainline denominations. (Regarding the correlation in the conservative churches, cf. David R. Gibbs, et al.:

"Doctrinal Orthodoxy, Salience, and the Consequential Dimension" [*Journal for the Scientific Study of Religion*, March 1973, pp. 33-52]. These authors show that the relationship between theological conservatism and social conservatism is strong where religious salience is high; where it is not high, the relationship may not exist at all or even be negative.)

Conservatives' Favored Position

The interpretation offered above suggests that members look to the Church more for comfort than for challenge. Are there any data to support it? Yes. In his article "Religious Belief as an Independent Variable" (*Journal for the Scientific Study of Religion*, March 1972), James Davidson describes his study of two Baptist and two Methodist congregations in Indiana in relation to this question. His conclusion: "The evidence indicates that a majority of the people in our sample derived some comfort from their religion, while less than a majority were socially active in their community for religious reasons. This finding supports the contention that religion today is oriented to personal and family matters more than it is oriented to social and community problems." One must not generalize from this limited situation to church membership in general, but so far as mainline churches have turned toward social action (and some would argue that it is not far at all), they have alienated and driven out those middle-class or other persons who are threatened by social change, who are individualistically oriented, whose religious convictions substantiate Herberg's thesis, and who also look to the Church to perform mainly comfort functions. Thus membership decline is at least in part the consequence of a *return to*, rather than a *falling away from*, strictness—if strictness means taking the faith seriously in terms of its implication for prophetic social action.

In addition, the conservative churches, especially the fundamentalist and pentecostal groups, benefited from the mainline churches' return to strictness on the social-action front. Not only does fundamentalism carry out the comfort function superlatively, it also deals with the prophetic or challenge dimensions of religious commitment by "swallowing them up" in eschatology. "Good works will not lead to salvation. Only faith in Jesus Christ holds this promise. One is safe with Jesus, and until one gets right with Jesus, all efforts to change the social order will fail. Besides, Jesus will transform the social order when he returns again in glory"—so goes the fundamentalist message. The challenge to social or collective responsibility is obliterated through indifference and strong emotional conviction. In short fundamentalism and pentecostalism counter the uncertainty of the times with a biblical literalism that offers both an explanation for all the earth's ills and a divinely revealed panacea for its salvation.

Hitherto fundamentalist or sect-type religious groups have been associated with the lower socio-economic strata. The Southern Baptists, the Churches of Christ, the Assemblies of God, and Jehovah's Witnesses still largely reflect their lower-class origins. Now however recruitment for these groups increasingly cuts across class boundaries and reaches into the working and middle classes as well.

I suggest that the growth of conservative churches has been and will remain a function of the institutionalization of mass evangelism. We live in a mass media world. The conservative churches have accepted this reality and have used it to their advantage. The institution of mass evangelism serves as a recruitment component of, or feeder system for, their local congregations. The conservative churches are highly competitive. They advertise and sloganeer, they give prizes and promise gifts, they sell hard and soft. They are constantly crusading and holding mass rallies, and they exploit fully the potentiality of radio and especially television. Moreover the conservative churches are excellent image-makers. And they are uninhibited in their use of the mass media to market charismatic personalties. In brief, in an America oriented to competitive free enterprise the fundamentalist groups have simply "outhustled" the mainline Protestant denominations. These have no such institutionalized mass evangelism component for addressing immediately, in settings outside church buildings, the comfort needs of large numbers of people caught up in threatening social change and in need of security in an anxious world.

As I said, the use of the mass media is increasingly bringing about an identification of middle-class life styles with conservative or fundamentalist theology. This is a new development in American church life. What will it mean for the future relationship between the conservative and mainline churches? To the extent that the latter move away from social action and toward strengthening the local parish, they will probably concentrate more and more on pastoral and maintenance functions. And to the extent that the local parish engages in social action at all, it will do so in more socially acceptable and traditional ways—as, for instance, by promoting local charity projects or by encouraging its members to participate in and influence other community organizations. On their part regional or national denominational offices and officials, separately or together in ecumenical fashion, will continue to deal with those broader institutional questions that the local parish could not conceivably confront because of its limited resources. Thus, whatever form they take, social action thrusts will be far less dramatic than in the past decade.

This means that social-class factors might aid in the stabilization of the mainline churches, for these will appear less threatening to members and potential members whose needs are primarily pastoral and family related. Even so, if the conservative churches continue to broaden their appeal and so to win over people from the higher socio-economic levels, the mainline churches might well experience a further decline in membership.

Downward Trends

The data given in the 1973 *Yearbook of American and Canadian Churches* (Abingdon, 1973) suggest that the trends of the past several years have scarcely changed. In 1972 (the year to which the data apply) 62.4 per cent of the American public were members of churches, as compared to 63.2 per cent the previous year. This is only a slight drop. It can be confidently said that three out of five Americans are still members of some church. But church growth is not keeping pace with population growth, even though in absolute numbers there were 343,689 more church members in 1972 than in 1971.

It is of course true that the *Yearbook* data may not be altogether reliable. Membership requirements among denominations vary greatly, and general membership statistics say nothing about the extent or significance of the members' commitment, about the nature of their religious beliefs or about the influence (if any) that these beliefs exert over behavior. But the *Yearbook* is our only source for national data on the churches, and is accurate enough for my purposes.

The 1973 *Yearbook* reports that, on the average, 40 per cent of the adult members attended church "within a typical week" in 1972. Because 62.4 per cent of all Americans are members of churches, the 40 per cent figure indicates that slightly fewer than three out of every ten Americans attend worship services weekly. This pattern continues the downward trend of the past several years.

The *Yearbook* also reports that both the Catholics and the Southern Baptists enjoyed membership gains in 1972—the Southern Baptists increased by 1.7 per cent. The United Methodist Church, the United Church of Christ, the Presbyterians (USA and US), the Christian Church, the Episcopal Church again suffered slight losses. Some of the more conservative churches also showed losses, and some showed lesser gains—a departure from the past decade's pattern of consistent growth. Thus the over-all pattern of decline in membership and attendance continues to obtain. But it is the conservative denominations that show whatever growth there is, while the mainline denominations keep on declining.

Whether and how long this trend will go on is hard to predict. But any forecast of possible future directions of American church life must be based on something more than an analysis, à la Dean Kelley, of the internal dynamics of institutional growth alone. Fluctuations in denominational membership are related to events in the larger American society and to the Church's response to them.

God's Arithmetic

Hans-Ruedi Weber

In the midst of much contemporary emphasis on "church growth" in mission, Hans-Ruedi Weber suggests what "may be on the fringe of heresy"—namely, that "the result of true evangelism may be the cutting down of the number of church members." The key question, he says, "is not how churches can grow numerically, but how they can grow in grace"—and discovering the cost of discipleship often results in a decline in church membership. Weber, a former missionary in Indonesia who is now director of the portfolio for biblical studies in the World Council of Churches, argues that mission in the New Testament is "not connected with statistics, but with sacrifice," therefore "we must leave this matter of statistics to God, and concentrate all our energy on discerning and serving God's cosmic mission of reconciliation." Our main concern in mission, he concludes, is "to become the representative number, to grow in grace and thus to be on the way to true maturity." "God's arithmetic," thus understood, "frees our missionary work from nervous fanatical activity and from the paralysis of defeatism." Dr. Weber's article first appeared in volume VI (Winter 1963) of *Frontier*, which is published by the S.P.C.K. in London.

"What will happen if we plan our evangelism project according to the insights we have now gained?" "Frankly, it may be that many among your present church-membership will leave the Church and that a few who are now completely outside the Church will join you." "You mean to say that as a result of this project we may in the end actually be fewer!"

This was the end of a conversation about evangelism that I held in California with a group of keen Lutheran laymen and pastors who were planning an evangelism project for the San Fernando Valley. In the course of our conversation we were led to that staggering discovery, which none of us was quite ready to accept, namely, that the result of true evangelism may be the cutting down of the number of church-members. Evangelism and outward church-growth will not necessarily go together. The renewed interest in church-growth and the stimulating studies of Donald McGavran are important, but they often use man's and not God's arithmetic as the measure of growth.[1]

We know little about how God uses and evaluates numbers, how He counts and measures. Nevertheless, the Bible reveals some astonishing things that are a paradox to our mathematical minds.

God's purpose is the salvation of *all*, of the total *cosmos*, yet, in order to achieve this, God elects, calls and converts a *few*. This began with Abraham. God judges all (Gen. 12:3a); moreover he wants all to be blessed (Gen. 12:3b). To this end he called and sent on a mission *one* man, Abraham, who, as God's man, was to bring crisis and benediction to all. It was promised to Abraham that he should become a great nation (Gen. 12:2), a promise fulfilled in the people of Israel. Yet the history of Israel is no success story. Sometimes the numerical growth and outward strength actually hindered Israel from being God's People. The story of Gideon's army is significant (Judges 7). The Lord said to Gideon: "The people with you are too many for me to give the Midianites into their hand, lest Israel vaunt themselves against me, saying, 'My own hand has delivered me.' " Even after a drastic cutting down of numbers the Lord had to say: "The people are still too many." Only when the army was cut down to 300 men was it ready to fight God's battle. The same happened later with Israel as a whole, as the prophetic message about the "Remnant" indicates. It is not the many who become the agents of God's mission of reconciliation for all, but the few who are so weak that they must put all confidence in God's strength.

The same paradox is seen in the New Testament. In order to save the *cosmos* God sends the One, his own Son. Christ calls a few, the representative twelve, and he sends them into the whole inhabited world to be witnesses of his cosmic redemption. The mission is entrusted to the few who live as aliens and exiles, as a Christian *diaspora* in this world, yet it is directed to *ta panta*. This Greek expression that occurs so often in the New Testament embraces not only all men, but also all powers and principalities, social structures, ways of thought and religions of this world. The few are given the promise of growth, and the author of the Book of Acts carefully reported the number of those who were added. Yet again the early history of the Church is no success story. Paul's and Peter's letters to the "younger churches" are full of records of persecutions. According to the Book of Revelation the outward victory is against God's people, and the Lord himself said that "many will fall away." Nevertheless, this cutting down of numbers does not frustrate God's purpose. By the One and the few he is bringing *ta panta* under the lordship of Christ. This is not only the message of the letters to the Ephesians and Colossians, but the main theme of the New Testament teaching as a whole.

Numbers and growth are important in God's arithmetic: not necessarily large and increasing numbers, but representative numbers and growth in grace. The representative few stand for all. Their mission consists not in propaganda in order that many may be induced to become like the few. Rather it consists in being *pars pro toto*, the part standing for the whole, being the light of the *cosmos*, salt of the earth, good seed sown in the field of the world. The key question is not how churches can grow numerically, but how they can grow in grace and so become God's representative number.

The New Testament answers this clearly. The quality of representation is gained in a life in Christ, paying the cost of discipleship, like him being spent (a word that in the New Testament had a sacrificial connotation, meaning literally "to be poured out as a libation"). Therefore, most New Testament letters to younger churches contain neither exhortations to organize evangelism campaigns nor methods of increasing numbers. These letters are prefaces to martyrdom, and mission is there not connected with statistics, but with sacrifice. Consequently, the deepest reason for Paul's apostolic joy was not his and the younger churches' success, but the conformity to Christ's suffering in the fulfillment of their ministry. Another New Testament answer to the question of the growth in grace is the biblical concept of maturity (*teleiotes*). This term has nothing to do with the self-complacent and static perfection of those who are satisfied, whose hopes and expectations are fulfilled. On the contrary, it contains the significant term *telos*, which means the end, the purpose and fullness. The mature are those who keep firmly to the promise that, in the end, *ta panta* will be God's. Maturity consists of the expectancy and singleness of purpose of those who seek first God's Kingdom and his righteousness. The few become that representative number of witnessess whose life and message brings the world into crisis and ultimately to its true end. The opposite of maturity is the attitude of those who want everything for themselves, who are tossed to and fro by every new current of thought or propaganda, who insist on living by their own merit and not by grace.

If the above considerations about God's arithmetic are true, we need a conversion from the widespread wish to become or remain a Christian majority to the biblical criterion of maturity. This does not necessarily imply a condemnation of every *corpus Christianum*, because it may well happen that, at a given time and place, God elects, calls and converts a majority to be his people. Nor does it mean a retreat of the few into a ghetto, for these few stand for all and are entrusted with a mission to all. What this conversion means is that we must leave it to God whether and when he wants to use our worship and witness in order to add to or cut down the number of his militant Church on earth.

The Western churches must free themselves from their assumption that the *corpus Christianum* is the norm, and the minority church living in *diaspora* the exception. On the other hand, small minority churches in the East must be freed from a ghetto-mentality that assumes that God is only concerned with the few and not also with all nations, religions and revolutionary movements. We may pray for the numerical growth of small Christian minorities and rejoice if new members are added. We must also pray for the renewal of large Christian majorities and not panic when God answers our prayer by cutting down our number.

Church history would seem to suggest that growth in maturity often fosters numerical growth in minority church situations,

while in majority situations it often brings about a healthy dimi-
nution of church membership, because many nominal Christians
discover the cost of discipleship. We must leave this matter of
statistics to God, and concentrate all our energy on discerning
and serving God's cosmic mission of reconciliation. Both a majority and a minority church can do this. They both have their
own particular temptations and opportunities.

It may be that God always provides a provisional homeland
for the Church, a *corpus Christianum* on which the world-wide
Christian *diaspora* can fall back, and from which it receives help.
Yet it seems more likely that in our age of universal history, with
its world-wide secularization, all Christians are called to be a minority. However this may be, our main concern is to become the
representative number, to grow in grace and thus to be on the
way to true maturity.

This vision contradicts the old theological saying *extra ec-
clesiam nulla salus* (outside the Church there is no salvation). It
is true that God has wrought the salvation of this world by the
death and resurrection of his Son, and that salvation is, therefore, intimately linked with Christ's body, the Church. The
Church is indeed the agent of salvation. But is she the community
of the saved outside which there is no salvation? Arnold B. Come
believes that neither the old doctrine of double predestination,
nor a shallow and optimistic universalism, nor a doctrine which
limits salvation to an ever-growing Church expresses the full
biblical message. He makes a distinction between the conversion
by which the few elect join the company of the agents of reconciliation, and the crisis of decision to which all are brought by
the witness to God's cosmic redemption. According to him, the
purpose of election is, therefore, not to restrict salvation but to
make it universal.

The Church is representative, *pars pro toto*. Its worship is
the foretaste of the cosmic liturgy, when the whole universe will
join in the praise which the few—standing for all—sing now.
Through worship this world is linked with God's Kingdom. Yet
the Church is also the people of God's mission. This people is
buried like seed, like leaven, like salt in the earth of common humanity. Both its silent as well as its outspoken witness brings a
ferment in world history by which everything is turned upside

down. Criteria of judgment are changed, and millions of individuals, as well as whole nations, races and cultures, are brought to the crisis of decision. This ferment does not create God's Kingdom, but it preserves and prepares the world for it.

These considerations may be on the fringe of heresy, yet they do justice both to the particularity of the Church and to the universality of God's grace that are found together in the Bible. They are one way of expressing what some Christians, fully involved in the industrial innovations, the Asian revolution and conditions behind the Iron Curtain, are discovering to be true. This vision frees our missionary work from nervous fanatical activity and from the paralysis of defeatism. It assigns us our place in God's mission.

NOTES

1. Dr. Donald McGavran founded the Institute of Church Growth and School of World Mission at Fuller Theological Seminary, Pasadena, California.

Christianity Suffers
from "Teacher Complex"

Kosuke Koyama

Kosuke Koyama, the Japanese missionary-theologian who taught in Thailand for eight years, gave this meditation in the chapel of Trinity Theological College, Singapore, as he was about to leave Southeast Asia to join the faculty of Otago University in New Zealand. Following the pithy style of his *Waterbuffalo Theology* (Orbis Books, 1974), Koyama quickly confesses that he does "not see much future for Christianity," because it has become so self-righteous. Christianity, he says, suffers from a "teacher complex"—more interested in teaching than in being taught, in speaking than in listening. He does "not think Christianity in Asia for the last 400 years has really listened to the people." Instead, it has a "crusade complex," and "has become a one-way-traffic religion" of "self-assertion." The Great Commission, by contrast, is—Koyama admonishes— "Christ-like-going," which is "intensely two-ways" and means giving up "one's right-of-way for the sake of the other." His meditation first appeared in the *CCA News* for November 15, 1974, published in Singapore by the Christian Conference of Asia. *Mission Trends No. 1* included Dr. Koyama's article "What Makes a Missionary? Toward Crucified Mind, Not Crusading Mind," which applies his thesis specifically to the missionary vocation.

The theme of this meditation is evangelism. I begin, however, by confessing that I do not see much future for Christianity. I should have some grave reasons for saying something of this sort, but actually, my reason is rather simple. It is because

Christianity has become so self-righteous that I do not see much future for it. It wants to teach. It does not want to learn. It is arrogant. It is suffering from "teacher complex." "God, I thank thee that I am not like other men, extortioners, unjust, adulterers, or even like this tax collector . . ." There is not much future in this type of religion. I realize that I am starting off this meditation with a very strong statement—quite an "unpastoral" approach.

Christianity is a religion. You may protest against this. "All right," you say, "if Christianity is a religion, it is a genuine and true religion over against other misguided, false and man-made religions. Christianity is a faith in the living God in Christ and therefore not a religion in an ordinary sense!"

Please remember that Christianity is not identical with Jesus Christ. A Christian is not Jesus Christ. Christians are supposed to be "Christ-like," but they are only rarely so. Whether we are discouraged at this or not, it is a fact. There is a distance between Jesus Christ and Christianity as we know it. "Not everyone who says to me 'Lord, Lord' shall enter into the Kingdom of heaven, but he who does the will of my Father who is in heaven" (Matt. 7:21). The religion in which Jesus Christ is called "Lord, Lord" is Christianity. But it is very possible that Christians (who call Jesus Christ "Lord, Lord") do not do "the will of my Father." This observation should not shock you. In Paul's letter to the Corinthians which was written about A.D. 53 or 54 the apostle spoke about divisions within the Church (1 Cor. 1:10-17). Division within the Church is not "the will of my Father." If we think everything was fine in the primitive Church but later degenerated, we have a carefree mythology.

Christianity is a historically developed religion just as Hinduism, Buddhism and Islam are. There is then no such thing as a divine, pure and uncontaminated Christianity. As a religion, Karl Barth says, Christianity with other religions must stand under the judgment of the Gospel of Christ. "There will be tribulation and distress for every human being who does evil, the Jew first and also the Greek, but glory and honor and peace for everyone who does good, the Jew first and also the Greek. For God shows no partiality" (Rom. 2:9-11).

This religion called Christianity is, it seems to me, most interested in teaching people, but not interested in being taught by people. It speaks to people, but it does not listen to them. I do not think Christianity in Asia for the last 400 years has really listened to the people. It has ignored people. Ignoring *things* is not so bad, but ignoring *people* is serious. It has listened to its bishops, theologians and financial sponsors. But it really has not listened to the people. It might have listened to God (?) but it did not listen to its neighbors. "Give me a drink"—Jesus sought help from a Samaritan woman (John 4:7). "What is your name?"—Jesus asked a madman (Mark 5:9). In the famous story of evangelism of the chief tax collector, Zacchaeus, Jesus said only, "Zacchaeus, make haste and come down; for I must stay at your house today" (Luke 19:5). He was observing. He was listening. In the synoptic Gospels, don't we get a strong impression that Jesus was not a talkative man, but that he was a careful listener?

Christianity, when we think of its activity in Asia for the last 400 years, has not listened to the Asian peoples. It has been busy planning mission strategy—this campaign and that crusade. People have become the object of evangelism since it is understood by Christians that people are "automatically" living in the darkness and they are untrustworthy, wicked, adulterous and "unsaved," while the believers are "automatically" living in the light and they are trust-worthy, good, not lustful, and "saved." "Teacher complex" expresses itself in "crusade complex." What a comfortable arrangement for the believers! What an irresponsible and easygoing theology!

Christianity has become a one-way-traffic-religion. It is true that Christianity has done much to benefit mankind but it would have done much more if we did not suffer from this "teacher complex." Let's be critical about ourselves. The Christian faith demands such self-criticism. Often this one-way setup has been justified by simply quoting the Great Commission of the Risen Lord: "Go therefore and make disciples of all nations, baptizing them in the name of the Father and of the Son and of the Holy Spirit, teaching them to observe all that I have commanded you" (Matt. 28:19-20). I do not understand this powerful sentence as a guarantee for "one-way-traffic." I believe it is for "Christ-like going" (take note that it is not just go, but "go therefore." That is to say, go on the basis of life and ministry of Jesus Christ, his love, his self-denial, his hope, his death, his resurrection) that we are to make disciples of all nations. "Christ-like going" is not "one-way traffic." It is intensely two-ways. And in this two-way-traffic situation with his people, he gave up his right of way! "The Son of man came not to be served but to serve, and to give his life as a ransom for many" (Matt. 20:28). At the last moment of his life he was mocked by the "church leaders." Please listen:

> So also the chief priests, with the scribes and elders,
> mocked him, saying "He saved others; he cannot save
> himself. He is the King of Israel; let him come down
> now   from   the   cross,   and   we   will   believe   in
> him."   (Matt. 27:41-42)

Then read Matt. 28:19-20 together with Matt. 27:41-44 (or with 16:24-25—then Jesus told his disciples, "If any man would come after me, let him deny himself and take up his cross and follow me. For whoever would save his life will lose it, and whoever would save his life for my sake will find it"). If we go we must be prepared to go the way of self-denial. We want to go, but we do not want to be mocked. Bishops, theologians and church leaders go as long as their spiritual, intellectual and ecclesiastical prestige is safely protected. Our shepherds are just like us. (Or do we mean—do we really mean—what we sing? "Faith of our fathers, holy faith, we will be true till death." Let's not sing what we do not mean. Lie begets lie. Soon we will hypnotize ourselves into believing lie is truth.) "Go therefore" is too dangerous and too risky!

The amazing thing—how utterly amazing—is that it is only in this way of giving up himself that Christ came to us. In his self-denial he came to us. In his dying for us he came to us. This is the heart of the Gospel. At the realization of this truth the Apostolic faith began. Meditation on the Crucified Lord—this is the theme of Christian spirituality and Christian missiology.

One-way-traffic Christianity is an ugly monster. This monster lives by self-assertion not by self-denial. Ugly? Yes. One-way-traffic human relationship is ugly. It is uglier than Count Dracula and Frankenstein's monster put together. I understand that "to be human" means to live in two-way traffic and "to be divine" means to give up one's right-of-way for the sake of the other in this two-way traffic.

I have lived my 43 years of Christian life (I was baptized when I was ten years old) without "crusading." I dislike this word as I dislike a cobra. I do not find it in the Bible.

My occasional crusades against my wife, children and friends have always ended in more unhappiness and alienation. I learned that by crusading I cannot run my own family. I don't think then that crusading has a place in the household of God. "Crusade" is a self-righteous pharisaic (holy war) military word. It does not belong to the language of the "Prince of Peace who died on the Cross." I refuse to sing "Stand up, stand up . . . ," because the hymn does not express the center of the biblical message: "in dying he came to us." It is therefore too cheap and too "ugly" to sing. There is a difference between Jesus Christ and General Westmoreland. I hesitate to sing "Crown him, crown him . . ." I believe there is no need to crown him. He has been crowned already by God. Otherwise, how is the Gospel possible? Don't crusade against Jesus Christ. Evangelism has not made any significant headway in Asia for the last 400 years because Christians crusaded against Asians. When did Christianity become a cheap military campaign? Who made it so? I submit that a good hundred million American dollars, 100 years of crusading with 100,000 "Billy Grahams" will not make Asia Christian. Christian faith does not and cannot be spread by crusading. It will spread without money, without bishops, without theologians, without plannings, and without "Billy Grahams," if people see a crucified mind (not crusading mind) in Christians.

What is this crucified mind? It is the mind of Jesus Christ. It is not a persecution complex. It is not a neurotic mind. It is not a stingy and condemning mind. It is not a paternalistic mind. It is a two-way-traffic mind. It is a mind of self-denial. It is a community-building mind. It is a mind of "in dying I come to you." It is a mind obedient to "go therefore." If we have this mind people will see it. People are perceptive. They will ask the secret of this crucified mind. And that is evangelism.

Our Christianity has become a one-way-traffic religion. Jesus Christ is not! It is not people out there who need repentance. It is we who need repentance. We are far more arrogant than people on the streets. We are bigoted. We are prestige minded. We are money minded. We want to be called "doctor," "bishop," "president." We are self-righteous. We want to teach but we don't want to learn. Christianity suffers from a "teacher complex." We are uglier than we think we are. We are becoming more and more blind because we say we can see (John 9:41).

Christianity is not identical with Jesus Christ. But Jesus Christ stands in the center of Christianity. At the moment of our repentance we see him standing among us. "Lo, I am with you always, to the close of the age" (Matt. 28:20). Because of this promise, the promise that brings forth our repentance, Christianity has a future. The future belongs to those who repent. As we repent, we begin to see our neighbors, their spirituality, their frustrations, their aspirations, to which Christ is ever speaking. "Blessed are the meek, for they shall inherit the earth" (Matt. 5:5). "The time is fulfilled, and the Kingdom of God is at hand; repent, and believe in the Gospel" (Mark 1:15).

What's Ahead for Evangelism?

Martin E. Marty

Using a working definition—"to evangelize means to meet people in situations where the Gospel of Jesus Christ is given the opportunity to change individuals and groups and to bring them toward wholeness"—Martin E. Marty reviews various models or styles of American evangelization from the past and shows that "not all American evangelizers did things the way Billy Graham or Oral Roberts do now." He also sees "some signs of a break with the past, so far as the role of the evangelizer" in America is concerned. For instance, "No longer do loyalties rooted in habit, blood-inheritance and undisturbed community hold together the evangelizing community." Another sign of the break is that "no longer does biblical religion have a monopoly," and "the ever-wider pluralism of choice alters people's way of looking at Christian options." When looking at some newer styles of evangelization, Marty acknowledges the possibility that "mere Christian 'presence' accomplishes the evangelistic task," but—he reminds the Church—"sooner or later the story has to be told." Dr. Marty is professor of the history of modern Christianity at the University of Chicago Divinity School and associate editor of *The Christian Century.* His book *Righteous Empire: The Protestant Experience in America* (Dial Press, 1970) won a National Book Award in 1972. This article was an address at the annual meeting of the U.S. Catholic Conference of Major Superiors of Men in 1974, and first appeared in the December 1974 issue of *The Lutheran* (Philadelphia), published by the Lutheran Church in America.

During the 1960s the social activist received attention in religious circles. Now in the 1970s the evangelist is back in the spotlight.

If ten years ago the good Christian was supposed to get out of the pew in order to work for justice and peace, now he or she is asked to ring doorbells for Jesus or go to rallies in his name. The Bible knows of no such either/ors, but our world does. So while the evangelistic forces currently enjoy their half of the inning, we ought to scurry back into the Christian and American pasts to find clues about the meaning of these ventures.

First, a working definition of evangelism is necessary. For me, to evangelize means to meet people in situations where the Gospel of Jesus Christ is given the opportunity to change individuals and groups and to bring them toward wholeness. Evangelism, in other words, is to "save" them and to situate them in the context of Christian community so that their lives will be enhanced. Then they can face together those questions of values, meanings and service that also have eternal dimensions.

The evangelizer is the human agent in this task. But the evangelizer and the people to be reached live in ever-changing situations and circumstances. American history reveals a succession of these.

A backward glance can be creative. It helps us to be free from today's stereotypes. Not all American evangelizers did things the way Billy Graham or Oral Roberts do now. Historical reflection also reminds us that we can change our way of thinking about evangelism without necessarily being untrue to an unchanging tradition. Finally, since something of most earlier styles somehow lives on among or around us, a look at what was conceived or done in the past will help today's Christians explain themselves.

Let me paint with a very broad brush and without much detail seven successive pictures of American evangelization.

1) The earliest images deal with evangelization as conquest, as the superimposing of a new religious culture on existing ones. Spanish, Portuguese, French Catholic and some of the British Protestant endeavors in the New World simply carried on some unlovely ancient Christian styles. They tried to use power and the sword to enlarge the Christian world.

Who bothered to understand the American Indians who were here already or the blacks who were brought here? Christians knew they were superior and that they had a right to impose themselves on others.

This heritage lives on in the terminology of some mass evangelism: people speak of having "crusades" for Christ. Why they need to choose the name of one of the least Christlike movements in Christian history to explain what they are about is not fully clear. But it hints at something disturbing.

2) This style remains creative; it is based on what evangelization meant among the English Puritan colonists in America. These fathers and founders considered the whole colony to be "the people of God," a covenanted community on the model of God's ancient Israel. They also knew that not all people "owned the covenant" or lived up to it. So evangelizing meant what today we would call "consciousness alteration" so that members of the community would see things in a new light. This mode lives on today whenever people show concern for the sensibilities of the whole (and half-faithless) American people *as people.*

3) The beginnings of modern-style evangelization in America derive less from the First Great Awakening of the 1720s-1740s (as we have just sideswiped it), and more from the Second Great Awakening that began about 1801. In a free society and on the frontier, preachers had to *compete* for people. They were pagans or "nothingarians" and evangelists came to help them "get religion." (H.L. Mencken reminds us that to "get religion" is an American concept and term.)

Churches took steps to rouse emotions, induce guilt, produce conversions. Out of these efforts grew the camp meetings, the anxious bench, the sawdust trail. In this period the evangelized were subsequently expected not just to chatter about their Jesus-experience but to go out and reform the world.

4) By the middle of the nineteenth century, later immigrants, many of them of Catholic or continental Protestant background, were crowding the cities and the backwoods. They came from European state churches and were often lackadaisical members. They needed to be corralled and cajoled into religious activity.

Evangelizers "met people at the boat," and shepherded

them in urban ghettos and rural valleys. They used the language of conversion on people who probably had always thought of themselves as having been Christian. Some day we may see the evangelization of the suburbs in the 1950s as an extension of this "meeting the boat" style.

5) This style picked up where the third one left off: the religious awakening and converting moved from frontier and forest to the cities. The urban and industrial setting produced rootless, alienated people. A century ago a number of evangelists found formulas for reaching them, and in mass revivals they promoted a new gospel of individualism, of rescue from the world.

Dwight L. Moody was the grand man of this movement; he was aped by lesser people, many of them entrepreneurs and exploiters. Now what mattered was a personal decision for Christ, of turning the back on the world, of obsession with "how'm-I-doing,-God." Needless to say, this manner of evangelizing remains with us.

6) The middle of the twentieth century saw evangelism partly bureaucratized, an element in the committee efforts of the churches. While the earlier five styles lived on, they tended to be fused now in a concept of evangelizing as programming for church growth. Energetic church extension boards sent agents, paid for by those already settled in churches, to start new congregations. Committees and programs were developed in parishes so that people would not have to rely on spontaneity but would have intensive schemes for winning new people.

The more conservative churches have thrived on this model. What are called the "mainline" churches have often grown relaxed or unsure about themselves in such efforts.

7) Finally, especially during the 1960s, some leaders took up strands that had been neglected in many earlier styles and tried to convince others that evangelism really meant changing people's social circumstances and working for human betterment. Conversion was played down, emotional experiences were shunned. No one can read the good Samaritan story or the parable in Matthew 25 (about serving "the least of Christ's brethren") without recognizing that the evangel has to do with the whole individual in whole societies. But the whole society is a

place of complex self-interests, and the Christian evangelizer does not have his or her way in it alone.

There was backlash to this style and there is now some retreat. Yet the people of the 1960s did reinforce the old idea that rescue from the world is not the only motif in historic evangelization.

While I have dropped clues along the way about heritages from these earlier approaches, questions are now in order about what might be learned from these activities that have shaped so many of our own.

Surprisingly, there are some common features. In all of them, evangelizers have worked with a clear Christian focus. "Evangel" is a particular word, rooted in a specific experience of God's activity in Christ. Generalized doing good or speaking inspirational language is not the same thing as evangelization.

Also, the evangelizers' activities have always been marked by intentionality. They rarely think of evangelization as an automatic spill-over of Christian life and work. They devise means and instruments for carrying out their purposes and find measures for determining success and failure.

To the concepts of focus and intentionality we add the language of community. Now and then we hear that a mere Christian "presence" accomplishes the evangelistic task. God can and does work through silence and is served by people who do not speak his name; the church can show forth his love without a lot of tract-passing and chatter.

But American evangelizers have also known that sooner or later the story has to be told and they use the language of specific Christian communities to do so. They never work wholly outside the context of such communities. Some of them relied on WASP culture, others on Catholic truth; many of them stretch the point and seem to strike out on their own. But sooner or later, again, they know that they and their converts have to "check in" to some part of the whole Christian church.

In American history evangelizers have always implied personal involvement between themselves and the evangelized. Mass evangelism makes such contact virtually impossible and church programming for evangelism often looks computerized. But even in those impersonal settings much is made of the need for personal sharing of God's love in Jesus Christ. Phillips Brooks once spoke of preaching as being "truth through personality," and most evangelizers have known that they have to risk themselves in building ties to people.

Finally, the history of American evangelism shows that most evangelizers have been rather nervous about "holistic" concepts. They are not sure that bodies have to be dealt with along with souls, physical needs with spiritual ones, whole communities along with isolated individuals. Such concerns would make their work more controversial; they might slow down the door-bell-ringers and emotion-wringers. But evangelizers can never quite get out of their systems the Gospel's portrayal of Jesus ministering to people's basic and total needs.

History informs us about today's evangelistic work; tradition can impose a dead hand on new efforts just as it can provide identity and clarity. But we do not live in the past and are not wholly determined by it. If we can point to seven earlier stages, we can assume that later ones are in the making. Recent American history points to some signs of a break with the past, so far as the role of the evangelizer is concerned. We can pick out a few signposts and landmarks.

No longer does a vivid sense of the whole covenanted community motivate Christian evangelism. America is too secular, too pluralistic. Now and then we hear about one nation "under God" and about a single "civil religion." But most of the time people are not being called back to the corral from which they strayed. They are approached as lonely individuals who do not yet know who they are or where they belong.

No longer does the protection of a ghetto provide all meaning for evangelized people. It is true that a glance at a religious atlas still finds some faith or other dominant in many parts of the country: Baptist in the deep south, Methodist in the upper south, Mormon in Utah, Lutheran in the upper midwest, Catholic on the coasts and in urban areas. But the atlas is capable of creating illusions.

People are not easily segregated when they are converted and they will continue to come into contact with people whose faith will not reinforce their own. For this reason the more aggressive and nervous conservative groups often try and succeed in efforts to build psychic walls around their converts. They thus prosper, if at the expense of some Christian virtues, while the high risk groups that send people back into open exposure in the world experience some erosion and leakage.

No longer do loyalties rooted in habit, blood-inheritance and undisturbed community hold together the evangelizing community. Today people can escape their own religious context and any others that they would like. In a frontier town or an urban ghetto someone was always watching, always predisposing people to act in specific ways.

This means that if one chooses to respond to an evangelistic call today, he or she ought to be capable of knowing what is going on and what the commitment involves.

No longer does biblical religion have a monopoly. Hare Krishna, the Unification Church, Transcendental Meditation, occult, African and many Eastern religions as well as marginally Christian groups often produce the most aggressive missionaries. A glance at an airport newsstand will show who is trying to evangelize through the printed page; rarely does historic Christianity make its pitch there. The ever-wider pluralism of choice alters people's way of looking at Christian options.

No longer does the religious assumption prevail. Once upon a time it was assumed that the good citizen would be a Christian or Jew or whatever—even if fewer went to church in the past than do now. But today's setting is sufficiently secular that people can pay no heed to the evangelizer and suffer no social stigma at all. Who will notice?

No longer does our culture predispose people to be assured that their conversion or awakening is "once and for all." Yes, the language of decision for Christ and of total commitment implies it. But too many converts have already been too many things. Anyone with eyes can guess that today's young Jesus freak or Pentecostal may have been "into" astrology or Zen last year and next year might move on into straight secularity, Fundamentalism, the Catholic alumni association or a hundred other options.

Not all evangelizers have to become historians, and historical awareness will not help solve all problems facing those who would evangelize today. But the presence of a variety of models in the short span of American history should free people from conformity to only a current version or two.

Evangelizing does not have to mean manipulating or exploiting people, turning the Gospel into a public relations machine, or computerizing conversions and then building insulation around the happy saved. It can proceed with full awareness of values and value systems in other cultures, with regard for those who do not respond and with new love for those who do.

We can expect that debates about the evangelistic community and about the role of evangelism in the task of meeting all human needs will continue. Crusades, wall-building, computerized mass evangelism, freaking-out for Jesus will go on. At their side will also be subtler but perhaps more durable efforts to see God's love in Jesus Christ spoken about and acted out in our ever-changing environment.

1. Evangelism by conquest: Enlist path

2. Evangelism by consciousness alteration—"see new light" "colonist America"

3. Evangelism not just for an experience but to reform the world. Start about 1801

4. Mid-1800s: Evangelism by "meeting the boat" (immigrants) helping them get settled.

5. Picked up from no.3: Personal decision for Christ. "How am I doing—Lord?"

6. Mid-1900s: Evangelism by "sending"

7. 1960s ⇒ Conversion played down: evangelism by changing social conditions

II: Priorities and Strategies

Church Growth in Africa

James Sangu

In this excerpt from his report to the 1974 Synod of Catholic Bishops in Rome, Bishop James Sangu, chairman of the Tanzanian episcopal conference, describes the vitality of the church in Africa and the continuing need for missionaries. His report was published in the October 24, 1974, issue of *Origins*, published by the National Catholic Documentary Service, Washington, D. C.

Christianity in Africa is experiencing the greatest numerical growth on a sustained basis (7.5 million Christians per year) of any continent or of any period of history. This startling fact is one of the many hopeful signs in analyzing the present state of evangelization in Africa. . . . Christianity in Africa is growing twice as fast as the population.

There are some who insist that for the young church of Africa to become quickly self-supporting it is imperative that expatriate missionaries should leave because their presence constitutes a hindrance to the growth of the Church in Africa. This is a narrow and misleading viewpoint. Missionaries are still needed and welcome. The establishment of the local Church demands that the local clergy assume more responsibilities and that expatriates be evermore willing to play a *supporting role*. Also, the presence of some expatriate missionaries would be an expression of the universality and catholicity of the church, the same as would be the presence of some African clergy in Europe, North America and other parts of the world . . .

We are confident that through the grace of God there will be a bright future for the Church in Africa. We dare to forecast that Africa will truly be the land of Christianity, the land of saints.

Evangelization
and Development

Samuel Rayan, S.J.

From India, Samuel Rayan, S.J., asks if working for liberation, humanization and development "is the task proper to a missionary, whether and how this could be counted as part of the Church's Gospel mission, and in what manner and measure it is related to evangelization." In discussing these issues Rayan maintains that "the unity of God's plan" does not permit a dualism or dichotomy of faith and life, material and spiritual, sacred and profane. For him, to evangelize "has to do . . . with the creation and revelation of the new brotherhood and sisterhood of Jesus' dream, with its realization and expression at all levels of life, including the economic and the political." He believes that "Jesus' own evangelizing ministry . . . can be spelled out in the language of liberation and development." In evangelization, therefore, "preaching and development work all converge to gospel human existence." Born in Kerala, India, Father Rayan has his doctorate in theology from Rome's Gregorian University, and is presently dean of the Jesuit theological faculty in Delhi, India. Since 1968 he has been one of the Catholic members of the Faith and Order Commission of the World Council of Churches. His paper, prepared originally for the American Jesuit Missions Conference in St. Paul, Minnesota, in August 1974, is reprinted from *Studies in the International Apostolate of Jesuits*, volume 3, number 2 (November 1974), published by Jesuit Missions, Inc., in Washington, D.C.

Introduction

The focus of this paper is on India. The paper proposes to

study the relationship between development and evangelization in the context of the Christian mission in India today.

New Trends and Questions

A Jesuit missionary, Belgian by birth, is working in three Indian states: Orissa, Karnataka and Tamilnadu. He does not preach, does not administer the sacrament of baptism, does not seek to make converts to the Catholic Church. He is concerned rather with what he calls community building. The following is how I understood his program as he described it to me in an interview.

Mine is action to help the exploited and neglected masses of people to become conscious of themselves, conscious that they are somebody, that they matter, and are to be counted. Call it humanization, if you like. For centuries now the poor in these places have been led to believe that they are nothing, they have no rights, they are part of nature and its processes, and tools of an economic system run for the benefit of the few who alone mattered. They must now be enabled to emerge as self-conscious, responsible, free individuals, shapers and not slaves of nature and economic realities, and architects of their own future. My work is meant to help them become persons. Some of its salient features may be pointed qut.

The starting point is the realization by all that alone and in isolation they are nobody; they can only be somebody together, in solidarity, as a community. Along with that goes the insight that a community, to be real and rich in fellowship, cannot be made up of homogenous men and women of the same caste status. It has to be heterogenous; different castes and the casteless have to mix, live side by side, draw water from the same wells, buy from the same shops and increasingly share life and collaborate in projects designed for their own common growth and well-being. But persons can scarcely be somebody and develop a community-consciousness unless they are at home somewhere, have an environment and react to it affectively and creatively. Refugees have no consciousness of being somebody; they have no home, no environment that speaks to them, or reflects their spirit, imagination, toil or tradition. Refugees are nobodies until they settle down, build a home and tame their surroundings. The dispossessed masses must have something of the world as their own human space. All this and all further growth calls for their liberation. They need to be liberated above all from fear—fear of the landlord, fear of insecurity, of taking risks, of failure, of their own voices and of speaking up. One can understand the poor man's fear of the landlord and higher castes when one remembers that for centuries he has been kept down by threat and had his hands crushed or legs broken for the least resistance or the smallest "theft." My program educates people spontaneously and collectively to resist every kind of injustice and inhumanity, to speak their mind, to protest and to demand land in reparation for injury done. It leads them to see that security is not in craven submission but in clear thought and courageous action, even when action involves risks. There is further need to liberate people from determinism, from belief in the inevitability of the *samsara* cycle of births and deaths, from helpless resignation to *karma* understood as fate, from undue dependence on horoscopes and the stars. This is achieved chiefly through diversification and possible change of employment. So people come to realize that they need not be doing what their forebears did in the way they did it. Diversification of work also means liberation of abilities into various fields of activity, leading to discovery of themselves through discovery of new talents, for they have been told for long and led to believe that their abilities were such and so much and no other and no more. Finally, it is necessary to release and develop the leadership potential of the community. The young people are enabled to identify and utilize leadership opportunities that are abundant in the life of the exploited masses. Leadership is stirred up through youth organizations that try to find out the truth about the community and its actual situation, and to be friends to all persons and foe to every form of inhumanity and injustice.

This is what this missionary has been trying to do for several years with the aid of all kinds of funding and organizing agencies, and—with large sums of money provided from these sources—he has been building villages in which the brahmin and the pariah live as neighbors, drink from the same well and work side by side. Certain factors in the program, like funds from abroad, or the too exclusive role of the missionary in decision-making, may have to be looked into critically and re-evaluated. But there can be agreement that on the whole the program is meant to be a process of liberation and humanization making for development. The real question many raise is whether this is the task proper to a missionary, whether and how this could be counted as part of the Church's Gospel mission, and in what manner and measure it is related to evangelization.

The question is of more than local relevance. It is being directed to many missions and missionaries doing developmental work in many parts of India, and perhaps to numerous church ventures and church people engaged in a struggle for human liberation the world over. A 1971 survey showed foreign and Indian Jesuit missionary involvement in small and large scale rural-development projects and food-for-work schemes; programs for construction of wells, bunds, houses, roads; projects for the distribution of bullocks, pumpsets, hybrid seeds, fertilizers and pesticides; schemes for recovery of land from money lenders, for irrigation and terracing of fields; organizing of credit banks, savings schemes, grain banks and cooperatives in order to eliminate middlemen, to liberate people from the clutches of money lenders, and to educate them to provident planning of their own economic and social life; running technical institutes, institutes for social service, agricultural training centers, land development banks, and serving in the campaign against hunger and disease, as well as in projects that include hospitals, dispensaries, nursing schools, orphanages, technical schools, training programs and socio-economic plans. And there are other missionaries than Jesuits committed to India's development. On the world scene there have been, in recent years, numberless interventions of national hierarchies, bishops' conferences, individual bishops, religious orders, religious men and women in concrete situations of social, economic and political import. They have analyzed situations, exposed facts, registered protests, joined picket lines, courted arrest, fasted, organized resistance, raised funds for development programs in preference to building cathedrals or canonizing saints, financed liberation movements, organized boycotts and sales in favor of developing countries and rights of peoples, and joined national and international agencies to struggle together for justice, equality, human dignity, peace, land reform readjustment of trade and tariff and to conscientize and awaken the silent masses.

With these facts before us we ask ourselves what relationship exists between them and the Gospel of Jesus or the Church's mission to communicate the message of salvation in Christ so that people may respond in faith and find wholeness. What relationship is there between eternal life and one's historical activity for earthly prosperity? How does faith in the Crucified link up with social action, political conflict and economic development? What is the meaning of the faith in a life committed to struggle against injustice and alienation? Or, what is the meaning of such commitment in a life of faith? Is the Kingdom of God bound up in any sense with the building up of this world and of human history? We also reverse the question and ask, what is the glad tidings we can meaningfully bring to the masses of men living in destitution and unfreedom, and to whole continents submerged in misery or blocked by oppression? In the face of widespread poverty and human degradation, what is the shape of love and service Jesus is demanding from his disciples?

The Wider Mission

A bishop in North India told me the story of a Muslim girl who, after her university studies, settled in a remote village and having lived through initial difficulties and risks, deployed in the village a many-sided program of social service. She soon won the respect, confidence and cooperation of the entire locality, and was able to see the village improve in various ways and lift itself up. Her idea, too, was to transform the village into a community of responsible people. At the end of five years or so she planned to leave; she had given all she could give in the circumstances.

But the people pressed her to stay. She consented to do so only if they agreed to withdraw all court cases and settle them amicably among themselves. They agreed and the girl decided to stay. The bishop who told me the story was delegating two nuns to stay with the girl for some time to study her work and learn its lessons.

This Muslim girl's work is likewise for liberation and humanization, laying foundations for development. Could it also be included within the scope of our inquiry? The thinking Indian Christian naturally inclines to do so, and to ask if this girl's work too is not a ministry of evangelization by which the Church of God is being built in spite of the fact that the girl is no missionary in the classical Christian sense of the word, and that her sense of mission is in no explicit way related to the Gospel of Jesus or to the work entrusted to his Church. The question in this instance has deeper theological implications for the understanding not only of evangelization but of the person and mission of Christ Jesus himself.

A similar question may be posed before the phenomenon of hundreds of dacoits whose ancestors resisted the British and who have been thwarting the efforts of the police to suppress them, choosing to heed the appeal of Gandhi's nonviolent disciples, Venoba Bhave and Jai Prakash Narain, and surrender to them, lay down arms and be willing to undergo trial in court and accept in peace and a spirit of penitence whatever sentence might be passed on them. The style of life that men like Venoba and Jai Prakash lead, the purity of their character and the ideals for which they stand have such impact on the minds of others that dacoits surrender themselves to them, rich men surrender land for distribution among the landless and young people offer their strength for free work on behalf of the needy. To the question whether such lives and the fruit they bear belong in the sphere of the Gospel, the answer is often a ready Yes. To the further question whether they belong within the process of evangelizing the world, is there a ready answer?

The Background

I do not know how central and vital you feel these questions to be, or how trite and marginal. To us in India and, I believe, to

Christians all over Asia, they are basic. The reasons for their being so may be gathered from the many factors that are leading to new thinking in India and Asia on mission and evangelization. If we are talking about evangelization in a concrete way, we cannot but take into account the experience of life that is India's at the moment. No word, not surely the Word of salvation, can be truly spoken to India today without in the very act speaking to its present experience, within which the mission is situated and from which its problems, challenges and embarrassments arise. Mission in India with its ideal of Church extension, its relief services and colonial educational system has been challenged since independence by numerous factors:

(1) by the people's commitment to nation-building through planned development. In this context are seen the inadequacy and the dangers of relief programs which concentrated on the victims of social evil, leaving the evil itself untouched.

(2) by secular ideologies like Marxism that are concerned with justice and human well-being on earth, and have created awareness of problems and needs unrecognized by churches and missions, and have succeeded in giving to marginalized masses a measure of dignity, freedom and hope that the churches and missions have not cared to, or been unable to give.

(3) by the secular historical hope thus aroused as against the eschatological salvation that has been the strong point of colonial missions.

(4) by the new positive approach in the Church and in the religions of India to the world and its values that may now be loved and cultivated for their own intrinsic worth and not merely for their service to religions and ecclesiastical ends.

(5) by the deepening preoccupation everywhere with the harrowing conditions of the life of the masses in the Third World and of the poor in all countries, with the forces and processes that exploit and oppress them and with action and struggle for their liberation.

(6) by the realization that existing economic arrangements in the world today in aid or trade or tariff are all geared to the benefit and profit of the already affluent Western (Christian?) countries to the detriment of nations struggling to develop.

(7) by its remembered association with the colonial system

from which it profited and to which is traced much of the bro-
kenness and malaise of these blocked and fettered lands.

(8) by the memory people have of the two great wars of the
century in which the colonial competitive enterprise culminated;
after all that cruelty and injustice, all that carnage and destruction, what honest message of human salvation could be expected
from the Christian West, or be offered by missionary movements
initiated by the West?

(9) by the striving of newly independent peoples to rebuild
their consciousness as nations, their national self and national
pride; and this means for India a revival of its ancient culture,
languages, traditions and symbols. In this context a great deal of
the classical mission with its pretensions to "civilize" began to
appear very much out of date and out of place.

(10) Pride in our national heritage has been particularly
keen in regard to spiritual and religious traditions. If the West is
rich in science and technology, India considers herself rich in
spirituality and wisdom. Proselytizing is therefore resented as a
slur on the religious patrimony of the people and as a new type
of colonial dominance if not a continuation of the old.

(11) A new awareness is growing among Indian Christians
of the universality of God's saving grace and the cosmic significance of Christ. From this results a fresh appreciation of other
religions as God's saving provisions within the one history of the
one humanity rooted and crowned in Christ. With that there
began to subside that type of missionary zeal that had been
whipped up by visions of the unbaptized dying and descending
into hell as leaves fall in autumn.

(12) Along with that and with a growing sense of the depth
of history, a new religious horizon is emerging that relativizes
the Church as a limited historical realization of the purposes of
God for humankind.

All this then naturally affected the concept of mission and
the practice of evangelization. Many missionaries felt that the
shaken or eroded credibility of the mission should be rebuilt with
a more effective witnessing than verbal preaching and relief
work. That is how the new style of missionary concern began to
grow, and an ever greater number of missionaries took to heavy
development projects, and programs of social revolution, eco-

nomic growth and structural change. Debate followed. An International Theological Seminar on Evangelization was held in October, 1971, and an All India Consultation in October, 1973. A survey of viewpoints among Jesuit missionaries was made in 1971. The first question posed for the survey was about the relationship between evangelization and development. The answers offered showed four different trends of thought.

No Part of Evangelization

For some, evangelization consists in preaching the Gospel with a view to bringing men and women of other faiths or no faith to an explicit acceptance of Christ and his Church. Other activities like relief and development programs or food and health services may be necessary as exercise of Christian charity in given circumstances, but form no part of evangelization proper. At the most they serve as a means of approach and contact.

This view rests on a theological and spiritual tradition which neatly distinguishes the religious from the profane, and sees a discontinuity between the natural and the supernatural. The earth does not evolve into heaven, nor does historical experience flower into eschatological salvation. Salvation comes through the Cross, through the uprooting of man from the world through death and the uprooting of the world in the cataclysm of the Parousia. Pilgrims on earth, we should not seek to build on the road, nor store up treasures which are bound to perish. We are sent to preach not earthly prosperity but Jesus Crucified. Jesus never spoke of development; his Gospel keeps its distance with regard to material goods; its eschatological perspective deemphasizes the world and temporal well-being. He showed no interest in structural change, and did nothing for the political liberation of his own people. He knew that the Kingdom of God did not consist in affluence, political freedom or human justice. One points occasionally to the West to prove that material prosperity, technical progress and advancement of science need not bring moral transformation or increase of faith or spiritual liberation. Wealth and well-being often degrade man and dull his sense of

God, while poverty and grief awaken it. There are missionaries who hold up as ideal the simplicity, piety and joy of the unlettered, exploited, half-starved villagers and slum-dwellers. Development activities divert the Church from her sole task of preaching Christ. They are a betrayal of her mission and a sign of her secularization.

Recently an Indian Jesuit whose mission led him into action for the liberation of *Adivasis* (aboriginal tribes) and *Harijans* (casteless and enslaved groups) from various kinds of oppression and harassment by caste Hindus, landlords and money-lenders has been shifted from his work site by his religious superior. If it was to avoid conflict and save the mission that the superior yielded to pressure from high places in the government, the action implies an abstract conception of evangelization and salvation unrelated to concrete experiences and situations of the people who are to be saved. Another Jesuit who wanted to contest a seat to the State Legislature in order to become the voice of the silent tribal masses was asked by superiors to go "lay" for the whole period of his political service. The Jesuit organization was apparently unwilling to be associated with the priest's eventual struggles with the powers that be on behalf of the downtrodden. Why so, if not for a conception of mission in which political action for the poor has no place?

The history of the Church in Kerala (South India) is a good illustration of this conception of mission. This Christian community started in the fourth century or earlier as a mission from Syria and has flourished in Kerala all these centuries with deep religiosity expressed in terms of church buildings, church worship, privileged clergy, pious practices, celebration of Saints and "Christian" names, but without in the least touching, leavening or transforming society, its caste structures, its economics of disparity and exploitation, its traditions of holding the masses in dependence and degradation. Even today this Church is preoccupied with clerical concerns, is anti-intellectual and traditional in thought and theology, is negative in its attitude toward the arts, and paternalistic and intolerant of freedom and of humanly rich emotions and relationships. Is the cause of this state of affairs to be sought in the Gnosticism of Syria, or in the allegedly world-denying traditions of Buddhism or Hinduism, or in the fact that the earliest Christian groups in Kerala were merchant colonies immigrating from western Asia?

For we must note that merchant and colonial missions tend to tailor the Gospel to suit the economic and political interests of their sponsors. As Philip Potter pointed out in his report to the Bangkok Assembly of the World Council of Churches Commission on World Mission and Evangelism, "the period of the western mission to the continents of colored people was a period of European and North American political and economic imperialism. There were features of the missionary movement which contributed to or reinforced the disease of racism and particularly white racism. Mission agencies have been and still are, to a greater or lesser degree, involved in this (cultural, spiritual, economic and political) domination. . . . Mission agencies and even national churches may be identified with the colonial power structures." Such missions could not proclaim the political and social message of the Gospel nor effectually announce the dignity of people, the equality of persons, fundamental human rights, freedom of individuals and peoples, social and national justice or international decencies; they could not do it without undermining the colonial system, fomenting revolt and cutting the ground from under their feet. Missionaries therefore confined themselves to "spiritual" things, letting the dehumanizing forces be, leaving the captain and the viceroy to enslave humans, and destroy the rhythm of growth and developmental potential of whole peoples and continents. They had to distinguish sharply between the sacred and the secular, preach an individualistic eschatological salvation, and a vertical, a-political, a-social, innocuous, supernatural Gospel. Churches born of such missions have as a rule remained uncreative and sterile.

Fruit of Evangelization

The second view agrees with the first in that it understands evangelization in terms of preaching and conversion, but differs from it by accepting that development activity is related to evangelization as its direct result and consequence. It holds that the preaching of the Gospel and conversion to Christianity has a

liberating and "civilizing" effect that therefore should not be
thought of in total isolation from evangelization nor entirely neglected by the preacher of the Gospel.

This position may be accepted in substance and principle as
far as the affirmation goes, provided evangelization is properly
understood and the claim made for it is not exclusive. It is valid
if evangelization is more than a matter of words, rites and impositions, if the mission itself is a felt presence of the Word made
flesh seeking a home among humans, and a clear appeal to men
and women that they too may realize the new style and quality
of life disclosed in Jesus. But to support it by factual data is as
difficult a task as to support the claim of a casual relationship
between the Christian faith of the West and the West's technological and economic ascendency over the rest of the world. In
fact the thesis seems to overlook such facts as the socio-
economic underdevelopment of Christian peoples in Latin
America and Southern and Eastern Europe; or the economic and
technical progress of Japan, which never let itself be broken by
colonial dominance nor disturbed by colonial missions; or India's
industrial and agricultural wealth, which was the dream of Europe
in the sixteenth century and the coveted goal of its East India
companies. The tilting of the balance in favor of the West came
about in the last 130 years, not through a more complete obedience to the Gospel faith in Northern and Western Europe and
in the United States, but through the gun, through colonial
plunder, slave trade, slave labor, child labor, racial discrimination, the creation of a dispossessed proletariat, and the destruction of the soul and life styles of many peoples.

Perhaps in the beginning of the Christian movement, the
Gospel brought a new sense of dignity and historical hope to the
enslaved and to the downtrodden, and pressed for new social
structures and new patterns of human relationships. The ideal
was realized partially and for a while in the experiments in community life within the Church. But the leaven lost its ferment as
the Church became increasingly assimilated to the State. In the
colonial era the conquering Christian armies, which secured and
supported the far flung missions of the time and utilized them for
their own political and economic purposes and destroyed them
when they did not serve imperialistic designs, were always there

to plunder, humiliate and dehumanize hitherto free and often economically advanced peoples who were in the end left emasculated, broken and blocked. What were once developing countries have, at the close of the colonial period, become underdeveloped and fettered in spite of the colonial brand of evangelization. Or perhaps due to it in part.

It is as a rule in the Christian communities of India—and, I believe, of other former colonies—one finds the greatest measure of alienation, westernization, denationalization and apathy, if not opposition, to national liberation movements. The clericalism of the Catholic system brought by the missions, its attempt to control everything through impositions and prohibitions, liturgies in dead languages, alien theologies, devotions, attitudes and style of leadership have acted as negative factors in the process of humanization and development. Even now missionaries lapse into actions and attitudes detrimental to human growth. Note for instance the use of the possessive and paternalistic "our" in the following quotes from missionaries working for the betterment of villagers and tribals. "Our Catholics belong to the outcasts group . . . . our Catholics belong to the case of weavers . . . . in the last 20 years our Catholics have improved. . . ." "This applies to our Christians . . . . our Christians learn to help themselves . . . . most of our Christians have been helped . . ." "Our Catholics have a desire . . ." "many of our Catholic children . . ." "I realize that unless our villagers are educated . . . our tribals will not be able . . ." Is it significant that this style of speech is peculiar to foreign missionaries?

Indirect Evangelization

The third opinion is that through works that liberate peoples, develop society and promote humanization, the values and attitudes of the Gospel are shared, its spirit and culture communicated. The quality of individual lives and of the social reality improves thereby and comes closer to the ideals of the Gospel. These services therefore constitute proper, though indirect, evangelization, while verbal presentation of the Gospel constitutes direct evangelization.

But if there are only words and they never become flesh and the reality they point to is in no measure made present, the Gospel can scarcely be said to have been communicated. If however work is necessary to incarnate the Word, both are mutually complementary, and equally direct or indirect. Together they serve the Kingdom, realize its values and "gospel" the world. If development is called indirect evangelization because the name of Jesus is not mentioned, or the Church organization is not benefitted, then the question will have to be raised as to what is a real name as distinct from a label, and whether the mission is the Church's service of itself or of the Kingdom of God.

The classic work of Jesuits in India, described as indirect evangelization, is education at school and college levels. This could be evangelization if it contributed to the nation's human and social development. But as a matter of fact, being a remnant of the colonial system, designed originally to serve British imperialist interests in India, the education to which Jesuits here are heavily committed caters for the most part to an elite upper-class minority, succeeds only in uprooting and alienating them from the nation and the masses, in enhancing their privileged positions and consolidating their powers of exploitation. The efficiency and influence of our educational institutions have been a factor in retarding the radical reform that is necessary. Our contribution to original thinking and research in education has been negligible, and our response to Gandhi's original contribution, analogous to Freire's and springing from a sense of Indian realities at grass-roots level, has been nil. Something perhaps in the direction of development-evangelization could be achieved if we were to invent and deploy a process of educating, awakening and organizing the masses to understand their situation and struggle for their liberation.

The Two Are Identical

Jesuits in Ranchi maintain that the relation between development and evangelization has never been a problem to them. In their view and work the two always belonged together; development work in fact grew out of evangelization. It is recognized that the Ranchi mission really began with Lievens' work of liberating tribals from oppression by landlords and helping them defend their rights in the courts of law. It advanced when Hoffman's Credit Bank saved them from money lenders, and the grain bank gave shape and consistency to their economic and social life. It remains, however, to ask whether the work of liberation and of social consolidation of the tribals would have been considered evangelization and progress of the Kingdom of God, even if few or no tribals had sought instruction in the faith and baptism. Or, would their failure to seek these have had to be viewed as insensitivity to a God-given sign? In other words, should or need peoples' acknowledged experience of God's justice and love, mediated through Christian action always lead to and express itself in visible and social membership of the institutional Church?

Indian and foreign Jesuit missionaries who are engaged in social and economic development in various parts of the country, bear witness to the validity of the Ranchi experience. Some of them wrote in 1971:

> When one is in the work of development, one is bringing the justice and love of God to one's brothers and sisters; if this is not evangelization, then I would like to know what it is. (J. Knecht, working with Food for Work Project in Bihar).

> I never read in the Gospels about Christ opening schools, teaching Aramaic, Hebrew or geography. I do read how he fed the hungry and cured the sick. It is true that "it would not be right for us to neglect the word of God so as to give out food" (Acts 6:3); but please read the rest and see how the Holy Spirit selected so many (and the "apostles . . . laid their hands on them") to carry out the social "apostolate" that we try to carry on. (J. Garcia, engaged in large-scale rural development, financed by USAID and CRS).

> In the particular field where I find myself I meet "Katkaris," seminomad *Adivasis* . . . . The missionary is "Christ" present among them. He loves them, prays to God about them, and helps them to solve their problems towards their unique destiny . . . . Looking at things in this way I

fail to see the difference between development and evangelization . . . In reality they are the same process of helping
people to reach their destination . . . . Cathechizing and
digging wells both are evangelization if we really want it to
be so. (A. Ribas, missionary among primitive tribal people).

If both development and pure evangelization are known to be
specifically Christian, they will both carry the Gospel message to the people and each will help the other. (D. Gordon,
Provincial).

Others equate development work with evangelization because it is a service of justice and freedom, a fulfillment of the
commandment of love, a lived and free self-identification of the
Church with the salvific event of Jesus Christ in that people are
led to overcome their self-centredness and laziness in obedience
to the call of God as manifested in the real needs and challenges
of the situation in which we live. Work of development is therefore an evangelizing witness to Christ.

Unity of God's Plan

Such missionary experience agrees with the theology of the
unity of God's plan. To appreciate this theology one should overcome the habit of thinking of reality in terms of the dualism and
dichotomy of the natural and supernatural, temporal and eternal, material and spiritual, sacred and profane. It is an error to
separate faith from life, to oppose religion to social involvement,
to reduce religion to acts of worship and moral duties alone. The
fact is that temporal duties and eternal salvation are so interlocked that to neglect the one is to endanger the other. It is
surely the risen Jesus and his Spirit that animate and promote
man's longings and strivings for a life on earth that is truly and
more fully human.

The dilemma of the sacred versus the secular is overcome in
Jesus. In him nature and grace are one. This mystery of his Person as well as his parables and his sacraments show that revelation and redemption are given within the profane world and its
simple realities and within ordinary secular history. And because

of Jesus the dilemma is also overcome in every person. God is met in Jesus and in the needy brother or sister. Experience of God is possible on earth only if meditated through relationship to the world of human beings. The bond linking people to God and the bond linking person to person are radically and indissolubly present in each other. Whatever is in the direction of humankind is in the direction of the image of God and therefore of God. Hence it is that Jesus set man at the center of religious and moral concern. The Sabbath and the whole world of the sacred represented by the Sabbath are to serve individuals and their well-being, even their well-being on earth. Hence also his new commandment that directs us to share among ourselves the love we have received from God and his Christ. It is in this complex relationship of willing to be loved by God and to love others that we are "evangelized" and saved. Action for humanity's well-being, liberation, humanization and development is the concrete form in which this love-relationship and Christ's presence are today actualized among us. Development service is love and therefore a saving experience to engage in, which is to evangelize.

Love is the point of union and continuity between the temporal and the eternal. The simple human love concerned with humanity's well-being is what blossoms into the life of the Kingdom. This is so because there is only one human history and a single human destiny of which all the dimensions have been taken up into Christ's incarnation and work of redemption. Because salvation lies embedded within world history, our historical destiny has its place within the horizon of salvation and creation is experienced as part of the saving process or a first saving act. To perceive this is to perceive the existential unity of salvation: salvation of the whole person, of spirit-in-history, of person-in-society, of the family of God on earth as well as the earth of God's family bearing upon it all the marks of human needs and labors, human thought, fantasy and creativity.

Therefore insofar as working for the earthly well-being and a better future on earth for one's neighbor is an expression of love, this commitment cannot be adequately distinguished from commitment to the Kingdom of God. Real human welfare and the building up of the earth are interior to the experience of salvation given to us in the Body of Jesus. To evangelize is to help transform heart, life, person, group, world and the entire network of human relationships according to God's own best wishes on our behalf. It is more than a matter of words, rites and registration in a church. It has to do with that special quality of life and relationship associated with the person of Jesus and with what He said and did; with the creation and revelation of the new brotherhood and sisterhood of Jesus' dream, with its realization and expression at all levels of life, including the economic and the political. Love and life, therefore, and preaching and developmental work all converge to gospel human existence on earth.

Jesus' own evangelizing ministry consisted in the disclosure and communication of the Father's love and forgiveness through healing, feeding and liberation of all persons and concerned response to human need. There is a considerable "secular, temporal, nonspiritual" side to his ministry. His work has not only an eschatological thrust, but a clear historical one that can be spelled out in the language of liberation and development. He emphasized the point that being neighbor to broken and needy individuals was integral to discipleship. It is the suffering and developing peoples who will judge how far we are their neighbors and Jesus' disciples.

I am suggesting therefore that the work of evangelization be taken as a unity comprising the missionary's life, work and word; the various activities of all the laborers in the field be viewed as part of a single whole. All the disciples together, with their entire task of witnessing, humanizing, preaching and loving make a single mission, of which the various components illustrate and interpret one another. The mission of the Church is a single mission multifariously shared; a single piece woven of numberless colors contributed by numberless hands. What services should come first, what aspects should have priority, what factors should receive emphasis and articulation cannot be determined *a priori* and in the abstract, but have to be settled in each concrete historical situation, the deciding factor being individuals and the community, their growth and development.

There is no other symbol of human development than the developing person in his or her creative liberty, his or her capacity to love and his or her ability to give and share. Development is the organization of the world in terms of people rather than of things, ideologies or laws. It consists ultimately in the blossoming of men and women as persons and as community. It involves and demands the creation of new relationships of love, respect, acceptance, freedom and fraternity between persons, peoples and continents. Development is human relationships tending towards total proexistence in love and towards the creation of a world-brotherhood and sisterhood to be realized and lived out at all levels of life and in every area of human activity. That defines for us the direction in which all development activity has to strive. And we note that it coincides with the main thrust of the Gospel.

Young People
and the Church

John Krol

If the challenge that the Church presents to young people today
"is to their appreciation of the values of authenticity and integrity, their rejection of whatever is 'phony,' " then—says John Cardinal Krol of Philadelphia—"it is also a challenge that the young
are turning back on the people of the Church. They are telling us
that we also must be clearly committed and authentic in our acceptance and preaching of the message of Christ." Cardinal Krol
urges the Church to "adapt its manner of preaching the Gospel
to make it intelligible and convincing to modern ears" by "finding a contemporary style for evangelization in which Christ's
timeless message can be expressed in a timely way." Cardinal
Krol sent this message in a letter from Rome while attending the
1974 Synod of Bishops that met to consider "Evangelization in
Today's World." The letter was published in the October 17,
1974, issue of *Origins*, the National Catholic Documentary Service, Washington, D. C.

In discussing evangelization isn't the Synod of Bishops trying to reinvent the wheel? After nearly 2000 years doesn't the
Church know perfectly well how to preach the Gospel?

The answer to the first question is no. The synod participants are quite aware that this particular "wheel" was entrusted
by Christ to the Church and need not be "reinvented."

The answer to the second question is yes and no. In one
sense the task of evangelization never changes. In another sense
it changes constantly. The Church cannot rest on the assumption
that methods of evangelization suited to times past are equally
suitable today.

The message of Christ never changes. But the world does.
Today it is changing with dizzying speed. Human beings change

along with it, adopting new attitudes, new values, new ways of understanding themselves and the world.

As this happens it is essential that the Church adapt its manner of preaching the Gospel to make it intelligible and convincing to modern ears. The message remains the same. The way in which it is communicated needs constant evaluation and updating.

How for example communicate Christian truth effectively to young people today? Many of them are anxious to find a better meaning to life than the hedonism and materialism of a consumer society. But many are also alienated from organized structures—social, familial and even religious. Many simply do not accept the Christian message as relevant for them.

It is easy—and misleading—to point the finger of blame: at the Church ("out of touch"), at parents ("insensitive"), at young people themselves ("immature," "unteachable"). But the problem goes much deeper.

When young people in today's world seek reinforcement for Christian beliefs and values, they have great difficulty finding it in the society around them. Many of the beliefs and values of the contemporary world are fundamentally opposed to Christianity.

Pluralism and secularization provide the context in which young people must form their beliefs and values today. These are problems enough for older people who grew up in an environment which tended to reinforce religious belief or at least did not challenge it openly and directly. They are grave difficulties for young people who must evaluate the Christian message alongside other competing messages presented in an almost overpoweringly attractive form.

There is no point in lamenting this situation or pretending that it is somehow possible to turn back the clock. Evangelization must be carried on in the world as it is, not as one might wish it to be.

Difficult as it is the new situation also provides a remarkable opportunity. Many social and cultural props of religious belief and practice have been knocked away. It is scarcely possible to be "religious" out of habit or conformity. One who is a Christian today is so out of personal choice and conviction. It is possible to foresee—or at least to hope—that a deeper and more intense form of Christian commitment will arise from this.

There is—or should be—an obvious appeal here for young people. The appeal is to their appreciation of the values of authenticity and integrity, their rejection of whatever is "phony." In communicating the Christian message to young people today the Church is not asking them to be conformists. It is challenging them to make an authentic personal commitment that once made will set them at odds with much of what passes for wisdom and for being "with it" in contemporary society.

If this is the challenge that the Church presents to young people, it is also a challenge that the young are turning back on the people of the Church.

They are telling us that we also must be clearly committed and authentic in our acceptance and preaching of the message of Christ. If the Church is to be an effective witness to Christ in the modern world it must be possible for people really to see Christ in all Christians.

The work of evangelization—especially of the young—is thus clearly a responsibility of every Christian. First of all it is a responsibility to give concrete witness to our faith by the way in which we live. If the young see Christ in us, they will be led to accept him and his message. If they do not, it may be that we will have helped make it even more difficult for them to know and love Christ.

Continued purification and renewal of the Church—the people of God—are needed. This does not mean abandoning the past. It means finding a contemporary style for evangelization in which Christ's timeless message can be expressed in a timely way. It means preserving ancient traditions and also incorporating new approaches. Pope Paul in an address at the start of the synod put it this way:

"It will be your task to bring face to face the traditional concept of the action of evangelization and new tendencies . . . There will certainly be a preferential consideration for the structures and institutions of the Church that have already been tested for centuries.

"But, without renouncing the past or destroying values that have been acquired there will be an effort to remain serenely open to everything good and valid to be found in the new experiences . . . You will make your own the Pauline motto: 'Test everything; hold fast what is good.' "

The Highest Priority:
Cross-Cultural
Evangelism

Ralph D. Winter

The "really horrifying fact," according to Ralph D. Winter, is that "the vast bulk of evangelistic efforts, even missionary activities today, are caught-up in the internal affairs of the various church movements," leaving four out of five non-Christians in the world "beyond the reach of the ordinary evangelism of existing Christian churches." This situation requires, in his view, a reordering of priorities and a renewal of emphasis on *cross-cultural* evangelism because "most non-Christians . . . are not culturally near-neighbors of any Christians." Dr. Winter discusses a shorthand terminology (E-O, E-1, E-2, E-3) that he has developed for describing the "different kinds of evangelism" in terms of cultural distance and difficulty involved. He concludes that despite the "wonderful fact that there are now Christians throughout the whole world," cross-cultural evangelistic "efforts coming from outside are still essential and highly urgent," whether from the Western world or not. A former United Presbyterian missionary to Guatemala, Dr. Winter is now professor of the historical development of the Christian movement, School of World Mission at Fuller Theological Seminary, Pasadena, California. Dr. Winter edited this abridged version of the two papers he had prepared for the 1974 International Congress on World Evangelization at Lausanne. The full text of the two papers is published in *Let the Earth Hear His Voice*, edited by J. D. Douglas (Minneapolis: World Wide Publications, 1975), or is available as a booklet, *The New Macedonia*, from the William Carey Library, South Pasadena, California.

In recent years a serious misunderstanding has crept into the thinking of many evangelicals. Curiously it is based on a number of wonderful facts: the Gospel has now gone to the ends of the earth. Christians have now fulfilled the Great Commission in at least a geographical sense. At this moment of history we can acknowledge with great respect and pride those evangelists of every nation who have gone before us and whose sacrificial efforts and heroic accomplishments have made Christianity by far the world's largest and most wide-spread religion, with a Christian church on every continent and in practically every country. This is no hollow victory. Now more than at any time since Jesus walked the shores of Galilee, we know with complete confidence that the Gospel is for everyone, that it makes sense in any language and that it is not merely a religion of the Mediterranean or of the West.

This is all true. On the other hand many, many Christians have as a result of all this gotten the impression that the job is now nearly done and that to finish it we need only to forge ahead in local evangelism, reaching out wherever the new worldwide church has already been planted. Many Christian organizations, ranging from the World Council of Churches to many U.S. denominations and even some evangelical groups have thus rushed to the conclusion that we may now abandon traditional missionary strategy and simply count on local Christians everywhere to finish the job.

While most conversions must inevitably take place as the result of some Christian witnessing to a near neighbor—and that is evangelism—*the awesome fact is that most non-Christians in the world today are not culturally near-neighbors of any Christians, and it will take a special kind of "cross-cultural" evangelism to reach them.*

Consider the great Batak Church in Northern Sumatra. Here is one of the famous churches of Indonesia. Its members have been doing much evangelism among fellow Bataks of whom there are still many thousands whom they can reach without learning a foreign language, and among whom they can work with the maximum efficiency of direct contact and understanding. Even so, the majority of the people in Indonesia speak other languages and are of other ethnic units. Thus, for the

Batak Christians of Northern Sumatra to win people to Christ in other parts of Indonesia is not the same as winning culturally near-neighbors. It is a distinctly different kind of task. It is another kind of evangelism—cross-cultural evangelism.

Or take the great church of Nagaland in Northeast India. Years ago American missionaries from the plains of Assam reached up into the Naga hills and won some of the Ao Nagas. Then these Ao Nagas won practically their whole tribe to Christ. Next, Ao Nagas won members of the nearby Santdam Naga tribe, who spoke a sister language. These new Santdam Naga Christians then proceeded to win almost the whole of their tribe. This process went on until the majority of all fourteen Naga tribes became Christian. Now that most of Nagaland is Christian—even the officials of the state government are Christian—there is the desire to witness elsewhere in India. But for these Nagaland Christians to win other people in India is as much a foreign mission task as it is for Englishmen, Koreans or Brazilians to evangelize in India. This is one very substantial reason why, so far, the Nagas have made no significant attempt to evangelize the rest of India. India citizenship is indeed one advantage the Naga Christians have as compared with people from other countries, but citizenship does not make it easier for them to learn any of the hundreds of totally foreign languages in the rest of India.

In other words, if Nagas decide to evangelize other peoples in India they will need to employ a radically different kind of evangelism. The easiest kind, when they used their own language to win their own people, is now mainly in the past. A second kind of evangelism was not a great deal more difficult—where they won people of neighboring Naga tribes, whose languages were sister languages. A third kind of evangelism, needed to win people in far-off parts of India, will be much more difficult.

Let's give labels to these different kinds of evangelism. Where an Ao Naga won another Ao, let us call that *E-1 evangelism*. Where an Ao went across a tribal language boundary to a sister language and won the Santdam, we'll call that task *E-2 evangelism*. (This E-2 task is not as easy and requires different techniques.) But then if an Ao Naga goes to another region of India, to a strange language such as Telegu, Korhu or Bhili, his task will be considerably more difficult than E-1 or even E-2 evangelism. We will call it *E-3 evangelism*. Note that we are classifying both E-2 and E-3 as *cross-cultural evangelism*.

Let us try out this terminology in another country. Take Taiwan. There are also different kinds of people there. The majority are Minnans who were there before a flood of Mandarin-speaking people came across from the mainland. Then there is the bloc of Hakka-speaking people who came from the mainland much earlier. Up in the mountains a few hundred thousand aboriginal peoples speak Malayo-Polynesian dialects entirely different from Chinese. Now if a mainland Chinese Christian wins others of his own kind that's E-1 evangelism. If he wins a Minnan Taiwanese or a Hakka, that's E-2 evangelism. If he wins someone from the hill tribes, that's E-3 evangelism.

Thus far we have referred only to language differences, but for the purpose of defining evangelistic strategy, any kind of obstacle, any kind of communication barrier affecting evangelism is significant. In Japan for example practically everybody speaks Japanese and there aren't radically different dialects of Japanese comparable to the different dialects of Chinese. But there are highly significant social differences that make it difficult for people from one group to win others of a different social class. In Japan as in India social differences often turn out to be more important in evangelism than language differences. Japanese Christians thus have not only an E-1 sphere of contact, but also E-2 spheres that are harder to reach. Japanese missionaries going from Japan to other parts of the world to work with non-Japanese with totally different languages are doing an evangelistic task on the E-3 level.

Finally, let me give an example from my own experience. I speak English as my native language. For ten years I lived and worked in Central America, most of the time in Guatemala, where Spanish is the official language, but where a majority of the people speak some dialect of the Mayan family of aboriginal languages. I had two languages to learn. Spanish has a 60 per cent overlap in vocabulary with English, so I had no trouble learning that language. Along with learning Spanish, I became familiar with the extension of European culture into the New World, and it was not particularly difficult to understand the lifeways of the kind of people who spoke Spanish. However, because Spanish was so easy by comparison, learning the Mayan language in our area was, I found, enormously more difficult. In our daily work switching from English to Spanish to a Mayan language made me quite aware of the three different "cultural distances." When I spoke of Christ to an American Peace Corps worker in English, I was doing E-1 evangelism. When I spoke to a Guatemalan in Spanish, it was E-2 evangelism. When I spoke to an Indian in the Mayan language, it was the even more difficult E-3 evangelism.

Everyone has his own E-1 sphere in which he or she speaks his or her own language and builds on all the intuition that derives from his experience within his or her own culture. Evangelism in such a sphere is not cross-cultural. Then, for almost all of us there is an E-2 sphere—groups of people who speak languages that are a little different, or who are involved in culture patterns sufficiently in contrast to our own to make communication more difficult and a separate congregational life desirable. Such people can be reached with a little extra trouble and with sincere attempts, but it will take us out of our way to reach them. *More important, they are people who, once converted, will not feel at home in the Church we attend.* In fact, they may grow faster spiritually if they can find Christian fellowship among people of their own kind. More significant to evangelism: it is quite possible that in a separate fellowship of their own they are more likely to win others of their own social sphere. That is, we must reach them by E-2 methods in order to enable them to win others by E-1 methods. Each of us has an E-3 sphere: most languages and cultures of the world are totally strange to us; they are at the maximum cultural distance. If we attempt to evangelize at this E-3 distance we have a long uphill climb in order to be able to make sense to anyone.

In summary, the master pattern of the expansion of the Christian movement is first for special E-2 and E-3 efforts to cross cultural barriers into new communities and to establish strong, on-going, vigorously evangelizing local churches and denominations, and then for that new "national" church to carry the work forward on the really high-powered E-1 level. We are thus forced to believe that until every tribe and tongue has a strong powerfully evangelizing church in it and thus an E-1 witness within it, E-2 and E-3 efforts coming from outside are still essential and highly urgent.

In view of the profound truth that (other things being equal) E-1 evangelism is more powerful than E-2 or E-3 evangelism, it is easy to see how some people have erroneously concluded that E-3 evangelism is therefore out of date, simply due to the wonderful fact that there are now Christians throughout the world. It is with this perspective that major denominations in the U.S. have at some points acted on the premise that there is no more need for missionaries of the kind who leave home to go to a foreign country and struggle with a totally strange language and culture. Their premise is that "there are Christians over there already." With the drastic fall-off in the value of the U.S. dollar and the tragic shrinking of many U.S. church budgets, some U.S. denominations have had to curtail their missionary activity to an astonishing extent, and they have in part tried to console themselves by saying that it is time for the national church to take over. In our response to this situation, we must happily agree that wherever there are local Christians effectively evangelizing there is nothing more potent than E-1 evangelism.

However, the truth about the superior power of E-1 evangelism must not obscure the obvious fact that E-1 evangelism is literally *impossible* where there are as yet no witnesses within a given language or cultural group. Jesus, as a Jew, would not have had to witness directly to that Samaritan woman had there been a local Samaritan Christian who had already reached her. In the case of the Ethiopian eunuch, we can conjecture that it might have been better for an Ethiopian Christian than for Philip to do the witnessing, but there had to be an initial contact by a non-Ethiopian in order for the E-1 process to be set in motion. This kind of initial multiplying work is the primary task of the missionary when he rightly understands his job. Hopefully Jesus' E-2 witness set in motion E-1 witnessing in that Samaritan town. Hopefully Philip's E-2 witness to the Ethiopian set in motion E-1 witnessing back in Ethiopia. If, for example, that Ethiopian was an Ethiopian Jew, the E-1 community back in Ethiopia might not have been very large and might not have effectively reached the non-Jewish Ethiopians. As a matter of fact, scholars believe that the Ethiopian Church today is the result of a much later missionary thurst that reached, by E-3 evangelism, the ethnic Ethiopians.

Unfortunately, most Christians have only a foggy idea of just how many different peoples there are in the world among whom there is no E-1 witness. But several recent studies have seriously raised this question: Are there any tribal tongues and linguistic units that have not yet been penetrated by the Gospel? If so, where and how many? Who can reach them? Even these preliminary studies indicate that cross-cultural evangelism must still be the highest priority. Far from being a task that is now out of date, the shattering truth is that at least four out of five non-Christians in the world today are beyond the reach of *any* E-1 evangelism.

Why is this fact not more widely known? I am afraid that all our exultation about the fact that every *country* of the world has been penetrated has allowed many to suppose that every *culture* has been penetrated. This misunderstanding is a malady so widespread that it deserves a special name. Let us call it "people blindness," that is, blindness to the existence of separate peoples within *countries*. This is a blindness I might add that seems more prevalent in the U.S. and among U.S. missionaries than anywhere else. The Bible rightly translated could have made this plain to us. The "nations" to which Jesus often referred were mainly ethnic groups within the single political structure of the Roman government. The various nations represented on the day of the Pentecost were for the most part not *countries* but *peoples*. In the Great Commission as it is found in Matthew, the phrase "make disciples of all *ethne* (peoples)" does not end our responsibility once we have a church in every country—God wants a strong church within every people!

"People blindness" is what prevents us from noticing the fascinating sub-groups within a country that are significant to the development of effective evangelistic strategy. Society will be seen as a complex mosaic, to use Donald McGavran's phrase, once we recover from "people blindness." But until we all recover from this kind of blindness, we may confuse the legitimate desire for church or national unity with the illegitimate goal of uniformity. God apparently loves diversity of certain kinds. But in any case this diversity means evangelists have to work harder. The little ethnic and cultural pieces of the complex mosaic that is human society are the very sub-divisions that isolate all Christians from four out of five non-Christians in the world today.

When John Wesley evangelized the miners of England the results were conserved in new worshipping congregations. There probably would never have been a Methodist movement had he not encouraged these lower-class people to meet in their own Christian gatherings, sing their own kind of songs and associate with their own kind of people. Furthermore, note that apart from this E-2 technique, such people would have not been able to win others and expand the Christian movement in this new level of society at such an astonishing rate of speed. The results rocked and permanently changed England. It rocked the existing churches too. Not very many people favored Wesley's contact with the miners. Fewer still agreed that miners should have separate churches!

At this point we may do well to make a clear procedural distinction between E-1 and E-2 evangelism. We have observed that the E-2 sphere begins where the people one has reached are of sufficiently different backgrounds from those of people in existing churches that they need to form their own worshipping congregations in order best to win others of their own kind. John, in Chapter Four, tells us that "many Samaritans from that city believed in Him [Jesus] because of the woman's testimony." Jesus evangelized the woman by working with great sensitivity as an E-2 witness; she turned around and reached others in her town by efficient E-1 communication. Suppose Jesus had told her she had to go and worship with the Jews. Even if she had obeyed him and done so she would have been handicapped in winning others in her city. Jesus may actually have avoided the issue of where to worship and with what distant Christians to associate. That would come up later. Thus the Samaritans who believed the woman's testimony then made the additional step of inviting a Jew to be with them for two days. He still did not try to make them into Jews. He knew he was working at an E-2 distance, and that the fruits could best be conserved (and additional people be won) only if they were allowed to build *their own fellowship of faith*.

A further distinction might be drawn between the kind of cultural differences Jesus was working with in Samaria and the kind of differences resulting from the so-called "generation gap." But it really does not matter in evangelism whether the distance is a cultural, a linguistic or an age difference. No matter what the reason for the difference or the permanence of the difference, or the perceived rightness or wrongness of the difference, the procedural dynamics of E-2 evangelism techniques are quite similar. The E-2 sphere begins whenever it is necessary to found new congregations. In the Philippines we hear of youth founding churches. In Singapore we know of ten recently established youth breakaway congregations. Hopefully, eventually, age-focused congregations will draw closer to existing churches, but as long as there is a generation gap of serious proportions, such specialized fellowships are able to win many more alienated youth by being allowed to function on their own. It is a good place to begin.

Whatever we may decide about the kind of E-2 evangelism that allows people to meet separately who are different due to temporary age differences, the chief factors in the immensity of the cross-cultural task are the much more profound and possibly permanent cultural differences. Here too some will always say that true cross-cultural evangelism is going too far. At this point we must risk being misunderstood in order to be absolutely honest. Throughout the world special evangelistic efforts continue to be made that often break across culture barriers. People from these other cultures are won sometimes one at a time, sometimes in small groups. The problem is not merely in winning them; it is in the cultural obstacles to proper follow-up. Existing churches may cooperate up to a point with evangelistic campaigns, but they do not contemplate allowing the evangelistic organizations to stay long enough to gather these people together in churches of their own. They mistakenly think that being joined to Christ ought to include joining existing churches. Yet if proper E-2 methods were employed, these few converts, who would merely be considered somewhat odd additions to existing congregations, *could* become infusions of new life into new pockets of society where the Church does not now exist at all!

A discussion of the best ways to organize for cross-cultural evangelism is beyond the scope of this paper. It would require a great deal of space to chart the successes and failures of different approaches by churches and by para-church organizations. It may well be that E-2 and E-3 methods are best launched by specialized agencies and societies working loyally and harmoniously with the churches. Here we must focus on the nature of cross-cultural evangelism and its high priority in the face of the immensity of the task.

It is appropriate, now that we have made these distinctions, to stop and see how many people fall into each category. The following table is not an exact tabulation, being in round *millions* of people. It consists, furthermore, merely of a series of educated guesses to illustrate the rough proportions of people around the world who are reachable by various kinds of ministries. The E-0 category is new here. It refers to the kind of evangelism necessary for the "Innermission" of bringing nominal Christians into personal commitment and into "the evangelical experience." In such activity there is a "zero" cultural distance. There is not even the so-called "stained-glass barrier" that is involved in E-1 evangelism (where one is not dealing with people in the Church but outside the Church and who are yet within the same cultural sphere).

		NON-WESTERN			GRAND
	WESTERN	Africa	Asia	Total	TOTAL
			(In millions)		
I. CHRISTIANS					
A. Committed—Nurture	120	40	40	80	200
B. Nominal—E-O Evangelism	845	76	58	134	979
	965	116	98	214	1179
II. NON-CHRISTIANS					
A. E-1, Ordinary Evangelism	180	82	74	156	336(12%)
B. E-2, E-3, Cross-Cultural					
Evangelism	147	200	2040	2240	2387(88%)
	327	282	2114	2396	2723
GRAND TOTAL	1292	398	2212	2610	3902

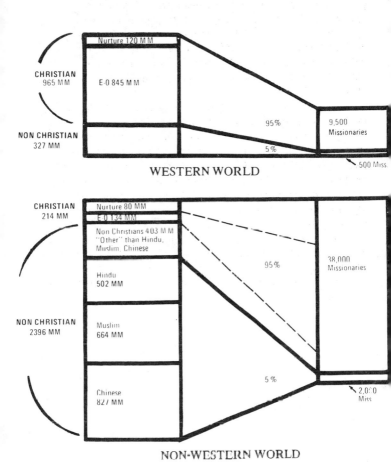

CHRISTIAN 965 MM
NON CHRISTIAN 327 MM

Nurture 120 M M
E-0 845 M M
95%
5%
9,500 Missionaries
500 Miss.

WESTERN WORLD

CHRISTIAN 214 MM
NON CHRISTIAN 2396 MM

Nurture 80 MM
E-0 134 MM
Non Christians 403 M M "Other" than Hindu, Muslim, Chinese
Hindu 502 MM
Muslim 664 MM
Chinese 827 MM
95%
5%
38,000 Missionaries
2,000 Miss

NON-WESTERN WORLD

The major point of this table and of this whole paper is that the total number of non-Christians (2,723 million in the table) are mostly in the E-2, E-3 cross-cultural category. We have spoken of there being "four out of five" who are beyond the reach of the ordinary evangelism of existing Christian churches. These figures make it actually 88%.

The really horrifying fact however is that the worldwide deployment of the active agents of evangelism does not at all correspond to these proportions. One observer has attested that 98 percent of all evangelistic activity in India today is focused on winning nominal Christians, that is, E-0 evangelism, including the work of the missionaries from abroad, while the vast millions of people in the great middle caste and Brahmin groups are virtually by-passed. In other words the bulk of evangelistic efforts even missionary activities, are caught up in the internal affairs of the various church movements rather than being focused on even the E-1 category of non-Christians.

The preceding chart utilizes only the Western and non-Western portions from the table above. It also breaks down the 2,396 million non-Western non-Christians into major ethnic-religious blocs, Chinese, Muslims, Hindus, and "Others." This allows us then to make an educated guess as to the deployment of roughly 50,000 Western Protestant missionary personnel. Even if the figures cannot be precise, the over-all picture is clear: the professional missionary today is not in most cases concerned directly with reaching non-Christians, and even if so only a few are focused on the three largest non-Christian blocs in the world today —Hindus, Muslims, Chinese.

Granting that in the long run most cross-cultural evangelists will not be Westerners let us underline the fact that the great bulk of non-Christians will not be reached apart from initial break-throughs that operate along the lines of the traditional and now almost extinct pioneer missionary. Let us look more closely at the great pockets of non-Christians in the world to see why this is true.

One of the great achievements in "mission lands" is the growth of the Presbyterian Church in Pakistan. In a land 97 percent Muslim it is noteworthy that several hundred thousand former Hindus are now Christian. However a converted Muslim will not feel welcome in the average Presbyterian Church in Pakistan. Centuries-old suspicions on both sides of the Muslim-Hindu fence make it almost impossible for Muslims, even converted Muslims, to be welcomed into the churches of former Hindu peoples. The present Christians of Pakistan (almost all formerly Hindu) have not been at all successful in integrating converted Muslims into their congregations. Furthermore it is not likely to occur to them that Muslims can be converted and form their own separate congregations. The tragedy is that, as a generalization, this kind of impasse postpones serious evangelism along E-2 lines wherever in the world there are any of the 664 million Muslims. However, far to the east of Mecca in certain parts of Indonesia, enough Muslims have become Christians so that they have not been forced one by one to join Christian congregations of another culture. And, far to the west of Mecca in the middle of Africa on some of the islands of Lake Chad, we have reports that a few former Muslims now Christians still pray to Christ five times a day and worship in Christian churches on Friday, the Muslim day of worship. These two isolated examples suggest that Muslims can become Christians without necessarily undergoing serious and arbitrary cultural dislocation. There may be a wide, new open door to the Muslims if we will be as cross-culturally alert as Paul was, who did not require the Greeks to become Jews in order to become acceptable to God.

Vast new realms of opportunity may exist in India too where local prejudice in many cases may forestall effective "near-neighbor," or E-1 evangelism. Indians coming from a greater distance might use E-2 or E-3 methods to escape the local stigmas and establish churches with the 100 or so social classes as yet untouched. It is folly for evangelists to ignore such factors of prejudice whose existence greatly increases the immensity of our task. Prejudice of this kind adds to cultural distance such that E-2 evangelism, where prejudice is deep, is often more difficult than E-3 evangelism. In other words, scholarly well-educated Christians from Nagaland or Kerala might possibly be more successful in reaching middle-class Hindus in South India with the Gospel than Christians from humble classes who have grown up in that area and speak the same language but are stigmatized in local relationships. But who dares to point this out? It is ironic that "national" Christians throughout the non-Western world are increasingly aware that they do not need to be Westernized to be Christian because they cherish for themselves the Christian liberty of self-determination, yet they may in some cases be slow to sense that the challenge of cross-cultural evangelism requires them to allow other people in their own areas to have the same liberty of self-determination in establishing culturally divergent churches of their own.

In any case the opportunities are just as immense as the task. If more than 600 million Muslims await a more enlightened evangelism, there are also 500 million Hindus who face monumental obstacles to becoming Christians other than because of the profound spiritual factors inherent in the Gospel. One observer is convinced that 100 million middle-class Hindus await the opportunity to become Christians but there are no churches for them to join that represent their dietary habits and customs. Is the Kingdom of God meat and drink? To go to the special efforts required by E-2 and E-3 evangelism is not to "let down the standards" and make the Gospel easy. It is to disentangle the irrelevant elements and to make the Gospel clear. Perhaps everyone is not able to do this special kind of work. True many more E-1 evangelists will eventually be necessary to finish the task. But the highest priority in evangelism today is to develop the cross-cultural knowledge and sensitivities involved in E-2 and E-3 evangelism. Where necessary, evangelists from a distance must be called into the task. Nothing must blind us to the immensely important fact that at least four-fifths of the non-Christians in the world today will never have any straightforward opportunity to become Christians unless Christians themselves go more than half way in the specialized tasks of cross-cultural evangelism. Here is our highest priority.

Evangelism in the Neo-Pagan Situation

W. A. Visser 't Hooft

Effective modern evangelism requires that we relate the Lordship of Jesus Christ to the existential concerns of people, and W. A. Visser 't Hooft suggests what three of these concerns are in the neopagan situation of the West. The content of our message he says should relate to our concerns about nature, about sex and about social justice if we are going to develop an adequate theology of evangelism. A lay Dutch theologian, Dr. Visser 't Hooft is the former General Secretary of the World Council of Churches and its Honorary President. His *Memoirs* were published by the Westminster Press in 1973. This article is part of a longer essay published in the January 1974 issue of the *International Review of Mission* (Geneva).

Even if I were able to develop a theology of evangelism in the neopagan situation it would be impossible to do so in a short article. But I should like to make a few suggestions. These have to do with the content of our message.

I do not believe that evangelism is adequately described as answering the questions that people are asking, however deep those questions may be. For evangelism is in the first place the transmission of God's question to humanity. And that question is and remains whether we are willing to accept Jesus Christ as the one and only Lord of Life. But I believe that we must try to relate God's question to the existential situation of people and show that as they answer God's question they find at the same time the answer to their deepest concerns.

Now it seems to me that for effective modern evangelism we need a much clearer and more explicit theology of nature than we have had thus far. The accusation that we hear from so many sides that the high-handed and acquisitive attitude to nature is due to the Old Testament tradition is untrue, for the Old Testament demands an attitude of reverence for God's creation and a practice of responsible stewardship with regard to use. But it is unfortunately true that Christians have neglected this teaching. The fear of a natural religion that tended to relativize or even supplant the revelation in Jesus Christ has too often led to a fear of any clear positive teaching about nature. The present-day evangelist must be able to make clear that it is not by returning to nature worship, which leads to sub-human and anti-human ideologies, but rather by rediscovering the meaning of Creation and by treating nature as a gift of God that we will overcome our present predicament.

Similarly the evangelist will have to restate the Christian attitude toward Eros. The general revolt against the traditional Christian position concerning sex is by no means simply a phenomenon of moral disintegration. It is fundamentally a protest against the devaluation of Eros that has been characteristic of the teaching of the churches. But here also the revolt leads to the destruction of the treasure that it seeks to defend. When Eros is no longer set in the framework of clear convictions about the responsibility of men to God and toward each other it ceases to enrich human life and plays havoc with human relations. Here again we have to re-read the Bible and to ask ourselves whether the pietist and puritan attitude towards sex has not neglected central truths of the biblical faith. Denis de Rougemont uses the telling phrase: "Eros saved by Agape." The evangelist addressing himself to a generation that is not worse than other generations but that has lost any sense of orientation in this field must be able to show that when the Bible speaks of faithfulness it does not do so in order to imprison man in a social institution that suppresses his vitality, but in order to allow him to receive one of the greatest gifts that God desires to bestow on man.

No modern evangelist will really speak to the condition of the present generation unless he relates his message to the issues of human justice. The polarization between Christians concerned with personal evangelism and those concerned with social justice is unbiblical and is at the same time an obstacle to effective evangelism. The prophetic message concerning righteousness in human relations is an essential part of the total biblical proclamation. To leave it out is to present a truncated Gospel. The evangelist must show that it is precisely the faith in a personal God and not the worship of the anarchic forces of nature that has produced a social conscience.

It seems to me that the confrontation with neopaganism is not only a frightening challenge but also a magnificent opportunity. For this confrontation forces us to proceed to a great spring cleaning, to a purification of the message we have given to the world, to a resourcement, throwing us back on the never-adequately discovered riches of the original Revelation.

Another Look at Key 73

Deane A. Kemper

In 1973 nearly 150 Catholic and Protestant church denominations and organizations in the United States and Canada joined in a common evangelistic effort known as Key 73 for the purpose of "Calling Our Continent to Christ." The official plan was "for a gigantic offensive in which every person in North America will be challenged with the claims of Jesus Christ." Looking back on the achievements and failures, Dr. Carl F. H. Henry—who first proposed such a campaign—wrote in the November 1974 issue of *The Reformed Journal* that "there is more truth than many evangelicals willingly recognize in the observation that Christian unity is crucial for effective evangelism." While this endeavor did not accomplish all that it planned—for reasons discussed—Henry concluded that Key 73 should "be buried with dignity and respect." But fellow evangelical Deane A. Kemper—a United Presbyterian on the faculty of Gordon-Conwell Theological Seminary near Boston—remonstrates in the January 1975 issue of the same journal .that, before burial, Key 73 "is in need of a more thorough autopsy than Carl Henry has given it." Kemper, whose field is communication and homiletics, offers a "dispassionate look at the very conception, design and execution of Key 73." Seeing it as "an evangelistic last hurrah best viewed in the context of the current wave of nostalgia," Kemper ends with an epitaph: "Let us remember Key 73 for what it was; an evangelistic Edsel, an idea whose time had truly passed." *The Reformed Journal* is published by Wm. B. Eerdmans Publishing Co., Grand Rapids, Michigan.

While I have no desire to hold to the fire the feet of my evangelical brethren who organized Key 73 or to join John Fry in calling down Divine judgment on "patent theological arrogance," I believe a campaign that so self-confidently trumpeted the inauguration of an effort "to raise an overarching Christian canopy" above the United States and Canada, to "share with every person in North America more fully and more forcefully the claims and message of the Gospel of Jesus Christ," and "to employ every means and method of communicating the Gospel in order to create conditions in which men [*sic*] may more readily respond to the leading of the Holy Spirit," is in need of a more thorough autopsy than Carl Henry has given it. What is needed today is not a listing of small gains or a recitation of individual failures of cooperating groups, but a dispassionate look at the very conception, design and execution of Key 73.

The Electric Gospel

The evangelical wing of American Protestantism has for the past several years been going through a programmatic phase. The Berlin Congress on Evangelism in 1966 was quickly followed by the Minneapolis Congress in 1968, the Jerusalem Prophecy Conference in 1971, EXPLO 72 in Dallas, Key 73 and the International Congress on World Evangelization, Lausanne 1974. For all the exotic locales and global emphasis of these confabs the leadership has been remarkably restricted to the same small group of American evangelicals—Harold Lindsell, Billy Graham, Carl F. H. Henry, Bill Bright, Harold Ockenaga—who promote and attend each other's conferences in much the same way that housewives in the neighborhood Kaffee-klatsch buy each other's Amway products, Tupperware containers, and Avon cosmetics. And while these men have been able to bring the resources of such large and influential bodies as the Billy Graham Evangelistic Association, Campus Crusade for Christ, *Christianity Today*, and the National Association of Evangelicals to their several projects, the danger of this kind of incestuous leadership is that of losing touch with the larger Church. When subjected to analysis, the programs of the last decade reveal a good deal of American evangelicals' talking to themselves.

Key 73 was without doubt the most thoroughly scrutinized, analyzed and demythologized evangelistic effort in the history of

Christianity. Indeed, if today's climate of religious journalism had prevailed in first-century Jerusalem we might well wonder if the Holy Spirit would have dared to show up for Pentecost. But we must hasten to add that, unlike Key 73, the Holy Spirit and the New Testament Church were able to do the work of evangelism without a cast-of-thousands-cost-of-millions super-spectacular show business media effort. It was the early lavish spending and massive publicity that provided Key 73 with a larger-than-life profile—a profile that provided a rallying point for those sympathetic to the cause and an ample target for those who were not. In short, the organizers of Key 73 had themselves to blame for their critics.

And the critics succeeded in making the more conspicuous shortcomings of Key 73 painfully apparent: jingoistic sloganeering ("Calling Our Continent to Christ"), incipient anti-Semitism ("Sharing Messiah with Jewish People"), overtones of American civil religion (that "overarching Christian canopy") and the construction of a mass media campaign that packaged and marketed the Gospel like a presidential candidate or an enzyme presoak. But to harp on these points is to belabor the obvious and overlook the significant. The public relations and promotional sins of Key 73 were those of any national campaign directed by slick professionals: an appearance of monolithicity, the offer of something for everybody, insensitivity in dealing with minorities, and oversimplification of complex issues. These practices are the stock in trade of advertising and promotion men. As such it is hardly surprising that Key 73 bore a more than passing resemblance to a new-car model year promotion or an Orange Bowl half-time show.

The Paper Monolith

It was these public relations excesses that gave Key 73 a larger-than-life image. The listing of 140 cooperating churches and organizations combined with print and electronic media publicity created the impression of an evangelistic juggernaut converting all in its path. But support of Key 73 in many sections of American Christendom was not unlike George McGovern's description of Richard Nixon's following: a mile wide and an inch deep.

Many early supporters, particularly in the United Methodist Church and the American Baptist Convention, lured to the cause by promises of emphasis on social justice as well as individual salvation, became disenchanted as successive Key 73 pronouncements stressed personal evangelism and virtually ignored social concerns. Still others hedged on their support when Jewish organizations voiced their criticism of the Key 73 manual, which singled out Jews as candidates for conversion while mentioning no other single religious or ethnic group, and a Key 73 filmstrip that established a dichotomy between two kinds of people—Christians and pagans. And one major group, the National Association of Evangelicals, which could safely be assumed to be in sympathy with the goals of Key 73, decided not to cooperate at all.

Nevertheless, the promotional effort of Key 73 and its seemingly omnipresent flaming dove symbol created an erroneous impression of a monolithic evangelistic effort. It was an impression that is, perhaps, summed up in the words of a Key 73 supporter to a meeting of churchmen and Jewish leaders in Boston in January 1973. "You people," he said to the Jews present, "are taking this thing a lot more seriously than the churches are."

A Favor for God

Those at the top of Key 73, however, viewed the operation with utmost seriousness. In fact, it is this air of seriousness combined with a pervading sense of moral purpose that separates the evangelical promoter from his cynical and worldly-wise secular counterpart. The professional adman looks for an angle, exploits a big name celebrity, drives a media wedge, or coins a catchy slogan, all in a day's work for the product/cause that happens to be paying his salary at that particular time. With solemnity and sincerity, the evangelical views his task as that of advancing the Gospel.

Because of this sense of mission the evangelistic promoter cries "Foul!" when his public relations-media effort is subjected to the same dissection and criticism as an advertising or political campaign. Thus, Carl Henry can dismiss as a rationalization a United Presbyterian spokesman's statement that his Church had not supported Key 73 because of "uncertainty whether the project involved a vote for Jesus Christ or for Billy Graham and President Nixon," on the grounds that "the Billy Graham Evangelistic Association was only one of many agencies cooperating in the movement." Without debating the issues involved in Mr. Graham's relationship with the former president, it can be said that Henry is rationalizing himself, as the evangelist's involvement in the founding and direction of Key 73 went far deeper than the mere listing of the association that bears his name as one of 140 cooperating bodies. In 1967 it was Mr. Graham along with Dr. Henry who jointly called the meeting in Washington that gave birth to Key 73. It was the Billy Graham Evangelistic Association, according to Henry, that provided $10,000 in seed-money to start the effort. And throughout the campaign the *imprimatur* of Billy Graham on Key 73 was widely publicized. Of the 140 groups constituting the Key 73 Central Committee it is simply a fact that some were more equal than others. To imply that the Billy Graham Evangelistic Association functioned equally with the Brunk Revivals Corporation, the Archdiocese of Dubuque, the New Mexico Inter-Church Agency, and the Ed Robb Evangelistic Association is nonsense.

When questioned concerning the use of certain methods the evangelical promoter argues the Great Commission and explains that he is performing the Divine task of creating an environment hospitable to the proclamation of the Gospel. The purpose of all that organization, promotion, marketing and advertising, it is argued, is to open the way for God to speak. When asked if this is not an attempt to manipulate the Holy Spirit, he replies hastily that the Holy Spirit *cannot* of course be manipulated and all that is intended here is to create a climate in which the Holy Spirit can work.

The evangelistic promoter goes to the marketplace and uses the techniques of the huckster, not to amass a fortune or elect a candidate, but to allow God to get in a word edgewise. The professionals in mass evangelism aren't exactly making God an offer he can't refuse, but they are giving him an opportunity that's too good to pass up.

The Last Hurrah

The last decade in which the evangelicals were truly at home was the 1950s. It was for all its Cold War crisis rhetoric a simple and secure time in which the lines between friend and foe and right and wrong were clearly drawn.

We knew who the enemy was because Joseph McCarthy and Richard Nixon told us about the villainous, godless forces lurking behind curtains of steel and bamboo in Eastern Europe and China (not to mention doors of mahogany at the State Department). The black man knew his place—and that place wasn't a house in the suburbs or a seat on the school bus. The censorious waxed indignant when Elvis gyrated on the Ed Sullivan Show. When Dwight Eisenhower fired his most trusted aide for accepting a fur coat the entire nation nodded in approval. And in the pseudo-revival of the 1950s, when church membership and attendance were higher than ever before, Billy Graham could visit any major city in the land and receive the solid backing of the local council of churches.

But like it or not, the wrenching 1970s are not the placid 1950s and there is no way of going back. Air Force One now touches down in Moscow and Peking, and we are assured that the great enemies of the Republic are not the Soviets and the Chinese but the Pathet Lao and the Cubans. James Foreman and Angela Davis obviously are not Amos 'n' Andy. The blatant sex of "Deep Throat" makes us wonder how anybody managed to get exercised over "You Ain't Nothin' But a Hound Dog." The vice president of the Eisenhower years somehow managed to escape infection by the sense of moral rectitude that characterized the general's administration. Cooperative evangelism today is a game played out by those sympathetic to conservative theological belief with the councils of churches sitting on the sidelines. It was the intent of Key 73 to bring the mainline churches of America back into the ballgame. Evangelicals set out to repair the membranous ecumenism of the 1950s for the purpose of saving souls.

But the major denominations have been on that route before and if some churches opted out of Key 73 and others managed to contain their enthusiasm and hang onto their wallets while going along it is not difficult to understand why. Two decades ago the evangelicals approached the councils of churches in cities throughout the land and said, "Come join us at the Cow Palace, McCormick Place, Madison Square Garden in a crusade for

Christ to win souls." And in a spirit that was often more ecumenical than theological in its sympathies the liberal churches signed up and provided the impetus that made Billy Graham an American institution. Ten years later in the great struggle for civil rights the liberals called to the evangelicals, "Come march with us in Birmingham, Selma, Cicero for the cause of human dignity." And the evangelicals responded, "We're too busy saving souls." When the liberals besieged the White House to demand an end to the killing in Southeast Asia, the evangelicals preached their moralizing sermons inside—and the rupture was complete. Cooperative evangelism, which was already showing signs of being threadbare, came apart at the seams and evangelical and liberal churchmen went their own ways.

Key 73 was then an evangelistic last hurrah best viewed in the context of the current wave of nostalgia. In a generation that has brought back F. Scott Fitzgerald, W. C. Fields, bow ties and cars with running boards, it should come as no surprise that there are those nostalgia buffs in the Church who wish to resurrect the good old days of cooperative evangelism.

Beyond Key 73

From the evangelical perspective there is a grave peril in Key 73 and its attendant reaction. That peril is of course that the infant may be discarded with the cleansing solution. A lesson of Vietnam was that war is too serious a matter to be left to the generals; a lesson of Key 73 is that evangelism is best not left in the care of evangelists.

The most significant shortcoming of those who brought us Key 73 was their failure to bring a sense of history to their task. They came naively as trickle-down evangelists, attempting to revive the church from the top. But just as Herbert Hoover's trickle-down economists failed to revive the economy in the great depression because recovery had to come from the grass roots, so Key 73 made no discernible impact on the Church. The Great Awakenings, the revivals of the nineteenth century, the surge in Church membership that followed World War II, and the continuing growth of Christianity on university campuses stemmed not from grand designs, elaborate structures, and expensive promotions, but from the work of the Holy Spirit in individual congregations, obscure pastors, small prayer meetings and local gatherings of concerned believers.

The history of the Church in America bears painful witness to the problems that invariably occur when the work of evangelism is entrusted to specialized professionals. We have evidence in the American Protestant experience of the progressive disintegration of revivalism. The Great Awakenings produced preachers of stature and integrity who were responsible for bringing thousands into the Church as well as founding institutions and programs that worked for the betterment of society.

The nineteenth and early twentieth centuries saw the rise of the professional revivalist who, in the classic manner of putting the cart before the horse, went about preaching in often frenzied attempts at producing revivals. The revivalist was usually judged by the number of converts he made, which led him not only into questionable tactics of persuasion but away from concern for the social order. Now in the late twentieth century those who would assume the mantle of the first American revivalists have removed themselves even one step further from the original model. Professional marketing, advertising and public relations people consult their data banks and demographic charts for the purpose of creating programs for evangelists to execute in order to usher in a revival.

Such is progress in the American Church. Where once we saw revivals producing preachers, we later saw preachers trying to produce revivals, and today we see Madison Avenue types producing preachers to produce revivals.

Evangelism clearly will survive Key 73 just as it survived the excesses of the Great Awakenings, the psychological manipulations of Charles G. Finney, the anti-intellectualism of Dwight L. Moody, and the moral shortcomings of Billy Sunday. What remains to be measured is the scope and intensity of reaction to Key 73. For if that reaction is intense and sustained, the fabric of American Protestantism may be rent anew and the bridges built between the ecclesiastical left and moderate evangelicals could be destroyed.

Four decades after the modernist-fundamentalist controversy we have arrived at last at a time when the descendants of the Macartneys and Fosdicks can come together for mutual

benefit. Recent declines in church membership and financial contributions have prompted the leaders of more than one major denomination to call on the evangelical minorities within their
ranks to initiate recruitment programs that will bring new
members into the churches. At the same time seminaries that
once were considered staunchly separatist are abandoning long-
held suspicions of their liberal counterparts and joining consor-
tiums of theological schools that include not only the Protestant
left but Roman Catholics as well.

Slowly but perceptibly the old stereotypes are breaking
down. Liberals are no longer viewed as one-dimensional social
gospelers who have abandoned faith, ignored the Bible, and embraced social concerns in a last-ditch attempt to justify their existence. Nor can evangelicals honestly be regarded as proof-text-
ing obstructionists, standing in opposition to the involvement of
the Church in the world while contending for sixteenth-century
orthodoxy. But stereotypes take longer to die than Wagnerian
heroes, and this new spirit of interaction on the academic level
has yet to be translated into full understanding within the larger
Church.

Tragically, neither the liberals nor the evangelicals seem to
understand what should be plainly apparent to both: the two
camps need each other. Simply stated, the mainline churches
have difficulty making converts and evangelicals are often unable
to retain the converts they make. Edward Fiske of the *New York
Times* offers this assessment:

> American religious liberalism has never been able to gener-
> ate much vitality on its own. Instead it has lived off the
> emotion of evangelicalism by providing theological depth to
> those rebels from evangelicalism who found it intellectually
> shallow.

Fiske cites Reinhold Niebuhr as an example of such a rebel, and
to the names of both Reinhold and H. Richard Niebuhr we could
add those of Fosdick, Nels Ferré, Harvey Cox, and countless
other leaders and scholars of the Protestant left whose first ac-
quaintance with the Christian faith came through an evangelistic
conversion experience.

In a recent lecture at Harvard Divinity School marking the tenth anniversary of the publication *Honest to God*, John A. T. Robinson expressed regret that for all of the discussion his book had provoked in Britain, he had never been able to enter dialogue with the evangelicals. He surmised that the reason the evangelicals had failed to rise to the bait lay in the rigidity of orthodox theology that is easily shaken by radical input. Bishop Robinson then paused and added wistfully, "You have to admire the evangelicals though. At least they are able to produce a second generation."

The liberal clearly has no less stake in evangelism than does the evangelical, and it is refreshing indeed to see a growing consensus on this point across the entire Protestant spectrum. It would be especially unfortunate if this new awareness were to be shattered by the gross imperfections of Key 73. Frankly, we must not let evangelism suffer for the shortcomings of evangelists.

"Religious liberalism," Fiske concludes, "appears to be going through a period of sterility, one in which there is no leader of Dr. [Reinhold] Niebuhr's stature to offer new directions." A barrenness of thought in the liberal camp is clearly felt on the other side; for in the absence of theological giants of their own, evangelicals have long looked to the left for creative scholarship. If the past is to serve as our example, new leaders and thinkers will emerge only as the work of evangelism continues and gifted people are brought into the Church. The strengths and weaknesses of the Protestant right and left in this country are such that there need not be competition and rivalry. Instead, the entire Church would be far stronger if we could draw from each other's strength with each side acknowledging its debt to the other.

Carl F. H. Henry has argued that Key 73 was "a weathervane of American religious fortunes"—and so it was in the same sense that the Ford Motor Company produced a weathervane of American automotive fortunes in 1957. Let us remember Key 73 for what it was; an evangelistic Edsel, an idea whose time had truly passed.

Six Theses:
Theological Problems
of Evangelism in the
South African Context

Manas Buthelezi

What are the prospects for evangelism—indeed for Christianity —in South Africa where a black majority in church and state is dominated and oppressed by a white minority? Lutheran theologian Manas Buthelezi—the only black South African with a doctorate in theology—offers six compelling "theses" that address this question. The basic problem, from his perspective, is that love cannot exist "where normal fellowship is banned," and this situation in South Africa has "created credibility problems not only for white men as messengers of the Gospel, but also for the Gospel itself." The task now, he proposes, is "for the black to evangelize .and humanize the white" who has "sabotaged and eroded the power of Christian love." The future of evangelism in South Africa according to Buthelezi is "tied to the quest for a theology that grows out of the black experience." Thus the black theologian must "discover a theological framework within which he can understand the will and love of God in Jesus Christ outside the limitations of white institutions." When Dr. Buthelezi's article "Change in the Church" appeared in *Mission Trends No. 1*, he had already been placed under a "banning order" for five years by the South African Minister of Justice who prohibited him from teaching or attending public gatherings other than church services and from publishing any material or even being quoted in South African publications. Since then the banning order against him has been lifted by the government, partly in response to internal and external pressure and protest by various church bodies. Now, Dr. Buthelezi continues his work as the Natal regional director of the interdemoninational Christian Institute. This article is reprinted from the June 1973 *Journal of Theology for Southern Africa*, published quarterly in Braamfontein, Transvaal, by the South African Council of Churches.

1. The future of the Christian faith in this country will largely depend on how the Gospel proves itself relevant to the existential problems of the black. This is so not only because the blacks form the majority in the South African population but also because Christendom in this country is predominantly black. Almost all the churches have more blacks than whites in national membership. This means that the whites currently wield ecclesiastical power out of proportion with their numerical strength.

2. The whites insofar as they incarnated their spiritual genius in the South African economic and political institutions have sabotaged and eroded the power of Christian love. While professing to be traditional custodians and last bulwarks in Africa of all that goes under the name of Christian values, the whites have unilaterally and systematically rejected the black as some one to whom they can relate with any degree of personal intimacy in daily life and normal ecclesiastical situations. They have virtually rejected the black as a brother or sister. Love can never be said to exist where normal fellowship is banned. Christian love is one of the most misunderstood Christian concepts in South Africa. This has created credibility problems not only for whites as messengers of the Gospel, but also for the Gospel itself. The days for the white to tell the black about the love of God are rapidly decreasing as the flood of daily events increase the credibility gap.

3. For the sake of the survival of the Christian faith it is urgently necessary that the blacks step in to save the situation. They should now cease playing the passive role of the whites' victim. It is now time for the black to evangelize and humanize the white. The realization of this will not depend on white approval but solely on the blacks' love for whites. From the blacks' side this will mean the retrieval of Christian love from the limitations of white economic and political institutions.

4. For this to be a reality it is imperative for the black to reflect upon the Gospel out of the experience as a black in order to discover its power as a liberating factor for him as much as for the white. The black needs to be liberated from white rejection so that white rejection may cease to be a decisive factor in the process of black discovery of human worth and potential. The black needs to see blackness as a gift of God instead of the biological scourge that white institutions have made it to be. The white will be liberated from the urge to reject the black in that this rejection will be rendered irrelevant and inconsequential.

5. The black theologian must therefore discover a theological framework within which to understand the will and love of God in Jesus Christ outside the limitations of white institutions. The black is the only one best equipped to interpret the Gospel out of the depths of the groanings and aspirations of fellow black people.

6. The future of evangelism in South Africa is therefore tied to the quest for a theology that grows out of black experience. It will be from this theological vantage point that the black will contribute to the understanding of Christian love and its implications in evangelism.

The Mutuality of
Evangelization:
Father Inocente Salazar

Fred Smith, M.M.

What should be the missionary's attitude and approach to the
religious beliefs and practices of persons of other faiths and cultures? Rejection—accommodation—adaptation—syncretism? In
a case study outlining the approach of the Maryknoll priest Inocente Salazar among the Aymara Indians of Peru, Fred Smith,
M.M., describes how mission became "the establishment of personal relations and the encouragement of dialogue" that resulted
in "a mutuality of evangelization." Instead of criticizing the
religious rites of the Indians, Salazar shared in their ceremonies
and developed a deep friendship with one of their leaders—a
blind "healer." There is an exchange of values and beliefs leading to "mutual enrichment"—where "the Church is enriched by
this culture and likewise enriches it." In the "mutuality" approach of Salazar, says Smith, "the Word of God revealed in
Christ stirs up the cultures of the world and, conversely, the Word
of God present in cultures brings the Church to a more profound
grasp of her own message." For a poignant portrayal of some of
Father Salazar's experiences, readers are referred to the award-
winning 30-minute color film, "The Healer" (Maryknoll Library
of Third World Films, Maryknoll Missioners, Maryknoll, N.Y.
10545). Fred Smith served for seven years as a Maryknoll missioner in the Altiplano area of Peru and now works with the Justice and Peace Office of the Maryknoll Fathers (Catholic
Foreign Mission Society of America). This report was published
simultaneously in Dossier No. 9, *In Search of Mission*, in the
IDOC Future of the Missionary Enterprise Project, and in

IDOC/International Documentation, No. 63, July, 1974 (New York and Rome).

I. Proclaiming the Word: Mutual Discovery

Throughout the history of the Church missionaries have often made serious mistakes with regard to the popular religion of the people to whom they preached the Gospel. The missionary often betrayed a patronizing attitude, looked upon the people as immature, and saw little value in their customs and religious practices. Pablo Joseph de Arriaga, writing in 1621, tells about the practice of the missionary with regard to the extirpation of idolatries in Peru. The missionary tried to convince the people of their errors and to instruct them in the mysteries of the faith. He explained to the Indians that up until then they had been sons of the Devil, and that they must now be converted in their hearts to the Lord their God. Then their idols were piled outside a village and burned.

Inocente Salazar, a Maryknoll missionary working among the Aymara Indians in the *Altiplano* of Peru, recalls his own experiences regarding local religious rites and practices. When he first encountered such practices as wine sprinkled over sacrifices to bring fertility to the earth, his first reaction was to speak out against these "idolatrous practices." But instead, he asked the people to invite him to assist in their religious ceremonies.

In the process he discovered that the Aymara people have a religion quite different from his own but with their own cultural expressions manifesting the richness of all human life and the diversity of ways of acknowledging God. Salazar came to recognize the presence of God among them revealing himself in ways foreign to himself but within the context of their reality and their human experience. The effect of all this upon his own understanding of the Gospel message was profound.

By presenting himself not as a teacher but rather as one who comes to learn with openness and respect he was able to earn the deep friendship of a blind "healer"—a kind of priest of the people—who continued to carry out their traditional rituals and liturgy. Mission then became the establishment of personal relations and the encouragement of dialogue. The result of this dialogue was a mutuality of evangelization to those involved. Through dialogue the people also came to hold their view of reality in a new way.

In this way the Church is enriched by this culture and likewise enriches it. The Word of God revealed in Christ stirs up the cultures of the world and conversely the Word of God present in cultures brings the Church to a more profound grasp of her own message. Proclaiming the Gospel is then on the way to becoming a redemptive Good News to a culture rather than the misguided destructive campaign that it has often been.

II. Acting on the Word: Christian Witness

Missionaries have often neglected an important part of witness. They have given the example of love and charity in terms of their own culture, such as bringing the sick to the hospital in their car, giving out food, money, clothing, medicine. Then they expected the people to do the same in terms of their own culture, but the kind of help that the people could offer seemed so inadequate compared to what the missionaries did that they remained forever dependent on them and did not try to develop forms of Christian witness within the context of their own culture and environment.

Salazar's approach has been to serve a catalytic role of one who permits and allows for action to take place among the people. His attitude is that of a person who has faith in people and the spirit of God in human beings. He usually approaches the people informally in small groups. In this case the missionary tries to express in the culture of his audience, with them rather than for them, what the message implies. He also looks for overlapping experiences between himself and the people. He comes as one who needs help but in relationship to others who also need help.

To overcome the tendency for the missionary to see things from his own point of view, he begins by knowing persons and their reality. Thus, he is less likely to impose his own way of thinking which creates a situation of "dependancy" of the people upon him. Therefore, he begins with life situations or "life blows" that people face in their daily living experiences. The particular methodology that Fr. Salazar has developed along this line is outlined as follows:

1. The people verbalize their self-identity as Aymaras and how they relate to others.

Salazar feels that this is what the Gospel is about; it teaches us to see who we are and how to relate to others. This focus is very person-centered; it begins with the reality of the people themselves, what they believe and what they do. What the people believe is very strong—it is what they are and what they act upon. This reality that the missionary confronts also causes him to reflect upon himself and to surface his own human relations; this, in turn, enables him to take a new look at the Church and to de-institutionalize it.

2. The people also surface their problems and try to define them.

They begin to see and understand their felt, real and basic problems. They define ways of overcoming some of their major obstacles, such as lack of knowledge, unwillingness and inability.

3. Finally the people learn how to organize themselves to work in common to resolve problems.

III. Creating Relationships: The "how" reveals the "what" of evangelization

The missionary has a vision that compels him to go and share it with others. He proclaims Christ through word and deed. His approach to the people however cannot merely be a strategy to bring the people around to a preconceived notion of his own regarding the Christian message. *How* the missionary relates to the people tells *what* vision he has of Christ. He is not merely an instrument who conveys doctrines to people, but he believes that Christ is alive today through his Spirit. A key difference manifests itself in the creating of relationships. Christ is not imposed as an object, but is a person revealed in and through relationships with other people. So the Gospel is announced, not just by word and deed but through personal relationships.

Salazar won the friendship of a local "healer," Marcelino. Marcelino's son died and in the face of this reality Salazar found overlapping experiences in face of death whereby he and Marcelino along with his community were able to exchange values and beliefs. There is a mutual enrichment here by bringing into communion the riches of the missioner's Christian tradition or situation. The relationship between the missionary and the peoples is what gives meaning to his message as well as theirs.

The next step is to create a relationship between the community thus formed through word and action that will survive the presence of the missionary. The missionary is essentially mobile. He is a pilgrim belonging to the sending church, and therefore always a visitor, a guest, a catalyst, but not a permanent leader of the receiving church. The very essence of his mission is to come from somewhere else with fresh points of view and challenge, as a sign and as a condition of the universality of the Church. The missionary's primary purpose is to assist in the development of the local church to the point where it is more autonomous and self-sustaining. But he realizes that his transcultural experience, especially in such a difficult region as the *Altiplano* of Peru, serves to stimulate his own personal maturing and growth in faith.

IV. Summary and Reflections:

1. Revelation of Christ Present in all Cultures:

—The recognition that God is present in and continues his revelation in all cultures. Before a missionary can be one with the people in the form of worship, he must *know*, *respect* and *experience* their forms.

—The missionary is one sent to discover the preparations of the Spirit of Christ in persons and cultures to bring about a conscious acceptance of the Gospel. He aims to work for the incarnation of the Gospel in every human culture without its being enslaved by any. He helps the people to come to an awareness of their dignity as children of God as well as their responsibility in relation to their present reality.

—The realization that God is encountered not in abstract principles but in the socio-economic, political reality of the present, mindful of its historical continuity.

2. The Mutuality of Evangelization:

—The need to accept people where they are, with nonjudgmental attitudes in the face of customs that are not understood.

—The need to identify with people on a personal level, but with the awareness of the missionary's pilgrim presence, his temporary function and the need for the people to accept the functions of leadership and Christian witness in the local church.

—The realization that as the missionary does not have all the answers, it is a two-way street between him and the people. There is a mutual revealing of God between them that ultimately enriches and helps each to become fully himself.

—The realization that all need liberation from the oppression of religion and that the missionary will be liberated together with the people as they grow together in faith.

—The recognition that development and evangelization go hand in hand.

3. Person Centered:

—This mission option is very person-centered. Persons are not merely on the way to God. Persons are the way. And Jesus is the Person.

The Gospel with Bread:
An Interview with
Brazilian Pentecostalist
Manoel de Mello

Roberto Barbosa

There is no consensus among Christians as to the proper relation between evangelization, liberation and relief work in mission. But a Pentecostal leader in São Paulo, Brazil, reminds Christians that the Gospel includes bread—in "a place of priority"—and much more. Therefore the Church should be concerned with "the total person," with "everything that benefits humanity," with "the whole truth." For Pastor Manoel de Mello, founder of the "Brazil for Christ" Pentecostal movement, the wholeness of the Gospel includes also the responsibility to denounce injustices by the government and to refuse "to collaborate with it when it is on a dangerous path." An ardent supporter of the World Council of Churches and an admirer of prophetic Catholic leaders such as Brazilian Archbishop Helder Camara, Pastor de Mello was arrested in his church in São Paulo on February 27, 1975. Detained on orders of the "Presidency of the Republic" he was released 30 hours later with no charges brought and no explanation given. This interview, reprinted by permission from the December 25, 1974, issue of *The Christian Century* (Chicago) is by the *Century's* regular correspondent in Brazil, Roberto Barbosa.

Manoel de Mello, 45, born 24th among 25 brothers and sisters, is the founder and principal leader of the 19-year-old

Igreja Evangélica Pentecostal O Brasil para Cristo (Brazil for
Christ Evangelical Pentecostal Church). One of Brazil's major
Pentecostal denominations, it is the only one belonging to the
World Council of Churches and its claimed adult membership is
larger than all combined Protestant denominations that have
been in the country for more than a century (Congregational,
Presbyterian, Methodist and Episcopal).

In the early years of his movement Mello was often denounced by representatives of the traditional Protestant churches
(he has been arrested 17 times). Although his Church has now
achieved respectability by joining the Evangelical Confederation
of Brazil and the WCC, his nonconformist views and especially
his prophetic utterances—a rarity among Brazilian Protestant
church leaders—set him apart as a key figure in Brazil's ecclesiastical scene. Although semiliterate, Mello has traveled and spoken throughout the world; he has made trips to the U.S. and
Russia and delivered an address before the Swedish Parliament.

I

**Q.: Tell us something about yourself and how you founded
your movement.**

A.: I was born in Brazil's impoverished northeast, in the
state of Pernambuco. Because our family was so large I scarcely
went to school at all. At the age of 17 I came to São Paulo like
thousands of other migrants. I was a construction worker until
1954 when I gave up my good job as foreman to become a full-
time evangelist with the American Foursquare Gospel Church.
My brief experience there convinced me of the need to begin a
movement with exclusively Brazilian roots. We have developed
our own worship forms and do not rely on foreign funds or personnel.´

**Q.: Does the Brazil for Christ movement use the criterion of
enrolled membership?**

A.: This kind of question still bothers me. I believe that the
enrollment of members is one of the things that has hindered the
growth of the evangelical church in Brazil. We think that a per-

son is a Christian only after we stamp him and give him a number. Man is born with a number. A friend told me that when man is born he already owes nine months' room and board. Everything is numbered—the room he's born in, the building, the doctor, everything. And we number him also so that he might go to heaven.

Q.: How many "numbered" ones do you claim?

A.: Here in São Paulo alone, more than 60,000. Nearly half a million throughout Brazil. But I make no distinction between brothers who are numbered and those who are not. A non-numbered brother came here yesterday. He's a university student. He comes to our Church with his fiancée. He's a Christian and gives a courageous witness. Even though he doesn't have a number, I am confident that he is saved.

Q.: Does your Church require baptism for membership?

A.: There are many persons who are Christians even though they are not baptized. I am in favor of baptism but not as an imperative. Even though Jesus said, "Whoever believes and is baptized shall be saved," in his own ministry there were those who were saved without being baptized. The best method is to preach the Gospel and let the person choose the hour to be baptized if he so wishes.

II

Q.: You claim to be building here the world's largest evangelical temple. What kind of program are you carrying out here?

A.: This building is more than a temple; it is an evangelical religious center. We carry on a religious program, yes, but also an educational program and a social one. As soon as it is finished, I intend to place the temple and other facilities at the service of all religious groups—including the National Conference of Catholic Bishops, if they wish to hold a eucharistic congress here. The Adventists have already held a congress here as did the Buddhists and a Japanese sect called Izein. I work in this open fashion not only because of my ecumenical conscience but also because only 40 percent of the funds for this temple comes from the Brazil for Christ movement. Catholics provided 30 per cent, and the other 30 per cent comes from other religious groups.

Q.: And that plaque outside, "We pay and you study"?

A.: As everyone knows, I never studied in regular courses. I studied in the "university of life," where I'm still enrolled and where I intend to stay until I receive my diploma. Education is at the base of everything, especially in an urban situation. We cannot expect that education will happen to others by miraculous processes such as mine. The Church must help. Because most of our young people are sons and daughters of migrants from the northeast like myself, the World Council of Churches has assisted me in setting up a program here that will help the young people integrate themselves into the new urban situation. The plaque means that we give partial or total scholarships for those who cannot pay.

Q.: Are you therefore trying to install a school in every sanctuary?

A.: That's right. Let me tell you of an experience I had in the Soviet Union. I got into a discussion with a police commissar and was arrested but later released through the intervention of a secretary of our embassy. One question I addressed to the police officer was, "Why do you close churches when you conquer a country?" He answered, "You are misinformed. Our party never closes churches." Then I began a heated argument, trying to convince him and repeating what I had heard. "No," he said, "that is false propaganda."

That officer then gave me the following explanation: "You have churches. You open them on Sunday for religious services. Then you close them and do not open them again until the following Sunday. When we dominate a country, we take the churches and install schools or museums or some other form of education. And then on Sundays we turn them back to the priest or pastor." And I agreed with him! For while in Brazil there is a need for thousands of additional classrooms there are thousands of empty churches throughout the week. According to our belief, the temple is not sacred. The temple is a building like any other. It is the people who are sacred. To help the people we want each church to be a school also.

Q.: How does this fit into your concept of evangelism?

A.: To begin with, more than 90 percent of Brazilians are

already converted. It is most difficult to find a Brazilian who does not believe in Jesus Christ as Savior, in God, and in the Holy Spirit. Paul was converted. And if anyone believes that Buddha is savior and later says that he's not—that the savior is Christ—he is converted. But in Brazil it is necessary to teach. What we need here is not evangelization and conversion but rather education and consciousness-raising. It is necessary to give to each person the consciousness of his own responsibility as a Christian. My preaching is for the purpose that each person have a genuine faith.

Q.: Father Sotero has said that "evangelism generates faith and catechization educates and makes conversion explicit." Is this the meaning of your words?

A.: I agree. That's what it is. Someone comes to my Church and says, "Pastor, I brought this couple to the worship service. They aren't believers." No, they are believers. You want to see? I ask, "Do you believe in Jesus Christ?" "Yes," is the answer. They all believe, but they do not practice the same faith. Let me add that we evangelicals have scared a lot of people away from the Kingdom of God because of certain expressions we have created: "So and so is not converted." "So and so is not saved." "So and so is not a believer." This scares people away.

III

Q.: And social action? Should this be a concern of a church, especially a Pentecostal one such as yours?

A.: Jesus once said, "Man does not live by bread alone . . ." He was saying that man does live by bread and also by the Word of God. Jesus did not want to put bread on a secondary plane. On the contrary, bread for him always had a place of priority. If someone knocks on your door and asks for food and you say, "God bless you. I'm going to pray for you. May Jesus cleanse you with his blood"—all this would be useless. And James even indicates that this might not be religion at all. I'm with James on this matter. The storage of bread without the Gospel is false. The storage of the Gospel without bread is false also. There are many churches that have the Gospel only; there's no bread. That's when the problem of communism and capitalism appears.

Q.: Explain to us how communism and capitalism enter into this matter.

A.: Communism is a storage of bread, but without the Gospel. It is therefore false. Capitalism is a storage of material things for a small group. Observe that capitalism accepts the Gospel, but only as a protective cape for its interests. But capitalism does not accept the distribution of wealth to those who need bread. It is therefore false. James says that it is false. The Gospel must be concerned with bread.

Q.: How, then, would you define the Kingdom of God?

A.: Is the Kingdom of God heaven? Is it a marvelous place, full of precious stones? No, no and no! The Kingdom of God is among us. It is here with us, right now. When the Church takes care of the total person, it is bringing about the Kingdom of God. We can live in the Kingdom of God or in the kingdom of Satan. In Matthew 10 Jesus says that he is going to give power to the preacher. He said that "In my name you will cure the sick, raise the dead, purify lepers, expel demons . . ." He said that all this is possible here on earth right now.

Q.: Does this explain the success of your movement?

A.: In part, for this is bread also. When I say Gospel with bread, I am saying Gospel with health and healing. This is part of the bread. The liberation of people is part of the bread. Bread is not only what you buy at the bakery to eat; it is everything that benefits humanity. By bread I mean education. I mean clothing. By bread I mean schools, hospitals. I mean a just salary. The respect for the human person. The rights of the human person. When I say "Gospel with bread," I mean Gospel with social justice, with the rights of man, with the Universal Declaration of Human Rights approved by the United Nations, that was signed by Brazil.

Q.: Do you believe that denunciation is also a part of the proclamation of the Kingdom of God?

A.: The Gospel is in itself a denouncing thing. It is a denunciating message. That's why the Gospel is not accepted in totalitarian countries. The Gospel cannot be proclaimed with half-truths, but only with the whole truth. That is why Jesus said that the Gospel must be proclaimed from the mountaintops. The Gospel cannot be proclaimed fully without denouncing injustices committed by the powerful. Preachers have the responsibility to denounce injustices and the errors that compromise the Gospel.

Q.: What do you mean by "errors that compromise the Gospel"?

A.: I refer to human promotion, the Gospel that involves man in society. If we announce the Gospel without denouncing, without publishing or proclaiming what is wrong—if we don't have the courage to point out injustices committed voluntarily or involuntarily—we are not following Paul's teaching. Paul denounced because he preached the whole Gospel. Christ confronted King Herod and denounced injustices committed under the guise of Roman intervention among the Israelites. I would subscribe to certain pronouncements of the Conference of Catholic Bishops, for they speak out against injustices in our society.

Q.: Do you believe that a lucid faith must be tied in to reality?

A.: The evangelical Christian is someone who is committed to the Gospel. Only through and by the Gospel can one determine all human attitudes in a given reality. The Christian therefore can't help but be committed to Christ and to justice.

IV

Q.: What do you mean by "evangelical Christian"?

A.: Everyone who believes in Jesus the Savior and who accepts the Gospel as normative for his faith. I am not even referring to my own Church or to any denomination. For me there is no Pentecostal Christian, no Methodist Christian, no Catholic Christian. I don't believe in this kind of labeling. There can only be an evangelical Christian—a Christian who accepts the Gospel, the Good News, no matter to what denomination he may belong. I believe that Pope John XXIII was a great evangelical Christian.

Q.: What has been the relationship of your movement with other churches?

A.: It was very hard in the beginning. We were misunder-

stood and severely persecuted even by the Evangelical Confederation of Brazil, of which I am now a vice-president. Our purpose
was to shake the accommodation of many traditional churches,
not to do away with them. The Conference of Catholic Bishops,
for instance, is today the only expression of serious criticism of
the acts of government. The ECB should do the same. This does
not mean being against the government, but simply refusing to
collaborate with it when it is on a dangerous path. From the
beginning those of us from the Brazil for Christ movement have
thought that Protestants have always been too timid and scared.
It is evident that an innocuous pronouncement by one group
tends to neutralize a courageous document by another.

To proclaim the Gospel does not mean staying behind the
altar simply saying that Jesus Christ saves. It means identifying
with the masses just as Jesus did. It means living with the people,
walking with them and saying that Jesus Christ wants them to
become human persons and to have the rights and privileges of
persons.

**Q.: And how is your relationship with the World Council of
Churches?**

A.: You mean do we regret being a member church? No. If
the renewal of membership were annual we would annually
renew our affiliation. We know that the WCC has a lot of shortcomings. Eugene Carson Blake once asked me, "Mr. Mello, in
what percentage do you approve of the World Council of
Churches?" I replied 60 per cent and he said, "I'm surprised, for
I might not approve of it as much." We are against some things.
We aren't clapping our hands for everything. But the WCC is a
place of dialogue; in it we have a chance to make the Pentecostal
movement known and to disseminate our points of view.

Ecumenism, my friends, has many defects. Only the Gospel
is perfect. But between ecumenism and the fundamentalism of a
certain Mr. McIntire, I would say that in ecumenism much is
biblical and that in fundamentalism hardly anything is. One day
Jesus spoke thus to the fundamentalists of his time, "Be careful,
for prostitutes will enter the kingdom before you do." Before condemning ecumenism one must examine it as I did for ten years before accepting it. We accept Geneva's leadership in the ecumenical movement for I have seen Israelis and Arabs sit at the same

table to dialogue, together with Americans and Russians, Cubans and Brazilians. Whoever has good merchandise wins, whoever has weak stuff loses.

Jesus did not avoid dialogue with Pharisees and Sadducees. He went to the homes of sinners. He let his feet be dried by the hair of a prostitute because Simon, the representative of the religious fundamentalism of his time, did not provide a towel for him.

V

Q.: What are your present theological concerns?

A.: Theological concerns—a matter to which the Pentecostal is allergic—are those I've already expressed. Our theological stance must be supported by the Gospels and the Pauline letters. Our theological preoccupation is to avoid confusing the sacred word of Scripture with the dogmatisms of men. Our Church rejects dogmatic formulations that are concocted to adorn the Gospel. The Gospel needs no adornments, nor is it in need of re-treading. We are wary of churches that set aside biblical for theological concerns, become tangled in laws and are consequently transformed into inquisitional tribunals.

Q.: And what is your view of the Catholic Church in Brazil's present context?

A.: Some of my views on that have already been expressed in answers to previous questions. Nevertheless I have a couple of things to add, maybe three. The most important is the biblical renewal going on within the Catholic Church. Catholics are distributing more Scriptures in Brazil today than all the Protestants. This is something new, praise the Lord! The Conference of Catholic Bishops has even endorsed the Portuguese version of *Good News for Modern Man*, which was published by our own Bible society! It is a shame that such cultured Protestants as the Presbyterians are condemning it. I am happy that my people can now read the New Testament more easily and can understand it better.

The second thing I would say about the Catholic Church

here in Brazil is that it is full of prophetic voices. There would have been no Reformation if these prophets had lived in Luther's time. Bishops and priests are not afraid to speak out. Even Archbishop Helder Camara admits that the Church had prostituted itself by its long association with Brazil's power elite. But the Catholic Church has returned to its people, the impoverished suffering masses throughout this enormous nation.

And third, no Protestant should sin against the Holy Spirit by doubting that these changes in the Catholic Church are the real thing. I meet regularly with Catholic Pentecostals! Yes, the Holy Spirit is powerful enough to change and renew even the Catholic Church. And as far as I'm concerned all churches should rejoice in this fact.

III. Common Faith and Divided Witness

The Dynamics
of Pluralism
in the Church

G. Emmett Carter

In this address to the Synod of Bishops meeting in Rome in October 1974, Bishop G. Emmett Carter, of London, Ontario, stresses the dynamic relationship between unity and diversity in the Church—citing the examples of Pentecost, the eucharist, the Gospels, and early Christian communities—as crucial for effective evangelization "in the new cultural pluralism of the technological era." Calling for unity without uniformity, the Bishop says that today the Church faces a twofold challenge: "She requires first, a strong central authority. . . . But secondly, the Church must simultaneously strengthen the other pole in this dynamic relationship by respecting the pluralism, initiative and legitimate autonomy of the local churches." Hearing "the voices of our brothers and sisters of Africa and Asia calling for understanding and trust and a chance to adapt the Gospel message to their indigenous cultures," he asks "whether matters of pastoral practice and discipline are not so socio-culturally conditioned that it is increasingly difficult for a central organization, however necessary, to take exclusive responsibility for overseeing them." The bishop's synod intervention is reprinted from the October 31, 1974 issue of *Origins*, published in Washington, D.C., by the National Catholic Documentary Service.

Unity and Diversity

A pilgrim gazing at the splendor of St. Peter's Basilica is impressed by the tremendous contribution a previous culture brought to the expression of Christian faith. But even from the oasis of St. Peter's Square the visitor cannot ignore completely the roar of traffic that recalls the temporal preoccupations and priorities of the new Rome surrounding the old. Two cultures coexist, compenetrate and raise a haunting question. What does a culture born of the Roman Empire have to say to the turmoil of contemporary Italian society on the eve of the 21st century?

As Pope Paul stated at his general audience August 28, 1974, "Pluralism is an ambiguous word. . . . There is a true and a false pluralism." The question of pluralism is indeed a difficult and complex one. Keeping in mind the possible ambiguities inherent in the term pluralism we must nevertheless come to grips with the reality underlying it. Otherwise our evangelization will lack that impact that comes only through a realistic incarnation in the modern world.

The main issues linked with pluralism seem to center around the two poles of unity and diversity. To some people unity demands uniformity. To others diversity takes priority even over solidarity. Some people see pluralism as a source of conflict and contradiction. Still others accept it as a necessary condition for human progress. It might profit our synodal discussions to study the issues in a broader context.

Pluralism as a contemporary phenomenon manifests itself at several levels:

a) Politically, the bipolarity of a world society dominated by two major blocks is evolving towards a pluralism of major world powers, as witnessed to by the increasing ascendancy of certain peoples of the Third World and by recent developments at the United Nations.

b) Minority groups in several countries are striving with increasing determination to express their relative autonomy both socially and politically. This applies to racial or ethnic minorities, social, political and ideological groups.

c) Another political issue is the vertical pluralism of social classes and the disparity between different socio-economic levels.

d) Economically, recent crises centered around primary resources, food, nuclear and fuel energy, finances point to the increasing need for world solidarity in the midst of pluralism.

e) Geographically, pluralism manifests its problems in re-

gional disparities, the contrast between urban ghettos and affluent suburbs, or rich metropolises ringed by zones of misery.

f) Demographically, we face the challenges of local clashes
among cultures, the dramatic increase in population, exploding
and imploding urbanization.

g) Socially, modern societies are becoming extremely complex, with an increasing pluralism of sub-cultures and sub-sys-
tems.

h) Increasing mobility and emigration force individuals and
peoples of many origins to communicate and live together in new
ways.

i) Ideologically, an increasing variety of models for human
society is proposed. Individualistic liberalism and collective socialism are challenged by new models based on divergent read-
ings of history and of social reality.

j) Religious pluralism is increasing as well, with the growth
of ecumenism, the meeting in dialogue of the great religions, the
proliferation of new sects, the search for new spiritualities, the
renewed religious quest of millions of young people.

Evangelical Discernment

Faced with these phenomena, several criteria for evangelical discernment are available to us:

Unity and pluralism of pentecost. There is one Lord, one
faith, one baptism. But the Holy Spirit endowed the Church with
the capacity to embrace all languages, cultures and peoples. Cornelius became a Christian without circumcision.

Unity and pluralism of the eucharist. The sacrament of sacraments assembles and unites master and slave, weak and powerful, white people and those of different colors. Besides its power
to build up the Church, the eucharist proved from the start its
ability to modify radically the patterns of society and to overcome every inequality or barrier between people and nations.

Unity and pluralism of the Gospels. Four Gospels emerged
from the one profession of faith in the Lord Jesus Christ in different communities of the primitive Christian Church. We must
recognize more effectively this original pluralism of universal

Christian community where unity is enriched and strengthened by diversity.

Unity and pluralism of grass-roots Christianity. What good can come from Nazareth? Jesus identified himself with the least of men and his followers demonstrated that salvation would indeed come from the poor. The basic human solidarity of those whose only possession is their common human dignity is the privileged soil in which the fraternity of the sons of God is expressed and realized. Gospel fraternity cuts through all divisions to find its radical inspiration and strength at this level.

Unity and pluralism of prophecy. History reveals the natural tendency of all human systems and societies to become exclusive. The Old Testament prophets fought against this inclination. Even after Jesus had commissioned his disciples to baptize all nations Paul had to confront Peter on this issue. The Church is not beyond temptation today. We must rediscover that prophetic dynamism of the resurrection that eliminates all barriers of race, color, sex or class (cf. Galatians, 3, 28) while respecting those same differences.

The New Pluralism: A Sharing

A new pluralism is emerging in the global village. Modern humanity searches for meaning in a secular society. The dichotomy between this secularized world and the cultural faith experience of most Christians results from our inability to distinguish the essential Gospel message from the cultural accretions that yesterday facilitated its incarnation. The Second Vatican Council recognition of the hierarchy of truths paved the way for a liberating experience. We can root the Gospel once more in the new cultural pluralism of the technological era.

We will prevent the formation of more Christian ghettos by avoiding both polarization and exclusivism and by bringing to each culture the deeper judgment or critique of the Gospel together with the universal enrichment that it provides. Realistic cultural insertion requires a mutual evangelizing of local churches sharing their manifold experiences of the paschal mystery.

An apologetic era identified oneness with uniformity. To be realistic, a church that numbers a half billion people and spans six continents in the most diverse historical context must face a twofold challenge. She requires first, a strong central authority with leadership capable of orchestrating the creative energies of the people of God immersed in the global family of mankind and leading it towards total unity. At no time do we need the Pope more than today. But secondly, the Church must simultaneously strengthen the other pole in this dynamic relationship by respecting the pluralism, initiative and legitimate autonomy of the local churches. They need the freedom to proclaim the one Gospel in a language comprehensible to each different culture. Refusal to accept new cultural understandings would cause our message of evangelization to remain a foreign language to people today.

With a view to the praxis of Church life we suggest some approaches through which authentic pluralism can be further incorporated:

1) A more trusting recognition of the diverse evangelical expressions proper to the various spiritual traditions and groups in the Church. The strength of the center always depends on the strength of the units. And the units will only be strong when they are challenged by confidence and responsibility.

2) In our secularized milieu people no longer move directly from the street to worship in church. We must recognize that their conscience and their faith mature progressively; and this requires various forms of belonging to the church. For example, a Gospel discussion group is not necessarily ready for the eucharist. Pastoral experiences with the young, with non-practicing Catholics or with unbelievers bear this out.

3) This openness to various expressions of faith and to more diversified fields of evangelization must be accompanied by a minimum of consensus among all the apostolic forces in the local Church, a consensus for instance about an order of priorities for means as well as for objectives. Sharing the same mission of evangelization, we must share precise common orientation at the local level.

We hear the voices of our brothers and sisters of Africa and Asia calling for understanding and trust and a chance to adapt the Gospel message to their indigenous cultures. The Holy Father in his speech in Kampala (July 31, 1969) recognized this need and we lend our support.

We raise the question whether matters of pastoral practice and discipline are not so socio-culturally conditioned that it is increasingly difficult for a central organization, however necessary, to take exclusive responsibility for overseeing them without in practice violating the relative and rightful autonomy of the local churches and episcopal conferences.

We are at a point when perhaps for the first time in history we perceive the signs of a human community emerging into a true and unified family. Signs are not yet reality, but they must not be neglected. What an opportunity for the Church, raised as a sign of unity among nations, to anticipate the gathering of the Kingdom and to set an example of oneness. It alone has the grace from the Lord to draw everyone to itself, even the least and the most helpless.

Evangelization in the Modern World

Philip A. Potter

After affirming that "the conviction of the World Council of Churches has been that evangelization is the ecumenical theme par excellence" and giving a summary of ecumenical thinking on evangelization, Philip A. Potter told the 1974 Roman Catholic Synod of Bishops in Rome, "The main focus of our concern for evangelization is . . . to discover what the evangelistic task is in today's world." It is the experience of the ecumenical movement, he said, "that the only way forward is the way of dialogue with the modern world." Furthermore "The real issue is not to ask whether cooperation in evangelization is possible between Roman Catholics and other Christians, but whether Christians of different confessions are so prepared to be exposed to each other, in faith and life, that they allow the Gospel to do its own explosive work in and through them. That is the ecumenical task and that is why evangelization is essentially an ecumenical enterprise." Dr. Potter, a Methodist minister from the West Indies, was general secretary of the Methodist Missionary Society in London. He then became director of the Division of World Mission and Evangelism, and since 1972 has been general secretary of the World Council of Churches, Geneva. His address to the Synod of Bishops first appeared in *Information Service* (No. 25; 1974/III) of The Secretariat For Promoting Christian Unity, Vatican City.

It is with a sense of deep joy and fraternal solidarity that I address you on the theme of the Synod of Bishops, "Evangelization in the Modern World." The invitation to a representative of the World Council of Churches (which comprises 271 member churches in more than 90 countries of the Orthodox, Protestant, Anglican and Pentecostal confessions) is a sign of the ecumenical spirit that exists among us all today—truly a miracle of God's grace to his people and to the world.

Already at Vatican Council II representatives of the World Council and of many member churches followed the proceedings as observers and were encouraged to make their contributions to the deliberations. Then in 1965, after the visit to the World Council of Cardinal Bea, of blessed memory, a Joint Working Group was formed between the Roman Catholic Church and the World Council. When His Holiness Pope Paul VI visited the World Council in June 1969 he referred to the many ways in which co-operation had taken shape. He spoke of "plans to find the possibilities of a common Christian approach to the phenomenon of unbelief, to the tensions between the generations, and to relations with the non-Christian religions." He went on to say:

> Such development supposes that at the local level the Christian people are prepared for dialogue and for ecumenical collaboration. Is it not for this that in the Catholic Church the promotion of the ecumenical effort has been confided to the bishops for their diligent promotion and prudent guidance (cf. *Decree on Ecumenism*, n. 4), according to the norms set down by the Vatican Council and given precision in the Ecumenical Directory?

In the five years that have passed since the Pope's visit our collaboration has been intensified, thanks to the tireless efforts of that intrepid ecumenical pioneer, Cardinal Willebrands, and of his devoted colleagues in the Secretariat for Promoting Christian Unity.

One of the significant landmarks in the relationship of the Roman Catholic Church and the World Council was the study undertaken under the auspices of the Joint Working Group on "Common Witness and Proselytism." [*See infra* p. 176.] This document was commended in 1970 to the churches for study. I only want to lift some sentences from it that are relevant for our consideration today:

Unity in witness and witness in unity. This is the will of
Christ for his people. . . . All Christian communions, in
spite of their divisions, can have a positive role to play in
God's plan of salvation.

The central task of the churches is simply to proclaim the
saving deeds of God. This then should be the burden of their
common witness; and what unites them is enough to enable
them in large measure to speak as one. Indeed all forms of
common witness; and what unites them is enough to enable
proclaim the Gospel to all men; they all find in the one Gospel their motivation, their purpose and their content.

Whether in witness or service, the churches are together
confronted by the fundamental issues of the nature and destinies of men and nations, and while they face these questions they encounter men of other religions, or men who are
indifferent or unbelievers who hold to a variety of ideologies.

It is in this spirit that the synod working paper states (and I
quote it in a rough translation): "The ecumenical movement
finds its origin, among other things, in the requirements of evangelization that call for unity among Christians. The Council has
considerably encouraged the Catholic Church, according to the
will of Christ, to institute a dialogue with the other Christian
churches and thus increase the concern for restoring unity among
all Christians." It is in this spirit that I have been invited to
speak to you today.

The conviction of the World Council of Churches has been
that evangelization is the ecumenical theme par excellence.
When the World Council was being formed it was agreed that
one of its major functions should be "to support the churches in
their task of evangelization." It was then stated: "The proposal
is based on the conviction that today more than ever evangelism
is the supreme task of the churches and that in this task they
should assist each other to the utmost of their ability." This was
endorsed by the first assembly of the World Council in 1948 that
declared, after surveying the situation of the world and of the
Church: "The evident demand of God in this situation is that the

whole Church set itself to the total task of winning the whole world for Christ." The Central Committee meeting of 1951 adopted a statement on "The Calling of the Church to Mission and Unity" in which the churches were reminded that the word *ecumenical . . .* "is properly used to describe everything that relates to the whole task of the whole Church to bring the Gospel to the whole world."

This conviction implies that the evangelization of the modern world can only be conceived and carried out in an ecumenical perspective and fellowship. That has in fact been the experience of the World Council and of the ecumenical movement. The ecumenical movement as we know it now had its origins in the World Missionary Conference in Edinburgh in 1910. From this conference sprang the International Missionary Council and the Life and Work and Faith and Order movements, all of which went into the formation of the World Council of Churches.

What has the World Council done during these years to support the churches in their task of evangelization? First of all, at its inauguration in 1948 the Council set up a Secretariat "to stimulate and assist the churches in meeting more adequately their responsibilities for the proclamation of the Gospel of Christ to all men everywhere in all their individual and social relationships." This Secretariat worked closely with the Department of Missionary Studies of the International Missionary Council until they were united after the integration of this Council with the World Council in 1961. Surveys on evangelism were made in the 1950s in Europe and North America leading up to a major consultation in 1958 on "Theological Reflection on the Work of Evangelism," preceded by a consultation on "The Role of the Laity in the Missionary Outreach of the Church." A parallel study was made in the 1950s and 1960s on "Churches in the Missionary Situation: Studies in Growth and Response," which included countries not only in the Third World but also in Europe and North America. Several volumes were published. In the 1960s there was a major emphasis on "Evangelism and the Structure of the Church," and "The Missionary Structure of the Congregation," which resulted in a report, "The Church for Others." There has more recently been a wide-ranging discussion on "Salvation Today" that was the theme of the conference at Bangkok at the end of 1972. The Faith and Order Commission has also conducted a study on "Giving an Account of the Hope that is in us." In both of the latter efforts Roman Catholics have played a very active role. I may mention too that each of the four Assemblies of the World Council have wrestled with the theme of evangelization in one form or another. The Fifth Assembly next year will have as its main theme, "Jesus Christ Frees and Unites," which is an evangelistic assertion and will deal with the topic "Confessing Christ Today."

What have we learned during these twenty-five years of reflection on the churches' work of evangelization?

The nature of evangelization. The declaration of the Second Assembly of the World Council is typical of ecumenical thinking on evangelization:

> Jesus Christ is the Gospel we proclaim. He is also himself the Evangelist . . . To evangelize is to participate in his life and in his ministry to the world . . . [Evangelism is] the bringing of persons to Christ as Savior and Lord that they may share in his eternal life. Here is the heart of the matter. There must be personal encounter with Christ . . . For on his relationship to God in Christ depends the eternal destiny of man.

There has also been general agreement on what evangelization is not. First, it is not propaganda or the purveying of a particular confessional doctrine or way of life or of a so-called superior Christian culture to the exclusion of others. At the last assembly of the International Missionary Council in 1957 it was explicitly stated: "The Christian world mission is Christ's, not ours. Prior to all our efforts and activities, prior to all our gifts of service and devotion, God sent his Son into the world. And he came in the form of a servant—a servant who suffered even to the death of the Cross . . . To seek first to safeguard the interests, the activities, the sphere of influence of our Church, our mission, our confessional body is in the end a denial of mission, a refusal to be a servant." Secondly, evangelization is not proselytism (in the pejorative sense). Here I refer to the important statement of the Central Committee in 1960:

> Proselytism . . . is the corruption of witness. Witness is

corrupted when cajolery, bribery, undue pressure or intimidation is used—subtly or openly—to bring about seeming conversion; when we put the success of our Church before the honor of Christ; when we commit the dishonesty of comparing the ideal of our own Church with the actual achievement of another; when we seek to advance our own cause by bearing false witness against another church; when personal or corporate self-seeking replaces love for every individual soul with whom we are concerned. Such corruption of the Christian witness indicates lack of confidence in the power of the Holy Spirit, lack of respect for the nature of man and lack of recognition of the true character of the Gospel.

The authority and urgency of evangelism. This was clearly stated in the document, "Theological Reflection on the Work of Evangelism":

The basic urgency of evangelism arises therefore from the nature and content of the Gospel itself and its authority lies in the recognition by all believers that they have been claimed by Christ precisely for the purpose of becoming his witnesses. The imperative of evangelism lies in the deeds of God which are its message, and its inevitability lies in the fact that they who evangelize are those who have been grasped by God's action and know that their witness in word, deed and oneness is the reflex of their faith-relation to their Lord. The love of Christ constrains them.

The dimensions of evangelism. The fullest expression of this element of evangelization was made by the document just quoted:

There is no single way to witness to Jesus Christ. The Church has borne witness in different times and places in dirrerent ways. This is important. There are occasions when dynamic action in society is called for; there are others when a word must be spoken; others when the behavior of Christians one to another is the telling witness. On still other occasions the simple presence of a worshipping community or man is the witness. These different dimensions of witness to the one Lord are always a matter of concrete obedience. To take them in isolation from one another is to distort the Gospel. They are inextricably bound together, and together give the true dimension of evangelism. The important thing is that God's redeeming Word be proclaimed and heard.

The goal of evangelism. Ecumenical thinking on the eschatological nature of the Gospel has deepened our understanding of the goal of evangelization. The Second Assembly in 1954 received a statement drawn up by twenty-five leading theologians and thinkers on "Christ—the Hope of the World." It described the Church's evangelistic task as "participation in the work of God which takes place between the coming of Jesus Christ to inaugurate God's Kingdom on earth, and his coming again in glory to bring that Kingdom to its consummation . . . Our work until his coming again is but the result of our share in the work which he is doing all the time and everywhere. The Church's mission is thus the most important thing that is happening in history. And yet because the mission of the Church points beyond history to the close of the age, it has this significance too, that it is itself among the signs that the end of history has begun. The hope of our calling is set towards the hope of his coming."

The evangelizing Church. It has been a datum of ecumenical thinking that the *raison d'être* of the Church as the whole people of God is evangelization. It is not only the task of specialists, societies or orders, but of the whole Christian community. This view of the Church is only slowly being comprehended. The Fourth Assembly asserted: "Mobilizing the people of God for mission today means releasing them from structures that inhibit them in the Church and enabling them to open out in much more flexible ways to the world in which they live. In this world we need to meet others across all the frontiers in new relationships that mean both listening and responding, both giving and receiving." It has also been our experience in the ecumenical movement that it is when churches in a local situation become deeply committed to evangelization in all its dimensions that they are driven to hear and begin to act on the prayer of our Lord "that they may all be one that the world may believe."

This summary of ecumenical thinking on evangelization can quite easily be paralleled by the massive body of thinking contained in the texts produced by Vatican II. I refer in particular to the Dogmatic Constitution of the Church (*Lumen Gentium*), the Pastoral Constitution on the Church in the Modern World (*Gaudium et Spes*), the Decree on Ecumenism (*Unitatis Redintegratio*), the Decree on the Apostolate of the Laity (*Apostolicam Actuositatem*), the Decree on the Church's Missionary Activity (*Ad Gentes*), the Declaration on the Relationship of the Church to Non-Christian Religions (*Nostra Aetate*), and the Declaration on Religious Freedom (*Dignitatis Humanae*). It is on the basis of the thinking of the Roman Catholic Church and of the World Council of Churches that we have been able to embark on cooperative efforts in many fields. I need mention only a few: The joint committee and secretariat on Society, Development and Peace (SODEPAX); the Christian Medical Commission; Urban and Industrial Mission; Dialogue with People of Living Faiths and Ideologies; Laity Formation; participation in the study of such themes as "Salvation Today" and "Giving an Account of the Hope that is in us," and the production of the study document "Common Witness and Proselytism." Experience has therefore shown that evangelization is now more than ever seen and practised in an ecumenical perspective and increasingly so in local situations around the world.

The main focus of our concern for evangelization is not to arrive at some consensus as to its nature, scope and goal, or indeed to affirm our common calling, but rather to discover what the evangelistic task is in today's world. This demands that we discern the signs of the times. What are they? During the first part of the Synod several bishops referred to some of these signs. I will try to mention a few in the knowledge that all the churches are called today to come to terms with these signs. No church has a monopoly of discernment or of wisdom. We are all compelled to listen to what the Spirit is saying to the churches.

Everywhere the process of secularization is going on. This process is the means by which people through science and technology liberate themselves from the forces of nature and gain their God-given dominion over nature in order to become truly responsible for their existence and not rely on some *Deus ex machina* or the surrender to Fate. The world is no more closed

and unchangeable, but open to the future and in constant transformation. This development did not happen automatically. It
was the result of biblical teaching and understanding. It is significant that the big leaps forward in secularization have taken
place in countries that were influenced by the Christian world
view. The whole biblical tradition is secular in purpose, enabling
people through faith in the God of time and history to dethrone
nature as an idol, an unknown capricious god, and to come of
age, as Bonhoeffer expressed it. The incredible advances in the
conquest of space, the vastly increased means of communication
both in travel and in the mass media have made the world a
global village. We are now more than ever in history members
one of another. We are now all neighbors on this planet sharing
a common destiny. Science and technology are providing the
possibilities for conquering disease, of dispelling ignorance, of
having enough to maintain the human species. We can even plan
ahead and mobilize resources to achieve our material designs.

   We Christians are adept at describing the other side of this
development. We are aware of the new material gods that people
have designed and made and to which they have given their
allegiance—the devotion to things, to having and consuming
more and more, to prospective rather than perspective, the use of
the enhanced power that people possess to increase war and destruction through armaments, the fact that our global village is
the scene of vicious and violent divisions more deadly than ever
in history, the greedy draining of our natural resources and the
devastation of our environment; indeed, the threats to our very
survival as the human species. All these things are contrived by
human beings and we carry inescapable responsibility for them
in all our societies.

   Another sign of the times is the search of millions of people
for ways of making life more humane. Everywhere there is the
struggle for liberation from injustice of every kind, from the
structures that imprison and warp both those who oppress and
those who are oppressed, from the idolatry of ideological and
social systems that resist change towards a more just, open and
human community, from the phenomenon of faceless men and
women who manipulate societies without having to be accounta-
ble, from the loss of purpose in work, leisure or social relations,
from the violation of human rights in all our countries, from the

paralysis of recurrent world monetary crises and uncontrollable inflation that make nonsense of people's capacity to manage their own creations, and from the resulting apathy, cynicism, alienation, despair and senseless violence.

Here again this struggle for justice and community finds its source in the biblical understanding that the structures of society are not fixed and ends in themselves, but must be subject to God's purpose of being the spheres in which people can fulfill their destiny to live a shared life in community. The awareness of millions of submerged people of this destiny is one of the new facts of our time. The attempts to suppress this awareness by ruthless power, supported by the complicity of many nations and through economic investment, only increase the human tragedy.

Now these two signs of people becoming of age by being more responsible for themselves vis-à-vis nature and the structures of society have given rise to other signs of the times.

Scientists, technologists and other savants are asking fundamental questions about their responsibility for what they produce or are asked to produce. Gone are the days when these intellectuals saw their task in neutral Promethean terms. For example, the World Council study on "The Future of Man in a World of Science-based Technology," which was brought to focus in a recent conference at Bucharest, drew the attention of Christians to the ethical and spiritual questions raised by their researches and discoveries. The pertinence of these questions is matched by the inadequacy of our present theological categories for dealing with them. Indeed, the scientists and planners of societies are now speaking of the need for a new asceticism with regard to the development and sharing of the world's resources.

Those who have embraced or live under the ideological system of scientific materialism are now conscious that the aim of a classless, just society is far from being achieved. In fact the revolutionary termination of the oppression of feudalism and uncaring capitalism has been replaced by the regimentation of people into industrial development with little regard for human freedom and participation, resulting in new forms of alienation. Rigid control of freedom of speech and expression has not been able to suppress the growing cry for a human face to socialism.

Over the past ten years we have witnessed the agonizing protest of youth who represent in a large number of countries the majority of the population. They have played a crucial role in challenging racial and social injustice and the demonic structures of our society whether in education, work, or human relations. In some countries they have been brutally suppressed. In more recent years youth have been expressing the spiritual hunger of our time. While many have taken off into mystical experience through drugs and Eastern religious practices, many more are earnestly seeking to find the spiritual resources in Christian faith and worship that will inspire and undergird their struggle for social justice. An example of this search is the significant Council of Youth inspired by the Taizé Community. [*See infra*, p. 277]. Contemplation and struggle are seen in dynamic, prophetic relationship. Others are attempting to overcome the anonymity and "privatization" of society by assembling in small, intense groups, some of them of a charismatic nature. The reemergence of faiths other than the Christian faith and the search for world community in justice and peace with Christians is yet another sign of the times.

The condition of the churches is itself a sign of the times. They are no longer a dominant and dominating force in society. The Constantinian era is over. Everywhere the Church is or is becoming a minority, a diaspora in society. Theological and ecclesiastical structures of thought and life that so often reflected and strengthened oppressive and unjust states are now discredited. The churches are being forced to discover their role as the body of Christ, the servant of the Lord, and as "the Pilgrim Church which goes forth boldly as Abraham did into the unknown future, not afraid to leave behind the securities of its conventional structures, glad to dwell in the tent of perpetual adaptation, looking to the city whose builder and maker is God" (WCC Third Assembly statement).

How do the churches read these signs of the times? How do these signs affect their work of evangelization today? It cannot be taken for granted that the churches do attempt to recognize and understand the signs of the times. Jesus himself warned the religious people and leaders: "When you see a cloud looming up in the west you say at once that rain is coming, and so it does. And when the wind is from the south you say it will be hot, and it is. Hypocrites! You know how to interpret the face of the earth and the sky. How is it you do not know how to interpret these times?" (Luke 12:54-56). It is possible to be able to be sensitive to the natural, traditional phenomena around us and yet be insensitive to the new and challenging issues of life-and-death significance for us. Jesus was himself the sign that illuminated all the signs of the times and yet people did not recognize him. We are less excusable, because we live in the reality of the finished work of Christ in his death and resurrection and in the dispensation of the Holy Spirit who enables us to discern and to act. This Synod of Bishops, the recent World Conference on Evangelization at Lausanne and the earlier Bangkok Conference on "Salvation Today" are genuine efforts to realize that this is a time of crisis, provoked by God's word and action in the cries and actions of humanity when decisions must be made which are of supreme significance for the Church's evangelistic task.

It is my own conviction that the signs of the times I have described among others constitute a genuine *praeparatio evangelica*. They demonstrate the ways in which human beings are on the one hand assuming their responsibility for their existence as made in the image of God, even if they do not know or acknowledge him, and on the other hand their increasing realization that they cannot achieve an authentic existence in justice and peace on their own. Even Marxists speak of the need for transcendent humanism. It is of course true that this recognition is not universal. There may even be a majority of persons who are indifferent or reduced to nerveless helplessness. But the hopeful sign is that even among these people there is an awakening of consciousness of their human lot. This is therefore no time for the churches to relapse into a feeling of fear and despair. Such pessimism is a denial of faith in our risen Lord and a misreading of the signs of the times.

But having said this, it remains true that a relevant evangelization will depend on a radical change of attitude, thinking, speaking and living in and among the churches. What then should be the form of existence of the evangelizing Church today? We have been learning in the ecumenical movement that the only way forward is the way of dialogue with the modern world. Dialogue is not an intellectual exercise, not a programme or a fashion. It is not a means of discovering how others think and speak so that we can adapt our ready-made, traditional dogmatic answers. Dialogue is a form of existence, the form of the incarnate Lord as a servant living among human beings, being open and vulnerable to them. It is the way of the Cross. Or as St. Paul puts it in his profound reflections in his letter to the Philippians, it means to know Christ, commit ourselves to him "in the power of his resurrection and the fellowship of his sufferings" (3:10). Jesus' ministry was one of dialogue with the poor and needy, the rich and the powerful, the sick and those who thought they were well, the religiously upright and the outcasts. It was in the dialogue of word and act, of debate and healing that the Good News was proclaimed. And the supreme proclamation was his solidarity, his life-giving dialogue with humanity on the Cross when he cried, "My God, my God, why hast thou forsaken me?" The authenticity of our evangelization will depend on our willingness to assume this faithful risk of suffering love with human beings today.

Such a costly dialogue also demands taking the others with radical seriousness in their particularities, their identities, their proper otherness. The Gospels do not give us a dogmatic presentation of God's revelation in Christ. Rather they tell a series of very diverse stories of Christ's concrete encounter with different human beings and groups.

As the Jewish philosopher Spinoza wrote: "The more we know things in their particularity, the more we know God." This means today that we must learn to respect people in their cultural and religious settings. Pluralism of life and response is not a danger to the uniqueness of the Gospel. Rather it makes possible the expression of what both St. Paul and St. Peter described as the many-sided grace or wisdom of God and affirms the true universality of the Gospel as it finds its form in the soil of different cultures. The Gospel by its very character challenges all peoples in their cultures and yet it is their culture that shapes the human voice which must answer the voice of Christ. There is no true evangelization that results in a copying of foreign ways of accepting Christ.

This carries two consequences for the evangelizing Church. First, evangelization is not a strategy that can be worked out by a synod of bishops, or by the World Council of Churches, or by a world fellowship of evangelicals. It takes place in a given place and with particular persons or groups. Therefore the base of evangelization is the local church, the whole people of God in the community as they worship, live and work among people in a dialogue of solidarity. What matters here is that there be a dialogue between local churches in mutual respect and correction in a collegiality of sharing and being enriched by "the grace of God in its varied forms" (1 Peter 4:10). Secondly, evangelization that occurs in a given place and among people in their particularities must take into consideration the whole of the existence of the persons and groups. Word and act, proclamation and service, theology and praxis, contemplation and struggle, patient hope and urgent engagement are inextricably bound together as the proper rhythm of evangelization.

But dialogue as the form of evangelization can be credible to those without faith only if the churches and Christians have learned to live this dialogue among themselves as a normal manner of existence. The real issue is not to ask whether cooperation in evangelization is possible between Roman Catholics and other Christians, but whether Christians of different confessions are so prepared to be exposed to each other in faith and life that they allow the Gospel to do its own explosive work in and through them. That is the ecumenical task and that is why evangelization is essentially an ecumenical enterprise.

The challenge facing the churches is not that the modern world is unconcerned about their evangelistic message, but rather whether they are so renewed in their life and thought that they become a living witness to the integrity of the Gospel. The evangelizing churches need themselves to receive the Good News and to let the Holy Spirit remake their life when and how he wills. As Monsignor Etchegaray said to the synod a few days ago: "A church that is being renewed in order more effectively to evangelize is a church that is itself willing to be evangelized . . . We lack not so much the words to say to people as credible persons to say the Word."

In reality evangelization, renewal and unity are intimately related as the common calling of all the churches. Evangelization is the test of our ecumenical vocation. The crisis we are going through today is not so much a crisis of faith as a crisis of faithfulness of the whole people of God to what he has offered us of his grace in the crucified and risen Lord and in what he demands in the wisdom and power of his Holy Spirit.

Common Witness and Proselytism

A Study Document

This document, prepared by a Joint Theological Commission, was received by the Joint Working Group between the Roman Catholic Church and the World Council of Churches at its meeting in May, 1970.

The document was elaborated by the commission on the initiative of the Joint Working Group. The commission held two full meetings (in Arnoldshain, Germany in 1968 and in Zagorsk/USSR in 1968). Various subsequent drafts were submitted to a wide group of consultants. This text was formulated in the light of comments received.

The Joint Working Group recommended to the parent bodies that it be offered to the churches as a study document for their consideration, saying, "Although there may not be complete agreement on everything contained in the document it represents a wide area of consensus on common witness and proselytism. It is therefore suggested that the churches in the same area study it together. The further examination of the theme of common witness will inevitably demand a fuller development of and agreement on the content of the witness Christians are bound to give to Christ and his Gospel." The document is reprinted from the January 1971 issue of *The Ecumenical Review* (Geneva).

Introduction

1. Unity in witness and witness in unity. This is the will of Christ for his people. The Lord has called all his disciples to be

witnesses to him and his Gospel to the ends of the earth (Acts 1.8), and he has promised to be with them always to the close of his age (Mt. 28.20). But for centuries in their efforts to fulfill this mission Christian communions have borne the burden of divisions, even differing about the meaning of the one Gospel. They have not been a clear sign of the one and holy people, so it has been hard for the world to believe (John 13.35; 17.21).

2. Today, moved by the Holy Spirit, the various Christian communions are seeking to restore the unity they have lost, in the hope that one day when they are fully renewed and united in faith and charity they may be better able to glorify God by bringing home to the whole world the hope of the coming kingdom. They are striving to overcome whatever indifference, isolation and rivalry have marked their relations to each other and thus distorted Christian witness even to that unity with which God has already blessed them.

3. This document is an attempt to state the implications of the obligation
—to bear common Christian witness, even while the churches are divided;
—to avoid in their mutual relations and in their evangelizing activities whatever is not in keeping with the spirit of the Gospel;
—to provide one another as far as possible with mutual support for a more effective witness of the Gospel through preaching and selfless service to the neighbor.

4. This document is offered to the churches. Its reflections and suggestions may serve as a basis of discussion among Christians in varied circumstances in order to arrive at a line of conduct where they live and witness.

MEANING OF THE TERMS:
Christian Witness, Common Witness,
Religious Freedom, Proselytism

5. *Christian Witness.*[1] Witness is taken here to mean the continuous act by which a Christian or a Christian community proclaims God's acts in history and seeks to reveal Christ as the true light that shines for every man. This includes the whole life: worship, responsible service, proclamation of the Good News— all is done under the guidance of the Holy Spirit in order that

men may be saved and be gathered into Christ's one and only Body (Col. 1.18; Eph. 1.22-23) and attain life everlasting—to know the true God and him whom he has sent, Jesus Christ (cf. John 17.3).

6. *Common Witness.* Here is meant the witness that the churches, even while separated bear together, especially by joint efforts, by manifesting before men whatever Divine gifts of truth and life they already share in common.

7. *Religious Freedom.* Religious freedom is not used here in the wider biblical sense (e.g. Rom. 8.21). It is pointing to the right of the person and of communities to social and civil freedom in religious matters. Each person or community has the right to be free from any coercion on the part of individuals, social groups or human power of any kind; so that no individual or community may be forced to act against conscience or be prevented from expressing belief in teaching, worship or social action.[2]

8. *Proselytism.* Here is meant improper attitudes and behavior in the practice of Christian witness. Proselytism embraces whatever violates the right of the human person, Christian or non-Christian, to be free from external coercion in religious matters or whatever in the proclamation of the Gospel does not conform to the ways God draws free men to himself in response to his calls to serve in spirit and in truth.[3]

Common Witness

9. There is a growing recognition among the churches that they must overcome their isolation from each other and seek ways to cooperate in witness to the world.[4] In face, however, of difficulties and obstacles, a clear basis and source of power and hope is needed if the churches are to embark on this common witness.

10. This basis and source is given in Christ. He is sent into the world by the Father for the salvation of mankind. There is no other name in which men may find salvation and life (Acts 4.12). Christian churches confess Christ as God and the only Savior according to the Scriptures and most adhere to the ancient creeds that testify to this central truth of faith.

11. Moreover, the churches believe that they live only by the divine gifts of truth and life bestowed by Christ. Most churches acknowledge that gifts of divine grace are a reality in other churches that also provide access to salvation in Christ. Thus all Christian communions, in spite of their divisions, can have a positive role to play in God's plan of salvation.

12. The churches have the privilege and the obligation of giving witness to the truth and new life that is theirs in Christ. Indeed both privilege and obligation are entrusted to the whole community of Christians to whom God gives a vital role in his plan for the salvation of the world.

13. Therefore Christians cannot remain divided in their witness. Any situations where contact and cooperation between Churches are refused must be regarded as abnormal.

14. The gifts that the churches have received and share in Christ have demanded and made urgent a common witness to the world. The needs of men and the challenges of a broken and unbelieving world have also compelled the churches to cooperate with God in deploying his gifts for the reconciliation of all men and all things in Christ. This common witness takes place in many areas of social concern, such as

—the development of the whole person and of all persons;

—the defense of human rights and the promotion of religious freedom;

  the struggle for the eradication of economic, social and racial injustice;

—the promotion of international understanding, the limitation of armaments and the restoration and maintenance of peace;

—the campaign against illiteracy, hunger, alcoholism, prostitution, the traffic in drugs;

—medical and health and other social services;

—relief and aid to victims of natural disasters (volcanic eruptions, earthquakes, hurricanes, floods).

15. Cooperation has also extended to include the production, publication and distribution of joint translations of the Scriptures. Moreover, an exploration is being made of the possibility of common texts to be used for an initial catechesis on the central message of the Christian faith. In this connection cooperation in the field of education and in the use of communications media is already going on in some places.

16. The cooperation of the churches in these varied fields is being accompanied by common prayer and common acts of worship for each other and for the world. Of particular significance is the "Week of Prayer for Christian Unity" that is now celebrated in many places around the world. This practice of common prayer and of acts of worship has greatly helped to create and develop a climate of mutual knowledge, understanding, respect and trust. The World Council of Churches and the Roman Catholic Church have contributed to this improved climate by their studies and guides to common prayer. This fellowship in prayer nevertheless sharpens the pain of the churches' division at the point of eucharistic fellowship that should be the most manifest witness to the one sacrifice of Christ for the whole world.

17. The central task of the churches is to proclaim the saving deeds of God. This then should be the burden of their common witness; and what unites them is enough to enable them in large measure to speak as one. Indeed all forms of common witness are signs of the churches' commitment to proclaim the Gospel to everyone; they all find in the one Gospel their motivation, their purpose and their content.

18. Whether in witness or service the churches are together confronted by the fundamental issues of the nature and destinies of men and nations, and while they face these questions they encounter men of other religions or men who are indifferent or unbelievers or who hold to a variety of ideologies.

19. But at this vital point of mutual engagement the churches become aware not only of their shared understanding of the Gospel but also of their differences. They all believe that Jesus Christ has founded one Church, and one alone; to this Church the Gospel has been given; to this Church everyone has been called to belong. Yet today many Christian communions present themselves to men as the true heritage of Jesus Christ, and this division among the churches greatly reduces the possibilities of common witness.

20. In the context of religious freedom and the ecumenical dialogue, respect is due to the right of churches to act according to convictions that they believe should be held in fidelity to Jesus Christ:

a) While it is indeed aware of its pilgrim condition, a church can be convinced that in it subsists the one Church founded by Christ, that also in it one can have access to all the means of salvation that the Lord offers, that its witness has always remained substantially faithful to the Gospel.

b) A church can regard itself as bound in conscience to proclaim its witness to its own belief, which is distinct from that of the other churches.

c) While the major affirmations of faith such as those that are formulated in Scripture and professed in the ancient creeds, are common to almost all the Christian confessions, different interpretations can sometimes call for reservations on this common character.

d) The teaching of certain churches can place limits on cooperation in social concerns, for example different positions on family ethics (divorce, abortion, responsible parenthood).

Nevertheless it is not enough to know the limits that the division of Christians places on common witness. The more the need of common witness is grasped, the more apparent does it become that there is a need to find complete agreement on faith —one of the essential purposes of the ecumenical movement.

21. Differences about the content of witness because of varied ecclesiologies are by no means the only obstacle to cooperation among the churches. The rivalries and enmities of the past, the continued resentments due to the memory of ancient or recent wrongs, the conflicts generated by political, cultural and other factors—all these have prevented the churches from seeking to bear a common witness to the world. Only the willingness to extend mutual forgiveness of past offenses and wrongs and to receive correction from each other will enable the churches to fulfill their obligation to show forth a common witness to each other and to the world.

22. There is however an understandable hesitation of a church to cooperate in witness where this may trouble and confuse its members. Among other reasons it may be due also to lack of contact and mutual understanding between the clergy and the laity of churches. In all such cases a patient and determined effort should be made to create conditions that favor cooperation.

23. A further obstacle to joint action in witness derives

from receiving and interpreting the Gospel in forms so exclusive
as to lead to a refusal of all discussion and an unwillingness to
recognize that the Spirit can operate in groups other than one's
own. This attitude is generally labelled "sectarianism" and such
exclusive and excluding groups are often called "sects." When
faced with this situation churches should first of all recognize the
challenge these groups present to them and examine themselves
as to their inadequacy in meeting the profound spiritual needs of
their members and of those around them. They must also guard
against the very spirit of sectarianism they so rightly deplore in
others. Rather should they strive to hear God's call to renewal
and to greater faithfulness to his message of salvation.

24. Moreover the churches should pay particular attention
to groups that seem open to receive those aspects of the Christian message that those communities have hitherto neglected.
The churches must thus always stand ready for dialogue and to
seize every opportunity to extend a fraternal hand and to grasp
the hand held out to them.

Proselytism and Relations Between Churches

25. Christian witness to those who have not yet received or
responded to the announcement of the Gospel or to those who
are already Christians should have certain qualities in order to
avoid being corrupted in its exercise and thus becoming proselytising. Furthermore the ecumenical movement itself had made
Christians more sensitive to the conditions proper to witness
borne among themselves. This means that witness should be
completely
—conformed to the spirit of the Gospel, especially by respecting
   the other's right to religious freedom, and
—concerned to do nothing that could compromise the progress
   of ecumenical dialogue and action.

26. *Required Qualities for Christian Witness.* In order that
witness be conformed to the spirit of the Gospel:

a) The deep and true source of witness should be the commandment: "You must love the Lord your God with all your
heart, with all your soul, and with all your mind . . . You must

love your neighbor as yourself" (Mt. 22.37 and 39, Lev. 19.18; Deut. 6.5).

b) Witness should be inspired by the true end of the Church —the glory of God through the salvation of persons. Witness does not seek the prestige of one's own community and of those who belong to, represent or lead it.

c) Witness should be nourished by the conviction that it is the Holy Spirit who by his grace and light brings about the response of faith to witness.

d) Witness respects the free will and dignity of those to whom it is given whether they wish to accept or to refuse the faith.

e) Witness respects the right of every person and community to be free from any coercion that impedes them from witness to their own convictions, including religious convictions.

27. Witness should avoid behavior such as:

a) Every type of physical coercion, moral constraint or psychological pressure that would tend to deprive people of personal judgment, of freedom of choice, of full autonomy in the exercise of responsibility. A certain abuse of mass communications can have this effect.

b) Every open or disguised offer of temporal or material benefits in return for change in religious adherence.

c) Every exploitation of the need or weakness or of lack of education of those to whom witness is offered, in view of inducing their adherence to a church.

d) Everything raising suspicion about the "good faith" of others "bad faith" can never be presumed; it should always be proved.

e) The use of a motive that has no relation to the faith itself but is presented as an appeal to change religious adherence: for example the appeal to political motives to win over those who are eager to secure for themselves the protection or favors of civil authority or those who are opposed to the established regime. Churches that form a large majority in a state should not use legal methods, social, economic or political pressure, in the attempt to prevent members of minority communities from the exercise of their right to religious freedom.

f) Every unjust or uncharitable reference to the beliefs or

practices of other religious communities in the hope of winning adherents. This includes malevolent criticism that offends the sensibilities of members of other communities. In general one should compare the good qualities and ideals or the weaknesses and practices of one community with those of the others, not one's ideals with the other's practice.

28. *Christian Witness and Relations between the Churches.* The Lord has willed that his disciples be one in order that the world believe. Thus it is not enough for Christians to conform to the above. They should also be concerned in fostering whatever can restore or strengthen between them the bonds of true brotherhood. Proposed suggestions:

a) In each church one is conscious that conversion of heart and the renewal of community are essential contributions to the ecumenical movement.

b) Missionary action should be carried out in an ecumenical spirit that takes into consideration the priority of the announcement of the Gospel to non-Christians. The missionary effort of one church in an area or milieu where another church is already at work depends on an honest answer to the question: what is the quality of the Christian message proclaimed by the church already at work and in what spirit is it being proclaimed and lived? Here frank discussion among the churches concerned would be desirable in order to have a clear understanding of each other's missionary and ecumenical convictions and with the hope that it would help to determine the possibilities of cooperation, of common witness, of fraternal assistance or of complete withdrawal.[5] In the same manner and spirit the relations between minority and majority churches should be considered.

c) Particularly all competitive spirit should be avoided by which a Christian community might seek a position of power and privilege, and concern itself less with proclaiming the Gospel to those who have not yet received it than with profiting by chances to recruit new members among the other Christian communities.

d) To avoid causes of tension between churches because of the free exercise of the right of every man to choose his ecclesial allegiance and, if necessary, to change it in obedience to conscience, it is vital:

(i) that this free choice should be exercised in full knowledge of what is involved and if possible after counsel with the pastors of the two churches concerned. Particular care is necessary in the case of children and young people; in such cases the greatest weight and respect should be given to the views and rights of the parents and tutors;

(ii) that the church that admits a new member should be conscious of the ecumenical repercussions and not draw vainglory from it;

(iii) that the church that has lost a member should not become bitter or hostile nor ostracise the person concerned; that it examine its conscience as to how it has done its duty of bringing the Gospel to that person. Has it made an effort to understand how one's Christian convictions ought to affect one's life, or rather was it content that he/she should remain a nominal and official member of that community?

(iv) that any change of allegiance motivated mainly by the desire to secure some material advantage should be refused.

e) Some points of tension between the churches are difficult to overcome because what is done by one church in view of its theological and ecclesiological convictions is considered by the other as implicit proselytism. In this case it is necessary that the two sides try to clarify what is really in question and to arrive at mutual understanding of different practices, and if possible to agree to a common policy. This can be realized only if the carrying out of these theological and ecclesiological convictions clearly exclude every type of witness that would be tainted by proselytism, as described above. Some examples of such tensions:

(i) The fact that a church that reserves baptism to adults ("believer's baptism") persuades the faithful of another church who have already been baptized as infants to receive baptism again is often regarded as proselytising. A discussion on the nature of baptism and its relation to faith and to the Church could lead to new attitudes.

(ii) The discipline of certain churches concerning the marriage of their members with Christians of other communities is often considered as proselytic. In fact these rules depend on theological positions. Conversations on the nature of marriage and the church membership of the family could bring about progress and resolve in a joint way the pastoral question raised by such marriages.

(iii) The Orthodox consider that the existence of the Eastern Catholic Churches is the fruit of proselytism. Catholics level the same criticism against the way in which certain of these Churches have been reunited to the Orthodox Church. Whatever has been the past, the Catholic Church and the Orthodox Church are determined to reject not only proselytism but also the intention even to draw the faithful of one church to another. An example of this pledge is the common declaration of Pope Paul VI and Patriarch Athenagoras I on October 28, 1967. The resolution of these questions, evidently important for the ecumenical movement, should be sought in frank discussion among the churches concerned.

29. *Conclusion.* These reflections and suggestions on common witness and proselytism will, it is hoped, offer the churches an opportunity of moving more quickly along the way which leads to the restoration of complete communion among them.

As they travel that path to unity the churches realize that Christian witness can never be perfect. They can never cease to strive for a deeper realization and clearer expression of the Good News of the unfathomable riches of Christ (Eph. 3.8) and for a more faithful living in accord with his one message. By fidelity to this striving the churches will grow together in witness to Christ "the Faithful and True Witness" (Rev. 3.14) in expectation of that day when all things will be perfectly reestablished in him (Eph. 1.10; Col. 1.20).

NOTES

1. Modern languages use several biblically derived terms that denote particular aspects of the announcements of the Gospel in word and deed: Witness, Apostolate, Mission, Confession, Evangelism, Kerygma, Message. We have preferred here to adopt "Witness," because it expresses more comprehensively the realities we are treating.

2. Cf. *Christian Witness, Proselytism and Religious Liberty in the Setting of the WCC*, of the Third WCC Assembly (1961); *Declaration on Religious Freedom*, of the Second Vatican Council (1965); *Universal Declaration on Human Rights*, of the United Nations (1948), esp. N. 18. Because the right to religious freedom operates in society these documents also mention rules that modify the use of it.

3. In certain linguistic, cultural and confessional contexts, the term "proselytism," used without qualification, has acquired this pejorative sense. In those other languages and contexts in which the term still retains its more original meaning of "zeal in spreading the faith," it will be necessary always to use "proselytism in the pejorative sense" or some phrase that denotes defective attitudes and conduct.

4. Cf. Second Vatican Council Decree, *Ad Gentes*, 6 and 15; and the proposals for "Joint Action for Mission" formulated by the 1961 New Delhi Assembly of the WCC and affirmed by the Report of Section II of the 1968 Uppsala Assembly.

5. In speaking of Joint Action for Mission, the World Council of Churches distinguishes three degrees of missionary collaboration: surveying the possibilities of missionary action; joint planning; and joint action. The meaning of common witness is wider than that of joint action for mission.

IV: New Perspectives on Other Faiths and Ideologies

Evangelization in the Asian Context

Stephen Kim

A Korean cardinal believes "the Christian message will remain an idiom foreign to our cultural soil" unless the Church recognizes and integrates the "valid spiritual values" in the cultural heritage and religions of Asia. In no way would this "lessen the fervor of evangelization," he says. "Quite to the contrary, it opens up new avenues." This excerpt from Stephen Cardinal Kim's position paper on "Principles of Evangelization in the Asian Cultural Context" for the Asian Bishops' Conference in Taipei, Taiwan, in August 1973, is reprinted from volume XI, number 4 (1974) of *Teaching All Nations*, published by the East Asian Pastoral Institute at Ateneo de Manila University in the Philippines.

We all recognize
that our countries of the East have been blessed
with a cultural and spiritual heritage
of the highest order.

We also recognize
that had those values been better understood
and better respected
much friction, including persecutions,
might have been avoided in the process of evangelizing.

These possibly unnecessary tribulations
did strengthen the faith and produce martyrs
in whom we take pride today.

However the basic misinterpretation
of Confucianism and Buddhism
helped to alienate the Church
from national cultural settings;
it impeded our long and diligent efforts
to implant the Gospel in our soil.

Against this background
it is most heartening to see
an ever-deepening understanding and recognition
of the eminent value of our cultural heritage,
and to see, late as it is,
an increasing number of Church scholars
going into such fields of research.

We must make a conscious and enlightened effort
to assume and integrate
those values and religious currents of thought
that have informed the life of our countries
through the ages.

Otherwise we shall continue to remain a minority,
unable to permeate the mainstream of our peoples' lives;
the Christian message will remain
an idiom foreign to our cultural soil.

* * *

Vatican II's teaching
that Christ's universal salvific will
is not limited to the visible unity of the Church
should in no way lessen the fervor of evangelization.

Quite the contrary
it opens up new avenues
by stressing the homogeneous continuity
of salvation history;
it should impel us
to study further the valid spiritual values
in Confucianism, Buddhism and other religions,
that are part of the Advent of Christ.

Those who become converted to Christ
shall no longer be told
that they must repudiate their past lives.

Having now found Christ
they are discovering the true face of God
whom they had sought and worshipped all along
according to the light of their conscience.

Conversion is not to be perceived as a rupture,
but as a step in maturation;
the fulfillment of man's innermost aspirations.

A New Humanity
in People's China

Donald E. MacInnis

How is "the hand of God" at work in the People's Republic of China? Donald E. MacInnis—head of the China Program of the National Council of Churches in the United States—sees a "religious" dimension in what is happening there, a spiritual struggle for "the hearts and souls of the people," with a "call for personal conversion" based on "the belief that a person's essential nature can be changed." MacInnis discusses the concepts of "conversion" and "universal salvation" in "the theology of Maoism" and describes Mao's advocacy of "continuing revolution" as a call in religious terms for "permanent revival." In the long run, however, a "Christianity incognito" is inadequate for the success of the secularized culture of People's China, says MacInnis, because it fails "to reach others for conversion in Christ." He maintains that "without commitment to the transcendent God by an identifiable, witnessing community of believers, 'secularization threatens to . . . [draw] everyone into the vortex of a nihilistic relativism.'" This paper was presented at the seminar in Bastad, Sweden, on "Theological Implications of the New China," in January 1974, sponsored by the Lutheran World Federation and Pro Mundi Vita, and is reprinted from volume 7, nos. 1-4 (1975) of *Holy Cross Quarterly*, published by College of the Holy Cross, Worcester, Massachusetts. In a postscript, Dr. MacInnis gives brief observations on his three-week visit to China in August and September 1974—his first time on the China mainland since serving as a teacher at Fukien Christian University in Foochow in 1948-49. *Mission Trends No.1* included MacInnis's article on "Theological and Missiological Implications of China's Revolution."

Visitors to China and scholars alike agree that enormous changes have taken place in China since 1949, with profound implications for the world in the years ahead. But neither scholars nor visitors agree on how to interpret the significance of those changes, either for the future of the Chinese people, or for other nations and peoples.

All visitors are impressed with the material changes in the face of the land and the improved standard of living for the workers and peasants. But their most vivid impressions, especially for those who have lived in old China, are the changes in attitudes, values and the spirit of the people. James Reston, senior editor of *The New York Times*, was overwhelmed by "the staggering thing that modern China is trying to do. They're not trying merely to revolutionize people and establish a sense of social conscience, but they're really trying to change the character of these people. The place is one vast school of moral philosophy."

Eric Sevareid, playing the role of skeptic, asked Reston in a trans-Pacific TV interview, "But you don't believe, do you Scotty, that they're going to succeed, by social means, political means, in changing the nature of the human animal? It's been tried before."

Reston replied, "Well, you know, Eric, you don't need to ask me that question. I'm a Scotch Calvinist. I believe in redemption of the human spirit and the improvement of man. Maybe it's because I believe that, or I want to believe it, that I was struck by the tremendous effort to bring out what is best in man, what makes them good, what makes them cooperate with one another and be considerate and not beastly to one another. They are trying that."[1]

Harrison Salisbury, another widely travelled senior journalist, concluded his recent book, written after an extended visit to China, with these words:

> There is—at least for a time—a New Chinese Man and a New Chinese Woman. They had self-respect and dignity. They are admirable in their fellowship, kindness and sense of self-sacrifice . . . . I had convinced myself that there was in China a new spirit among men, a contagious spirit, one on which China could build.[2]

Canadian Prime Minister Pierre Trudeau said to Premier Chou En-lai in Peking, October 1973:

> Your government has awakened a spirit in your people as few governments in the history of the world have succeeded in doing: a spirit of cooperation, of involvement, of community and individual betterment, of self-discipline. The social experiment you are conducting in this country has already demonstrated its successes. Its interest to Canadians is found in the fact that it emphasizes in many respects—though by no means all—goals identical to those held by us.[3]

An American visitor after a China visit in 1973 wrote in a letter to a friend:

> As a Christian I was deeply impressed by what I perceived in China as a strong Christian ethic in the fabric of the Chinese society and the teachings of Chairman Mao. It appeared that the people were attempting to apply the teaching of Christ to their lives and society without having known about Christ or his ministry.[4]

Hosea Williams, well-known black American civil rights leader, an advocate of non-violent means for social change, and former close associate of Dr. Martin Luther King, reported after his visit to China in 1971:

> The Chinese poor people are not only controlling their own schools but their children are receiving an education relevant to their needs. They are being taught to cultivate their talents to the best of their ability and taught not to use those talents for selfish gains but rather to give those talents to the social environment. As a result, that environment will become the best for all of its inhabitants, which embraces the principle that the strong are responsible for the weak. *To us, this is Christian education.*[5]

The end of alienation: *Is there a new humanity in China?*

Alienated man is an abstraction because he has lost touch with all human specificity. He has been reduced to performing undifferentiated work on humanly indistinguishable objects among people deprived of their human variety and compassion . . . . Marx asserts that communism is "the complete return of man to himself as a social (i.e. human) being . . . . ." It is "the positive transcendence of all estrangement—that is to say, the return of man from religion, family, state to his human, i.e. social mode of existence." In communism the breach is healed, and all the elements which constitute a human being for Marx are reunited.[6]

Disheartened by the moral squalor of the political and social scene in the West and despairing of hope for salvation through our seemingly impotent religious and social institutions, hope flares anew for mankind's future as we consider China's revolutionary experience. Questions immediately arise:

—Are the reports of transformed hearts and spirits empirically verifiable?
—If true, are the New Man and New Woman an authentic and lasting conversion or will "human nature," the imperious ego, at some later date overcome the communitarian values that now motivate the Chinese people?
—What are those values; are they cognate with traditionally accepted values in the West?
—By what methods are those values instilled and sustained?
—Are those methods and values transferable from Mao's China to nations of the West and the Third World? What relevance is there in the Chinese experience for the rest of mankind?
—What theological "truths" emerge from the Chinese experience?

We need to ask *ourselves* questions as well. Are we so conditioned by our class nature, by our Christian loyalties and by our commitment to political and social values based on instilled traditions of individual rights and liberties, that we are unable to look at China's revolution objectively? Or conversely are we so despairing of those same institutions and traditions that we look uncritically to the "China model" for a way out of our own morass?

Moreover, as Christians we ask if such profound and basically "spiritual" changes can take place without the witness and leadership of an authentic religious community. Is there something less than true conversion here, a disingenuous veneer of rhetoric and social practice masking the same old grasping human nature? Or is it true, as some observers believe, that China has created its own secular religion with a dynamic for moral transformation that outperforms the institutional religions? As Hosea Williams reported after his visit:

> We studied how the poor had been taught to develop self-respect, self-reliance, self-pride and how they took their bare hands and dug out of a mountain of despair a secure, productive future. We studied how the Chinese people are trying to develop leadership devoid of opportunism and Uncle-Tomism, leadership that remains loyal to the needs of the masses . . . . We therefore ask America: due to religious hypocrisy, is it possible that God has become so disgusted with the "believers" that he has decided to turn the moral future of mankind over to nonbelievers? Is it possible that Christianity is too important to be left in the hands of today's so-called Christians . . . ?[7]

Striving for scholarly objectivity, the phenomenological approach is bypassed for an examination of Marxist theory. One scholar, ending his comparative study of Russia and China at the year of 1949, finds both merits and inadequacies in the secular religion analogy:

> Marxism-as-prophecy, that is, as secular religion, has its merits. They include the recapture of a vision of the wholeness of man (though it corrupted the Christian vision), the comprehension of man's need for both knowledge and faith (although it confused the two with one another), the perception of man's willingness to surrender individual pride to something greater (though substitution of the party for the Church, and of history for God was not quite successful), the faith that the individual man (even though Communists un-

dertook to compel alterations in man's nature that no human agency can produce) can be changed.[8]

But, fascinating as they are, the religious analogies in Marxism and Maoism are only suggestive at best. They lead us back to fundamental questions about man and society—theological questions: What is God's intention for mankind? How is he at work fulfilling creation today? What is the relation between social justice and salvation in a secular context?

Development of People—the Religious Dimension

In July 1970, 180 delegates from 19 Asian nations, representing the three historical branches of Christianity and the Buddhist, Moslem and Hindu communities of Asia, met for eight days at the Asian Ecumenical Conference for Development to examine together issues of liberation, justice and development for Asian peoples. Their conference message said, in part:

> Our concern for development is the consequence of our faith . . . . In the suffering of the poor and the exploited we see the suffering of Christ. Where the sick are healed the hungry are fed and the captives are set free, where individuals and communities are reconciled and nations live in peace and cooperation with one another *we see the hand of God at work.*[9]

But that is not all. The Workshop on Theological Perspectives of that conference affirmed the traditional Christian view that "the meaning and destiny of human life are not exhausted by the potentialities open to human beings in development *within history** that is subject to the power of sin and decay and death. We believe that persons in Christ are destined to communion with God in this life and in the life to come. As Christians we have the task to participate in human development, to proclaim the hope of man in the Gospel of Jesus Christ, and to offer worship to the Lord of glory."[10]

While the members of this workshop agreed that "as Christians we are concerned in human development that we understand as the development of peoples in their dignity as persons and the achievement of freedom, justice and peace in the human community," they were not satisfied with a limited "realized eschatology" theology alone. "Christians need a *transcendent perspective* over development, which is necessary for a prophetic relation to it, in view of God's larger hope and purpose for mankind."[11]

Here are two poles around which this paper is organized. On the one hand there is a profound appreciation of the progress toward fulfillment in China today of the moral imperatives of the prophetic tradition and the claims of the Gospel for social justice for all the people. On the other hand, in view of progress toward liberation, justice and development for China's people in a totally secular context, a reappraisal of our own conviction that religious or transcendent values and experience embodied in a worshiping community are essential to fulfill the total needs of the whole person and society. It is my thesis that no nation or political order, however successful in reorganizing social institutions for maximizing social justice, can achieve the full humanization of its people without the meliorating presence of a "sacred community" in the midst of the secular community, and that China can be no exception in the long run.

The surviving religious community in China is apparently isolated from the political and decision-making process, while many of the traditional believers have found faith substitutes in a totalist system of secular values and practice.

The report of a Japanese journalist who visited a photographic exhibition at the People's Art Museum in Peking during the Cultural Revolution illustrates the impotence of traditional religion in the face of powerful secular forces for social change.

> One picture shows an old woman destroying a statue of a bodhisattva. The caption explained that when an earthquake occurred it was not the Buddhist saint but Mao Tse-tung who helped her. The next picture showed her destroying the old charm to give place to a portrait of Mao Tse-tung, and a new portrait of smiling Mao in military uniform was hung in the old family Buddhist shrine.[12]

There is no reported evidence of the survival of Buddhism in

China as a people's religion still being practiced. Although there are eyewitness reports of a spontaneous revival of Buddhist popular religious practice during the brief "anarchy" period of the Cultural Revolution in 1967, recent visitors to a number of temples and monasteries in various parts of China agree on the total absence of lay worshipers, and the presence of only a handful of clergy.

But the "religious" dimension is not absent in People's China. On the contrary, the "struggle between two lines" that characterized the Cultural Revolution counterposed the Maoists' "mass line," or the primacy of persons, against the revisionists' advocacy of bureaucratic routinization and maximized rationalization of the political and productive economies. For Mao the voluntarist principle is central: without changing the hearts and minds of individuals, society cannot be changed. "The people and the people alone are the motive force of history."[13] The opening sentence of the 16-point *Decision of the CCP Central Committee Concerning the Cultural Revolution* reads: "The current great proletarian cultural revolution [CR] is a great revolution that *touches people to their very souls*, representing a . . . new stage of the development of socialist revolution in our country."[14]

This call for personal conversion (in contrast to the technocrats' stress on institutionalizing revolutionary change) is immediately followed by a warning to those who would block social change and personal conversion by promoting revisionist values:

Although the bourgeoisie have been overthrown, yet they attempt to use the old ideas, old culture, old customs and old habits of the exploiting classes, to *corrupt the mind of man and conquer his heart* in a bid to attain the goal of restoring their rule. On the other hand, the proletariat must squarely face all challenges of the bourgeoisie in the ideological sphere, and use its own new ideas, new culture, new customs and new habits to *transform the spiritual aspect* of the whole society.[15]

A Manichaean polarity is manifest here, a virtual cosmic struggle between the forces of good and evil for the *hearts* and *souls* of the people, a *spiritual* struggle. These are the actual words of the Central Committee of the Chinese Communist Party! This is not classic Marxism-Leninism, for it reverses the process of social change: people's hearts and society's values can be changed, they say, *prior* to the final attainment of communism. Individuals' spiritual values and social nature are not rigidly fixed by economically-defined class criteria nor is social change bound to historically determined stages of development. New men and new women make revolution, not vice versa. Here is what has been called the "Yenan syndrome," the "revolutionary romanticism" of the Maoist vision: the belief that a person's essential nature can be changed, that the process of change is not fixed and immutable but can be hastened, and that the new men and new women are the subjects of revolution, not the objects.

A New Psycho-Cultural Identity

People's China is not just another in an endless cycle of China's imperial dynasties. Profound changes have transformed the psycho-cultural identity of the Chinese people. No future change in leadership can ever totally reverse that, although Mao's advocacy of "continuing revolution," and repeated exhortations to "fight revisionism" reveal a fear and awareness of the dangers of back-sliding. The Cultural Revolution was far more than a political campaign or power struggle. The goal was a massive reaffirmation of revolutionary commitments and Maoist values—a call to the masses to accept the unprecedented fact of their liberation from a role of subservience to a leadership role and to affirm in practice the Maoist collective values. They, not the party, were the ones to lead the nation, he affirmed. "Serve the people" and "Fight self, repudiate revisionism" emblazoned the banners of the cultural revolutionaries. For three years and longer the nation was convulsed in an internal "spiritual" struggle that dwarfed in magnitude—with the possible exception of the Taiping Rebellion—anything that had preceded it in human history. In one phase alone tens of millions of educated urban youth in a move to proletarianize the hearts and minds of intellectuals, as well as to diffuse trained leadership throughout the backward areas, have been shifted permanently to rural and frontier work assignments. The CR was a profound, all-embracing and excruciatingly risky summons to China's working classes for self-recognition and self-acceptance—a call to put into practice the liberation they had already achieved. At the same time it was a call to all China's people to maintain an optimum pitch of "proletarian cultural revolution" indefinitely—in religious terms, permanent revival. (The full name for the CR was the Great Proletarian Cultural Revolution.)

There are intriguing questions raised by terminology alone. For example, what do the Chinese Communists mean by soul (ling hun), spirit (ling hsing), personal transformation (kai tsao), ghosts and demons (niu kuei she shen), human nature, liberation, happiness? What did Mao mean when he referred, during the CR, to the "dark aspects" of the people? Was this his term for "original sin"?

> In the past we waged struggles in rural areas, in factories and in the cultural field; we carried out the socialist education movement, but all this failed to solve the problem because we did not find a form, a method, to arouse the broad masses to expose our dark aspect openly, in an all-round way from below.[16]

Mao's sombre thoughts about future "revolutionary successors," revealed to Edgar Snow in 1965, his belief in permanent revolution and the need for repeated cultural revolutions and his relentless drive for transformed persons suggest no Utopian romantic, rather a veteran realist. The current campaign against both the Confucian heritage and the dangers of cultural corruption from the West support this view: the "four olds" (old ideas, habits, customs, culture) were obviously not totally replaced by "four news" during the CR.

Liberation: An Event and a Process

We begin with common assumptions of the historical background for China's revolution: that a long-term process of internal weakening and disintegration was exacerbated by a "century of humiliation" at the hands of foreign imperialist powers, bringing misery and suffering among the people; that liberation in 1949 has been followed by spectacular achievements in reintegrating the nation, in transforming the economy and in equalizing the distribution of the products of the farms and industry; and that education, public health and other social services are enjoyed on a far more equalitarian basis than has ever prevailed in China before.

China has been engaged in development, that is in socialist nation-building since liberation—October 1, 1949. Liberation means many things in China. In 1949 it meant liberation from the "two mountains" which burdened the Chinese people, the mountains of foreign imperialist exploitation and feudal oppression. Chairman Mao's words proclaiming the founding of the new People's Republic in reality proclaimed the liberation of China's people: "The Chinese people have stood up!" Liberation for all Chinese is a date, a turning-point in history. History for People's China began October 1, 1949. (However, the Gregorian calendar is officially used in China today and the years are calculated from the birth of Christ.)

Liberation however is more than a date, more than an event commemorating victory after years of struggle and civil war. Liberation is a process. Women became free/are becoming free of traditional bonds. Peasants became free/are becoming free of external and internal limits for self-realization. Party cadres became free (in early rectification campaigns)/are becoming free of tendencies toward commandism, dogmatism and authoritarianism. Even bourgeois intellectuals and former capitalists or landlords can be liberated from wrong attitudes.

As Mao wrote in his electrifying "Report on an Investigation of the Peasant Movement in Hunan" (1927):

A man in China is usually subjected to the domination of three systems of authority: (1) the state system (political authority), ranging from the national, provincial and county government, down to that of the township; (2) the clan system (clan authority), ranging from the central ancestral temple . . . down to the head of the household; and (3) the supernatural system (religious authority), ranging from the

king of hell down to . . . . all the various gods and spirits
belonging to the celestial world. As for women, in addition
to being dominated by these three systems of authority, they
are also dominated by the men . . . . These four authorities
—political, clan, religious and masculine—are the embodi-
ment of the whole feudal-patriarchal system and ideology
and are the four thick ropes binding the Chinese people,
particularly the peasants.[17]

Mao's vision comprehends far more than a transformed
socio-political economy. "The Chinese people have stood up!" Is
this what the Asian Ecumenical Conference for Development
meant when delegates declared in their final message:

We understand development as a *liberating* process that enables persons and communities to realize their full human
potential as purposed by God. Wherever human life is oppressed, enslaved and dehumanized there is underdevelopment.

Even in the economically poor countries on which our attention was largely focused, people are crying not for food
alone; they need and demand freedom, dignity, justice and
participation as well. Their quest is for "integral human development."[18]

The Conference's Workshop in Influencing Structural and
Institutional Change agreed that "the most important goal of development is the *liberation of people from external and internal
forces* that inhibit and prevent the realization of their full potential as human beings with dignity and integrity. This goal of
human development subsumes the specific objectives of distribu-
tive justice, economic progress and national integration. . . .
The major value that facilitates the attainment of development
goals is the emphasis on human dignity that will promote the *liberation of humanity*."[19]

Three years later another church consultation on development concluded that the economic upgrading of whole communities depends primarily neither on funds nor on skillful management, but "the self evident truth that persons one by one must

become part of the movement toward freedom and self-development, or they will become instead the victims of rapid change, and the corporate approach will have become fruitless." (The Division of Overseas Ministries Role in Development, NCCC USA, Dec. 10, 1973.) The purpose of decentralization of small industries in China; of shop, school and street committees; and of basic-level management of commune production teams is liberation-by-participation.

Who Are the People?

The Ecumenical Conference in proclaiming the moral imperative for human dignity and the "liberation of man" embraces implicitly all persons without distinction of class. People's China holds a fundamentally different ordering of values. No individual has "inalienable rights" aside from rights and duties inherent in membership in a class or group. Moreover, although in Maoist social theory a person holds the central place in historical development, only "the people," as defined by class, make history.

In 1945 Mao said, "The people, and the people alone, are the motive force in the making of world history."[20] At other times he also said, "The masses are the real heroes, while we ourselves are often childish and ignorant."[21] "The masses have boundless creative power"; "We should go to the masses and learn from them."[22]

Mao is credited with numerous contributions to the theory and practice of Marxism-Leninism. One of these—perhaps the most significant and fraught with meaning for the people of China—is Mao's belief that *all* people can be used to build socialism, that members of any class (not just the industrial proletariat) can become "spiritual proletarians" once their attitudes and values have been transformed and they have committed themselves by total involvement to the collective values and tasks of new China. As modified by Mao, the "dictatorship of the proletariat" has become the "people's democratic dictatorship"—a much broader concept that can encompass those of any class who qualify; that is, those with right attitudes and those able to demonstrate in social practice their right to be of "the people."

During the wartime years when support was needed from any quarter and when their bases were located far from any urban proletariat the Chinese Communists accepted peasants, students, intellectuals—even bourgeoisie—into a "proletarian hegemony with a coalition of classes." Mao's populist concept of the New Democracy and the United Front was written into the 1954 Constitution. During the early period of the People's Republic, national capitalism coexisted with socialized industry and commerce. Numbers of peasants still worked their own farms, gradually coming together into cooperatives and finally into agricultural communes—where today they work alongside rehabilitated former landlords, young men and women graduates of urban middle schools and cadre-bureaucrats from the cities sent to the countryside to learn, by short-term labor in the fields and shared peasant living, the values of the rural proletariat.

A person enters society and adds his part to the motive force of history only as a member of "the masses." In 1949 Mao named four classes as belonging to "the people":

Who are the people? At the present stage in China they are the working class, the peasantry, the urban petty bourgeoisie and the national bourgeoisie.[23]

In a later rendering, foreshadowing the trend that climaxed in the Cultural Revolution, Mao gave primacy to the first two classes: "The people's democratic dictatorship is based . . . mainly on the alliance of the workers and peasants."[24]

In the 1966 *Decision* of the CCP's Central Committee, the vanguard of the Cultural Revolution was defined as a coalition led by the workers and peasants, together with "soldiers, revolutionary intellectuals and revolutionary cadres," and particularly "large numbers of revolutionary youngsters."[25] By 1968, the Red Guard youth movement had fragmented into myriad factions and the vanguard position shifted to the "triple alliance" revolutionary committees formed by workers and peasants, revolutionary cadres and revolutionary soldiers. Workers and peasants became leading members of the new revolutionary committees at every level, including the universities. Since then the "mass line," together with a steady reiteration of Mao's admonition to "remember class struggle," has predominated in directives and instructions.

> To link oneself with the masses one must act in accordance with the needs and wishes of the masses. All work done for the masses must start from their needs and not from the desire of any individual, however well-intentioned. . . . There are two principles here: one is the actual needs of the masses rather than what we fancy they need; and the other is the wishes of the masses, who must make up their own minds instead of our making up their minds for them.[26]

There is a seeming contradiction here. If "universal salvation" belongs to the theology of Maoism; that is, if anyone, regardless of class origins, can become by transformation of class viewpoint a member of the proletariat, then why are the workers and peasants apotheosized? According to the Chinese themselves, 95 percent of the people have "democratic rights"—that is, they are of the "people." This leaves 5 percent or 40 million people without democratic rights, that is without the rights of full participation in building the new China. While equalitarianism is a goal for People's China, the time for that has not yet arrived.

Equalitarianism Postponed

In the Kutien Resolution (1929) Mao condemned "absolute equalitarianism" and "ultra-democracy." To prematurely implement Communist values is adventurist, Utopian. Mao himself found this out in the Great Leap Forward. The question is how far to permit inequalities and how to justify inequalities during the period of transition to Communism? For now, some are more equal than others.

"Remember past bitterness!" Every child born since 1949 has heard countless stories relating bitter tales of exploitation and suffering at the hands of the former oppressor classes. In the early period after liberation the elimination of the landlord and capitalist classes was necessary to advance the interests of the working classes. To survive, the landlord or capitalist had to give up his property and privileged status. To participate in the new China, he had to give up his bourgeois attitudes as well.

To promote the interest of "the people" means in a class society to give priority to raising the levels of living and of self-determination of the most deprived and oppressed groups. In China these were the urban workers and poor peasants. Mao's ideological quarrel with the Soviets centers in opposing views of the meaning of socialist revolution: for the Soviets, the revolution is over; for the Maoists, the revolution continues and class struggle continues. Moreover, in a future generation when the former exploiting classes are all gone, Mao believes that bourgeois ideas will still be lurking in the shadows to tempt and corrupt the people. The spiritual needs of the least advantaged classes, as well as their economic and welfare needs are therefore accorded top priority in policy determination and goal setting.

Maoist Values, Both Spiritual and Material

"The Foolish Old Man Who Removed the Mountains" is the title of one of Mao's three most-read essays. The other two are "In Memory of Norman Bethune" and "Serve the People." In the first Mao rewrites an ancient Chinese fable in which an old man believes that with the help of his sons and their descendants two mountains can be dug away. In the fable God was moved by his persistence and took away the mountains on the backs of two angels. In Mao's version the people take the part of God. "If they [the people] stand up and dig together with us, why can't these two mountains be cleared away?"[27] Anything is possible if the people are motivated and mobilized. Maoist values are collective values, calling for sacrifice of private goals and for cooperation in the larger goals of the community. The individual is pressed to subdue selfishness and to give himself to the public good.

"Serve the people" is a brief encomium written by Mao to memorialize the death of Chang Sze-te, a common soldier who was killed when a kiln collapsed while he was making charcoal for the people. "To die for the people is weightier than Mount

Tai. . . . Comrade Chang died for the people."[28] Death, in a secularized society, can have meaning; immortality is guaranteed for those whose memory lives on in the hearts and lives of those he served.

Norman Bethune was a Canadian doctor who died of septicemia contracted while performing battle surgery for Communist soldiers during the anti-Japanese war. "What kind of spirit is this that makes a foreigner selflessly adopt the cause of the Chinese people's liberation as his own?" Mao wrote, "[His] spirit, his utter devotion to others without any thought of self, was shown in his boundless sense of responsibility in his work and his boundless warm-heartedness towards all comrades and the people. Every Communist must learn from him. . . . We must all learn the spirit of absolute selflessness from him . . . With this spirit everyone can be very useful to the people. A man's ability may be great or small, but if he has this spirit, he is already noble-minded and pure, a man of moral integrity and above vulgar interests, a man who is of value to the people."[29]

China's socio-economic goals during the transition to Communist equalitarianism begin with a secure basic living standard pledged for all the working classes, a guaranteed level of economic and social security. Jan Myrdal reported recently from Liu Ling village in Shensi on that commune's "five guarantees": enough food, enough clothes, enough fuel, an honorable funeral and a decent education for everyone's children.[30] No mention here of spiritual values, or of "absolute selflessness" and "boundless warm-heartedness toward all comrades." But these are implicit in the basic guarantees. For how are these five guarantees to be achieved? Only by implementing collectivist values. The revolutionary dramas, the story-tellers' tales, the recounting of "past bitterness" are daily reminders that, under the old, every-man-for-himself system, the five guarantees applied only to a privileged minority.

Mao has reversed the Marxist order: Maoist values do not grow forth *from* socialist revolution; rather, socialist revolution succeeds only when preceded by conversion of the masses to proletarian, communitarian values—dedication, self-sacrifice, frugality, temperance, selflessness, honesty, uprightness, service to others. In August 1967, Mao Tse-tung issued a call, "Train a

Larger Number of Revolutionary Vangards":

> We must train a large number of revolutionary vanguards
> who have political vision, militant spirit and readiness to
> make sacrifices. They are frank, honest, active and upright.
> They seek no self-interest; they are completely dedicated to
> national and social emancipation. They fear no hardships;
> they are always firm and brave in the face of hardships.
> They are never boastful; they covet no limelight. They are
> unpretentious, realistic people. With a large number of peo-
> ple like this, the tasks of the Chinese revolution can be easi-
> ly fulfilled.[31]

If Maoist communitarian values precede rather than follow
socialist revolution then where and how do they originate?

Conversion: The Making of New Men and New Women

The Maoist view of man rejects a doctrine of universal
human nature. In his "Talks at the Yenan Forum on Art and
Literature" (1942), Mao said:

> Is there such a thing as human nature? Of course there is.
> But there is only human nature in the concrete, no human
> nature in the abstract. In a class society there is only human
> nature that bears the stamp of a class; human nature that
> transcends classes does not exist.[32]

For Mao there is no such thing as genus "man"—only a
given, concrete, particular person. In Mao's philosophy, the centrality of the theory of contradictions—that is, the theory that
objects are never static but always in process of transmutation—
means that the nature of any given person is always changeable.
According to Marxist theory, changes in human nature are the
result of new social relationships and new consciousness following socialist revolutionary changes. The Maoist modification of
Marxist theory lays greater stress on every person's capacity for
inner-directed change in response to mental stimuli, rather than

response only to social, economic and natural forces. Mao believes that conversion to new values can be hastened, that human value changes are not tied to a rigid historical determinism.

This explains the Maoist emphasis on varieties of education and indoctrination. From the first year of the new regime onward the expansion of the school system and experimentation in varieties of both academic and moral education have commanded high priorities. One primary function of education in China is to train citizens in skills and knowledge that will contribute to increased production and nation-building. But ranked with equal importance are values and attitudes acquired in the classroom, in political study, in discussion and criticism sessions and in social practice—that is, in actual productive labor.

Writing in 1949 Liu Shao-ch'i identified two aspects of human nature:

> Man has two essences; one is man's natural essence, including his physical constitution, cleverness, state of health, instinctive capacities, etc. . . . ; the other is man's social essence, including his psychological state, thoughts, consciousness, viewpoints, habits, demands and so forth.[33]

It is the second essence, man's social nature, that commands the attention of China's educators and all others concerned with correct thinking and attitudes. It was primarily fear that the school system and particularly the institutions of higher learning were breeding a new class of "intellectual mandarins" that brought on the Cultural Revolution. The village people said that sending a child away for advanced education in the city was like "flying a pigeon on a foggy day"; he would never come home again.

Experimental correctives are now being implemented in the schools at every level: preferential admissions criteria for children of workers and peasants, augmented political training, mandatory manual labor for students in factories and farm communes, textbooks completely rewritten, closing the gulf between teachers and pupils, new participatory roles for students and nonprofessional peasant-worker teachers, and decentralization of the entire school system.

In Mao's words:

> People's thought is always concrete, varied and continually
> changing and developing. Our educational work can only be
> efficacious if we implement a variety of educational works,
> meticulously contrived in accordance with the thought con-
> ditions of each individual.[34]

But education for new values or thought transformation
transcends the classroom. Thoughts are remolded in all forms of
social practice: in manual labor, in "struggle-criticism-transfor-
mation" meetings, in political study groups, in extracurricular
activities of all kinds. "It is man's social being that determines
his thinking."[35] Based on this rationale, multitudes of cadres, officials and intellectuals have since the Cultural Revolution engaged in mandatory manual labor, either in May 7th Cadre
Schools or in short-term labor stints; tens of millions of educated
urban youth have been shifted to permanent work assignments in
rural regions, and every student from kindergarten through professional schools regularly engages in productive manual labor
linked with the schools. Visitors have observed kindergarten students salvaging cork inserts from used bottle caps, primary students assembling transistors, and students of architecture doing
manual labor on building projects.

The continuing campaign to end the "three differences" between mental and manual labor, urban and rural dwellers, and
industrial and agricultural labor is part of this all-encompassing
program for changing values. The goal is not only to narrow the
actual wage- and living-standard differentials, but to change attitudes that carry over from the Confucian tradition of an elitist
educated minority ruling the illiterate laboring majority. Beyond
that is the very pragmatic goal of accelerated nation building by
an aroused, motivated people with new skills, awareness and a
sense of purpose. According to Peter Seybolt, a specialist on
China's education:

> The stated objective of the CCP education program empha-
> sizes the importance of mass education for a revolution that
> aspires to nothing less than a total transformation of human
> society. The primary goal of education according to Mao

Tse-tung is to change man's consciousness so as to change the world in which he lives. Education efforts are guided by the belief that man's consciousness is shaped . . . by his material environment, but he is naturally endowed with the rational capacity to formulate ideas that, when put into practice, can change that environment. The engine of change is man's own effort, his labor, both mental and physical.[36]

Final Comments

Many questions remain unanswered. There is no way to test or evaluate the rate or durability of conversion to new values or of transmission of those values to children and youth. Empirical data indicate that the Chinese people are in fact living and working together cooperatively to a degree unknown in other modern nations. Are they doing this without coercion or material inducement? Moreover, is this collective life-style transferable to the advanced industrial nations of the West or to other developing nations? Observers and Chinese alike agree that the "China model" is designed to work in China, that it is an indigenous model still being developed by the Chinese people and that it is not designed for export. Nor could the present system have worked in preliberation China without revolutionary changes in the superstructure and infrastructure of China's traditional society. Yet while the China model for revolution and nation building may not be transferable intact, China's example is proof to all oppressed peoples that it can be done, and the Chinese themselves are supremely confident that the people's self-liberation everywhere will come in time. The Marxist eschatological vision, with both domestic and global implications for tomorrow's world, must be a central motivating factor for personal commitments to today's disciplines in People's China.

Who can disagree with the Asian Ecumenical Conference for Development: "Where the sick are healed, the hungry are fed and the captives are set free, where individuals and communities . . . live in peace and cooperation with one another we see the hand of God at work"? But beyond the material and social changes, where is the fulcrum above history, the persons and communities within this secularized society with commitments and perspective beyond the immanent and immediate present? In the words of the Ecumenical Conference's Workshop on Theological Perspectives: "Christians need a transcendent perspective over development that is necessary for a prophetic relation to it in view of God's larger hope and purpose for mankind."

How does one visualize that "larger hope and purpose" in the context of People's China? The secularization process for China was in part a rejection of primitive superstition and social irrelevance in the traditional religions, and of cultural imperialism and sterile pietism as perceived in the Christian churches. Secularization is a rejection of religious solutions for China's human and social problems, finding in humankind alone the source of salvation. This secularizing trend in China, based in the Confucian tradition, can be found in all the reformist, modernizing and revolutionary movements that followed the collapse of the Manchu Dynasty in 1911.

Some may choose to speak of Christ incognito at work in China today, but this will be seen by the Chinese as a last-gasp kind of reverse imperialism, an attempt to co-opt an historical process. Moreover the institutional church to the degree that it survives in China bears slight resemblance to the former mission-aided churches. Christians there, like their secular neighbors, have doubtless been converted from the "four olds," including the old-style church. This does not necessarily mean giving up their faith; it does mean that there can be no retreat to former ways. Secularizaton and loss of all former this-world securities force the Christians to a radically new understanding of their role in society. An American theologian writing on the topic of "conversion," said:

The Church now is seen as the historically tangible vanguard and explicit expression of what is a present yet hidden reality to all men. The task of conversion from *all* religions must therefore be concerned with the development of the type of Christian who can survive the permanent secularization of the world. This will be possible insofar as conversion fulfills itself as a truly secularizing act wherein the person is called to differentiate himself from all antecedent authority and assume his freedom in Christ.[37]

But this freedom in Christ cannot be a guise for pure anonymity of the Christian in a secularized culture. Christianity incognito will fail to reach others for conversion in Christ and total isolation will desiccate the faith of the individual. An identifiable community, the Church as the body of Christ, is needed within society at large. Without commitment to the transcendent God by an identifiable, witnessing community of believers,

> secularization threatens to become a self-standing secularism, sucking everyone into the vortex of a nihilistic relativism. At the same time, [Christian] conversion . . . . offers the basis for a new identity transcending but not annulling the old, and a new destiny whereby each person may participate in God's promise to "make all things new."[38]

God's creation is still unfolding; his promises are being fulfilled in China and in today's world.

NOTES

1. CBS, August 31, 1971, in *The New York Times*, September 1, 1971.

2. Harrison Salisbury, *To Peking and Beyond: A Report on the New Asia* (New York: Quadrangle, 1973), p. 301.

3. Hsinhua; Peking, October 15, 1973.

4. Personal letter to the writer of this paper.

5. Hosea Williams, Press Release; Atlanta, Georgia, October 29, 1971. Emphasis added when italics appear in quotations.

6. Bertell Ollman, *Alienation: Marx's Conception of Man in Capitalist Society* (New York: Cambridge University Press, 1971), pp. 134-35.

7. Williams, *op. cit.*

8. Donald W. Treadgold, *The West in Russia and China: China 1582-1949* (New York: Cambridge University Press, 1973), Vol. II, p. 189.

9. *Liberation, Justice, Development*, Report of the Asian Ecumenical Conference for Development; Tokyo, July 1970 (no publisher listed), preface.

10. *Ibid.*, p. 50.

11. *Ibid.*, p. 51.

12. K. Takahashi, cited in Donald E. MacInnis, *Religious Policy and Practice in Communist China* (New York: Macmillan, 1972), p. 286.

13. Mao Tse-tung, *Selected Works* (Peking: Foreign Languages Press, 1961), III/257. (Hereafter *SW*)

14. *Decision of the CCP Committee Concerning the Great Cultural Revolution*, translated in Survey of the China Mainland Press, August 16, 1966 (No. 3761) Sec. I.

15. *Ibid.*

16. Hsieh Sheng-wen, *Peking Review*, March 28, 1969, p. 11.

17. *SW*, I/44.

18. *Liberation, op. cit.*, p. 1

19. *Ibid.*, p. 34.

20. *SW*, III/257.

21. Mao Tse-tung, *Quotations* (Peking: Foreign Languages Press), p. 118.

22. *Ibid.*, p. 129.

23. *SW*, IV/417.

24. *Ibid.*, p. 421.

25. *Decision, op. cit.*, Sec. II.

26. *Quotations, op. cit.*, p. 124.

27. *SW*, II/271.

28. *SW*, III/177.

29. *SW*, II/337.

30. Myrdal and Kessle, *China: The Revolution Continued* (New York: Pantheon, 1970), p. 50.

31. *People's Daily*, Peking: August 30, 1967, p. 1. In Jerome Ch'en, *Mao Papers: Anthology and Bibliography* (London: Oxford, 1970), p. 145.

32. *SW*, III/90.

33. Donald Munro, "The Malleability of Man in Chinese Marxism," *China Quarterly*, Vol. 48, October/December, 1971, p. 613.

34. *China's Youth*, No. 2, 1960, in Munro, *op. cit.*, p. 636.

35. Mao Tse-tung, "Where Do Correct Ideas Come From?" in *Four Essays on Philosophy* (Peking: Foreign Languages Press, 1963), p. 134.

36. Peter Seybolt, "The Yenan Revolution in Mass Education," *China Quarterly*, No. 48, October/December, 1971, pp. 641-42.

37. James T. Laney, "Conversion from Other Religions," in *On Conversion: Four Views* (New York: Board of Global Ministries, United Methodist Church, 1968), p. 23.

38. *Ibid.*, p. 26.

POSTSCRIPT

One looks at America with an altered vision after visiting China. A Chinese visitor to the United States last year was astonished at our casual waste of food and resources. I too see our profligacy now in poignant clarity, a way of life that seems spiralling out of control. Our various crises are grim enough; but so were China's in the late 1940s. Signs in New York's subways shock: DIAL 911 FOR RAPE and FIGHT DRUG ABUSE. Why should New Yorkers be afraid to walk in Central

Park without a dog? We freely walked the streets of China's great cities at night with no sense of fear. Young girls strolled arm in arm, children played games, mothers cradled babies while talking quietly with neighbors, old men played chess under the street lights.

The overwhelming response one brings home from a three-week visit inside China is a renewed sense of hope. The Chinese we saw in an intensive tour of five cities and three rural areas were the picture of ruddy health, the markets were stocked with food, everyone—even the elderly—had jobs or meaningful tasks. If 800 million Chinese, living on the same land area as 200 million Americans can produce food, clothing and the basic needs of life without foreign aid and can share them equitably with all their people, then so can we and so can all the people on Spaceship Earth. But it will require some personal sacrifices and some collective sharing—both qualities of the life style we saw in China.

It is clear that the Chinese success in transforming their economy and way of life is due to more than a central political authority. True, politics is pervasive; but it seemed to be a participatory politics—far more so than ours. The prodigious achievements in changing the face of the land and the economy are the result of intensive and sustained man- and woman-power, motivated to work for goals beyond personal profit and self-advancement. There is a tangible spirit of collective purpose and communitarian ethic—a social milieu that makes a place and purpose for everyone. Decisions are made by committees at every level; everyone belongs to a committee, group, team.

While that could soon prove oppressive to us, accustomed to the option *not* to participate, the people pressures on food and resources in China make mobilization of human resources an imperative; the same will surely be true here at some early date.

Returning to China after 25 years was an exhilarating and deeply moving experience. In our conversations with dozens of Chinese of all ages we felt a powerful spirit of purpose, energy, enthusiasm. We tried to find its sources. What is the motivation that mobilizes an entire nation to "serve the people"?

There is material security at a minimal but adequate level for all. The working class has been elevated to a position of dignity and respect. Women, peasants, workers and ethnic minorities have been liberated from deprivation and exploitation. There is a national identity and purpose, an awareness of China's role in the world and a pride in China's self-reliance.

Finally there is a new values system. The central value is communitarian, a surrender of self: "Serve the people"; "Fight self, establish the common good"; "Remember class struggle." There is an eschatological dimension, a commitment to goals beyond self in today's society and tomorrow's history. And there is the recapture of a vision of the wholeness of persons, a belief that the individual can be changed, transformed, converted. All these we felt throughout our China visit.

Participation:
The Changing
Christian Role
in Other Cultures

Wilfred Cantwell Smith

A Christian missionary, according to Wilfred Cantwell Smith, should be one who is a deliberate, joyous and welcome participant in the religious history of others. As the model of what he has in mind for the modern missionary, Smith nominates Martin Buber, a Jew. Without preaching or trying to convert or dominate, Buber had something to say that enabled Christians to learn through him about God. Christians therefore welcomed him— just as Japanese Buddhists, for instance, welcomed Paul Tillich and wanted to learn from him. This collaborative style of participation by Christians—working by invitation and in cooperation with those of other religious communities—would be multilateral. According to Dr. Smith, "We have no right to send missionaries to any group from whom we are not ready to invite missionaries." We are moving, he says, into a new phase—"the unitary religious history of mankind"—in which not merely a person or group may participate in the religious evolution of another tradition, but "where eventually each will participate in all." Dr. Smith, whose essay is taken from the April 1969 *Occasional Bulletin* of the Missionary Research Library, New York, is an ordained minister of the United Church of Canada. He began his career teaching at Forman Christian College in Lahore, Pakistan. On returning to the West he established and directed (1951-63) the Institute of Islamic Studies at McGill University, Montreal, and later was director (1964-73) of the

Center for the Study of World Religions at Harvard University. Currently he is McCulloch Professor of Religion, Dalhousie University, Halifax, Canada. His published works include *Islam in Modern History, The Faith of Other Men* and *The Meaning and End of Religion.*

In "Participation," I would venture to suggest, we may have a theme that could prove serviceable in the cause of missionary thinking for our day. This concept may provide a helpful new way of looking at the role of the missionary; and indeed, if this does not sound too pretentious, perhaps also at the whole modern Christian and human religious enterprise. At least, I suggest that the matter may prove worth exploring.

I would define the missionary as that person who deliberately sets out to participate in the history of another community. If he be a medical or educational or technical missionary, then his participation is in the mundane sector of that community's evolution. Yet neither he nor we nor they are so naive or so dichotomizing as to suppose that the mundane history is not relevant to the religious and vice-versa; that the medical or educational or technical changes that he may introduce have no spiritual overtones or undertones. A fortiori, the more evangelical or theological or in any way self-consciously theoretical missionary is participating more directly in the cultural—that is, the religious—dimension of the community among whom he works; even if no more explicitly.

I have spoken of the missionary as a deliberate participant because the rest of us also participate unconsciously, often in spectacularly consequential ways. The degree to which Western ideas, techniques, institutions and processes are transforming the history, including the religious history, of the rest of the world as well as of ourselves is obvious, even if frightening. The Wall Street banker and the Pentagon planner, as well as the technological innovator in agricultural machinery in Moscow or the American mid-West, are of course playing a role in the religious history of the Islamic and the Hindu and the Buddhist movements, however unconsciously and however ineptly.

Even at the cultural level, however, and even at that of strictly religious ideas a Westerner knowingly or carelessly may sig-

nificantly affect religious thought and practice, sensibility and
concern in Asia. Theodor Herzl is clearly an eminently significant figure in Islamic history. A Toynbee or a Tolstoy has been
consequential in not only Christian thought. At a more homely
level, any local citizen who invites an Asian student on a local
campus into his home, or fails to invite him, may thereby turn
out to be playing some small role in the religious evolution of
Asia. Human history, including its religious history, is an in-
tricate and delicate web of human relationships.

Yet all this is incidental and you may feel that it is taking us
too far afield. Let us return to the missionary who deliberately
and conspicuously and flatly plants himself down in the midst of
an alien community and sets about explicitly to foster religious
changes. It is fairly easy to contend that even in the nineteenth
century and even though he was not aware of it in actual historical fact, the chief consequence of the presence of the Christian
missionary in Asia was the role that he played in the religious
history of the non-Christian world.

His participation was unwitting and uncouth. So gawky was
his intrusion that the primary and at times explosive consequence
was one of vehement reaction and antithetic rebound. I need not
stress and certainly need not elaborate that there was also a positive role where participation in Asian history—perhaps particularly in the mission colleges—opened new horizons, elicited
new aspirations, new motivations, which presently became incorporated within the ongoing religious traditions in the lands concerned. The role of C. F. Andrews in the life of Gandhi is one
striking illustration. An instance of a quite different emergence is
the Ramakrishna Mission, whose form certainly and some of
whose content it could be argued are historically to be explained
in terms of Christian missionary activity. That does *not* mean
that they are any less Hindu; only that the participation was to
that extent effective.

The consequences were sometimes in line with and sometimes in strident resistance to or in recoil from what was being
intended; yet whatever form they took, the fact remains that the
historical consequences of the introduction of Christian missionary endeavour into the development of the other communities may be conceptualized most truly in terms of their function

within the indigenous religious movements of the Orient.

Of course the ideological framework within which most of the missionaries then operated and the groups in the West that sent them was to an extreme degree individualistic. It is difficult now for any of us to imagine how utterly it was presupposed at that time that an individual person could be shifted, as a brand snatched from the burning, out of one sociological and cultural and historical complex and incorporated into another (the proselytizing process by which "a Muslim" became "a Christian" or the like) without any thought being given to sociological, institutional, economic, psychological, religious-historical and other ramifications of such radical displacement. Of course no one can weigh in a scale the eternal destiny of a single soul against the historical, mundane dislocation of a million persons, and I do not wish to become involved in a theological argument as to the cosmic validity or significance of an individual conversion. All I would say on this point is that the proselytizing process too may most fruitfully be envisaged as an act by which an individual person no longer chooses to participate in the historical religious tradition and community in which he was brought up, but to participate instead in another one. This is what intercommunity conversion is. To recognize it so would be an advance. (There is another sort of conversion, to which we shall come presently: conversion *within* one's own community and tradition.)

However that may be, the over-all number of outward conversions was small; and so far as observable consequences in this world are concerned the nineteenth century Christian missionary movement's role in the religious history of the planet is to be measured and conceptualized primarily in terms of the playing of a role in the history of one tradition, of intruders, or shall we simply say participants, from another. And in the twentieth century, or at least this latter part of it, with our new understanding both of what we are doing and of what Muslims, Hindus, and Buddhists have been and are doing I suggest that the role of the Christian missionary may become self-consciously what it has always been in fact. The theological question then becomes: What is the truly Christian role that a participant may play in the evolution of another culture?

It would take me too far afield and doubtless also be too

controversial to try a theological answer to that. I shall merely mention my own conviction that the correct theological answer, given our new understanding, could mean a Christian missionary who was not merely a deliberate but also a joyous, and not merely a joyous but also a welcome participant in the religious history of the rest of mankind.

The idea of a missionary being religiously "welcome," even invited, is strange, so accustomed has one grown to the notion that a Christian missionary is plotting to undermine and to destroy the religious processes in which those to whom he goes have been participating. That this should be so is an index of our stupefaction. I would affirm it as a basic principle worthy of all credence and of all new policy decisions that no missionary is worth his salt unless what he has to say is welcomed by the leaders of the group among whom he works, so that they want to hear more; and if he is talking at the religious level then he must be welcomed by the religious leaders.

Does this sound "way out" and ludicrously romantic? Am I dreaming about something far into the future? By no means. This stage has in fact already been reached. Only on the whole it is happening under auspices other than those of the traditional missionary boards; and sometimes perhaps it is hardly even noticed by them that this in fact is where the action is. For Tillich is being read in Tokyo, Buber in Boston, and Aurobindo in Oxford. Radhakrishnan, as Hendrik Kraemer correctly pointed out, is virtually an apologist for the Hindu orientation; yet we invite him to the Harvard Divinity School because we want to hear what he has to say. Suzuki was invited to participate in the life and thought of Union Theological Seminary and was welcomed there. Tillich was welcomed in Tokyo and is studied assiduously by Buddhists, because Buddhists hope that he will be able as a Christian to throw light on Buddhists' problems. These hopes are not absurd; neither are they disappointed.

My salient example is one of the most successful, as well as one of the most admirable, as well as one of the most welcomed interfaith participants of the modern age: Martin Buber. Here was a Jew, profoundly Jewish, who had something to say to Christendom and said it. Christians agreed that he had something to say and read him studiously and with profit. They learned from him, or should we rather say learned through him, about God, about themselves, about the Christian tradition in which they were participants. They welcomed him, applauded him and asked him to come back to give them more. I nominate Martin Buber as the model of the modern missionary par excellence.

But you may reply he was not preaching Judaism; not trying to convert; not trying to dominate. Of course not; and this, indeed, is precisely the point. He was not trying to dominate and the Christian Church must repent in dust and ashes for the domineering, agressive element in that phase of the Christian missionary movement that is now virtually or hopefully at an end. He was not trying to proselytize; it is legitimate to use the word "convert" in that other sense in which every true Christian hopes to be truly converted every morning; namely, to be converted more closely, and still more closely, to God and to the truth. In this sense, many of us have been converted again and again by Buber into being Christians of truer piety. He was not preaching Judaism; and it is a sorry evangelist, as the fundamentalists have long since known, who does not know the meaning of the aphorism, "We are not preaching Christianity: we are preaching Christ."

The counterpart today to the issue in the early Church about circumcision and the Jewish law is the question of baptism and Church membership. The first Christians had to face the question: Does acceptance of the Good News mean that he who accepts it must become a member of our Jewish community? Must he participate in our processes? The answer "yes" was given, but fortunately the answer "no" prevailed. The modern counterpart question is: Does what God has to offer to the world through the Christian Church entail others opting for participation in our religious history? Let us hope that the missionary wing of the Church will not be the last section of it to recognize that here too the answer most true to the heart of our message is still that of joyous freedom.

The theological facet of this position is decisive yet I leave it unformulated just now; I will glancingly touch on parts of it in my concluding section, but chiefly I have been writing on it elsewhere and I do not wish to repeat myself here. A programmatic or administrative facet I may however attempt to formulate in a way that will for some be maybe more provocative than the theological and perhaps more immediately illustrative. And as you will see, theology will be implicit.

The suggestion is this. Opportunity for a Buber-like participation of Christians, deliberate, self-conscious, constructive, in the life and thought of other communities is growing and can therefore begin to be planned. It can and therefore should be planned in consultation and collaboration with those with whose destiny the participant is to be involved. I mean that the selection, the training and the activity of Christian participants in the process of specifically Islamic history can and I think will be done by Muslims and Christians sitting together and discussing it constructively and implementing it jointly, or participants in Hindu development, by Hindus and Christians jointly, and so on in each case. I do not know whether this will develop in such a way that from "participant" so conceived, working by invitation and in cooperation, the "missionary," an older concept, will diverge—and perhaps presently peter out, or whether rather the missionary movement will move in this collaborative direction. (In a sense one might interpret my whole presentation of the concept of participation as of an actual burgeoning development, while the question of whether it is relevant to missions—or missions will be relevant to it—is left to you to decide.) I do not know whether mission boards and mission secretaries are yet ready to call and pay for a planning conference on Christian missions to India to which an equal number of Hindus and Christians will be invited. I seriously suggest that it could be not merely significant but fruitful. And not merely fruitful but right.

I am thinking here not in terms simply of social welfare work (although in the planned-parenthood movement there is an incredibly profound as well as important realm for activist-cum-theoretical collaboration), or any evading of crucial theological and centrally religious issues. To imagine so is to underestimate the seriousness and authenticity of persons of other faiths who after all are at least as concerned with the central and the ultimate issues as are we. A conference such as I suggest would be fruitful; it would not be dull.

Of course, such a cooperative conference would have to be

called not as a gesture, but genuinely and because one had deeply seen that what God wants accomplished by Christians in India tomorrow can be discovered in no other way. We can begin to participate helpfully only when we recognize that we have first much to learn.

In the conference idea, as I have said, new theological ideas are implicit. It was in part the mission field that spurred the theologians into ecumenical awakening; conceivably it is in part from the mission field also that those pressures will arise—and those insights and delights—that will help the theologians towards a more serious awareness of what the modern world is really like.

The fundamental prerequisites for a participant, apart from grace and faith (I leave them undefined), are from the Christian side, humility and love and towards the religious tradition of those among whom he finds himself, a profound respect and the ability to perceive God redemptively at work through it. Being myself an academic I am tempted to stress also that he should have a good deal of knowledge about the second tradition, yet this is less important at the start than that respect and that perception. Without these and the openness and sensitivity that they imply, the missionary movement must be called off. With them its day has just begun.

We have spoken of the Ramakrishna and other missionaries now serving in Christendom. I come back to that, and lest our own preconceptions of what a missionary is should make that idea rather frightening let me refer also to such illuminating and helpful writings as a recent critique of Christian ethics by a careful and serious Muslim, published by a Western university press, and a bruited commentary on The Gospel of Saint John by a Hindu, a commentary reverent, perceptive, novel. No true appreciation of Christian participation in other developments is available except to those who as Christians (and I stress that qualification: "as Christians") can see others' participation in our Christian development as something not only to be understood but to be welcomed, and not only to be welcomed but to be sought. If this seems too radical, let me recall that haunting injunction that we must do unto others only what we would that they do also unto us. We are not accustomed to taking this seriously at an interfaith level but we have to learn. We have no right to send missionaries to any group from whom we are not ready to invite missionaries.

The old concept of missions was unilateral. Some of you know that in my theological framework I propound a new concept of mission that is multilateral and theocentric. Certainly participation is to be apprehended as a reciprocal and worldwide process.

We come then to my final point. At this stage of the argument I would like to conclude by generalizing the participation theme. I suggest that in each community the religious person participates in that ongoing historical process of which the contemporary life of community is the current phase. As one's community comes out of its inherited past and moves into an uncertain future, the present members constitute that present phase as each plays a part in the company of one's fellow members and in the constant presence, dimly or deeply perceived, of that transcendent power in whom we all live and move and have our being. It is the quality of his participation that gives his life its religious significance. It is through that participation that God chiefly acts in human history.

Secondly, I suggest that people may, and many unwittingly and obscurely do, participate incidently or obliquely, for good or ill, in the ongoing process of a neighboring community. I further suggest that a few persons may play this kind of role self-consciously and deliberately, constructively and graciously, joyously and humbly, with fear and trembling and yet with good rapport.

Finally, I suggest that a profoundly new phase has begun in the religious history of mankind, a phase on which the whole world today seems to be embarked. Not merely is it one in which one person or group may participate in the religious evolution of another tradition; we are reaching a point where eventually each will participate in all. The new emergence is the unitary religious history of mankind.

One may not like the word "religious" here, and it may not survive; it is hardly likely that the term "spiritual" will be more widely appealing; maybe we should call it simply the humane history of mankind. A number of observers of the local scene here in the West have been greatly impressed by the convergence between the Christian and the secular. Never having been a victim of their segregation in the poor sense, I am not too enthusiastic about the new confounding of the two in a poor sense. Anyway, I am more impressed by the coming convergence—I do not say fusion—of the Christian and the Hindu and the Buddhist and the Muslim. This convergence is actually happening in ways whose depth and intricacy and novelty are beyond comprehension. We may be frightened by it, or bewildered, or exhilarated; in any case one has to try to understand. To my mind there is no question but that the human religious configuration throughout the world is entering a profoundly new phase.

I have observed, for instance, that a static notion of an "Islamic religion" gives way once one looks more closely to a dynamic notion of Islamic history, to the Islamic process in history in which Muslims have been participating. I may add that on still fuller inquiry, as our knowledge and perception of the religious history of the globe increases, the notion even of Islamic religious history gives way to the truer concept of *an Islamic strand in the religious history of mankind.* Given the hostility among communities, ranging from open warfare on the battlefield to intellectual and emotional boundaries of stupendous rigidity, I am not unaware of the boldness of this concept. Yet I press it, as that towards which we are inescapably moving. What is happening around the earth today or at least beginning to happen is the incredibly exciting development that will eventually mean that each person, certainly each group, participates in the religious history of mankind.

This is already happening in college classrooms; and is already happening in some churches, in the sense that for good or ill the religious life of an individual is beginning to be thought and lived in the light of the religious heritage of all the world. It began to happen some while ago in the sense already mentioned that what Westerners do and think constitutes for good or ill a consequential force in the religious life of Asia. Something approximating it has been happening all along in China and Japan, where Westerners have never understood how a man can "belong to two or three religions at the same time," as they ineptly phrased it, but where the situation can more truly be conceptualized by saying that Chinese and Japanese have participated in a process constituted by more than one tradition. Once one thinks of it, it turns out that we in the West have long participated in a complex process constituted by the Christian and the Greco-Roman humanist traditions in elaborate interaction; most Western Christians would feel grievously out of place in an Ethiopian Christian church for example, representing the Christian evolution in a process less adulterated by the other Western factors.

I do not mean that Christians will cease to be Christian or Muslims Muslim. What I mean is that Christians will participate as Christians in the religious history of mankind; Muslims will participate in it as Muslims; Hindus as Hindus; Buddhists as Buddhists. I am a Presbyterian and will never shake off my delightful Calvinistic Puritanism until the day I die; yet the community in which I participate is not the Presbyterian but the Christian. I participate as a deliberate though modified Puritan in the Christian community and the Christian process. In much the same way I choose to participate as a Christian in the world process of religious convergence.

One of the things that I have learned from my Christian heritage is that part of Christian truth, by which I mean part of the ultimate truth of the universe, is that all mankind is ultimately one community. It is my delight to find that this is part of the Islamic truth also, and of Hindu truth, and of Buddhist. I take history seriously, and the notion of historical process seriously: the task of one age is not necessarily that of another. One of the tasks open to us today, and beckoning to us, is to participate in God's creative process of bringing into actual reality what has until now been an ideal reality only, that of a worldwide human community. The missionary assignment for the next phase of human history is to take the leadership in this participation: to help realize in fact the vision that we can begin to see, wherein we all participate in each other's processes of moving towards God. Not that I have forgotten that the initiative is his: each separate tradition is the process of response to God's initiative, and the current phase is our response to his bringing of the religious communities of the world into mutual involvement. To responsible missionary leaders (among others) is offered the task of guiding that response.

All human history is *Heilsgeschichte*. Not the history of Israel only, the old or the new, but the history of every religious community. This has always been true, but we are the first generation of Christians to see this seriously and corporately and to be able to respond to the vision. We are the first generation of Christians to discern God's mission to mankind in the Buddhist movement, in the Hindu, in the Islamic, as well as in the Jewish and the Christian. Having discerned it, let us not fail to respond to it.

All human history is *Heilsgeschichte*. The most important missionary task of the Church, at least of its missionary leaders, is probably to lead the Church to seeing this so as to enable it to respond, so that Christians may participate, not fortuitously or ineptly, but intelligently and Christianly in the salvation history of all people.

Appendix

Bangkok:
Salvation Today
Conference, 1973

The world conference on "Salvation Today," called and organized by the Commission on World Mission and Evangelism (CWME) of the World Council of Churches, was held in Bangkok, Thailand, December 29, 1972, to January 8, 1973, in connection with an assembly of the Commission. It brought together some three hundred participants from sixty-nine countries. Bangkok was the eighth in a series of influential mission conferences that began with the Edinburgh World Missionary Conference in 1910, and included Jerusalem in 1928, Madras in 1938, and—the most recent previous conference—Mexico City in 1963. Documents presented and produced at Bangkok were published in the *International Review of Mission* (Geneva) for April, 1973. An interpretive volume about the Bangkok conference, *Salvation Today*, was written by Arne Sovik (Minneapolis: Augsburg Publishing House, 1973). See also *The Evangelical Response to Bangkok*, edited by Ralph Winter (South Pasadena, California: William Carey Library, 1973).

Bankgok Section I:
Culture and Identity (excerpt)

On Conversion and Cultural Change

A. It is very difficult to describe the existential experience of conversion—whether personal or corporate, as an event or as process—in terms that do justice to rational thinking as well as other levels of consciousness. In order to express this experience one has to seek other ways of communication than just report language. (That is why we wrote a number of prayers and affirmations that are added to this report.)

Conversion as a phenomenon is not restricted to the Christian community; it finds its place in other religions as well as in certain political and ideological communities; its forms may vary. The content of the experience differs according to the person or to the ideological system within which the person or the group is converted.

Conversion is a comprehensive concept: it changes the person's or the group's thinking, and perspectives on reality and action. It relates a person to people who have similar experiences or who are committed to the same person or ideology.

The Christian conversion relates to God and especially to his Son Jesus Christ. It introduces people into the Christian community, the structure of which may differ greatly from one culture to another, and which will always include a great variety of persons. Christian conversion gathers people into the worshipping community, the teaching community and the community of service to all men. Even if Christians are not called out of their culture and separated from the society in which they were born, they still will form cells of worship, of reflection and of service within their original cultures.

Personal conversion always leads to social action, but here again the forms will greatly differ. We heard action reports that gave us some idea how diverse the consequences may be. In the one case, people who had never known an identity of their own formed a very closely knit group within which intensive social care for each other developed. When such a group grows it almost inevitably enters into the full civic life at the local level; if it grows further it will acquire political power, which may align to either conservative or progressive political platforms. Where conversion takes place among the destitute and powerless, the sustaining community will tend to begin to empower the poor and oppressed.

But it is also possible that conversion means a calling out of people away from what is regarded as an oppressive power structure or even away from a type of social action that is regarded as dehumanizing or superficial.

It is important that the community of those converted to Christ is so sustained by the study of Scripture and the work of service that renewal of the conversion experience is possible.

Our group was unanimous in thinking that conversion is always related to the place and the circumstances where it occurs; therefore we recommend that detailed study be made of the form and consequences of conversion in different situations.

The relation between conversion and social change may be clear, but the relation between social change and conversion is much less easily described. It may be that secular conversion experiences remind the Christian community of elements in their own life that need to be renewed; it may also be that conversion phenomena within a new cultural situation will force Christians back on their unique identity and make them oppose the cultural development; their conversion in such instances is away from the prevailing cultural situation. To generalize about these various possibilities would hardly be helpful.

B. People everywhere are seeking experiences of community, whatever the name—cultural revolution, subculture or counterculture. The relation of the Christian community to such a search cannot be described without serious consideration of each of these scenes. We have learned in our group that the line between culture, subculture and even counterculture is not as sharp as these groups themselves often proclaim. People move from one to the other without observing strict sociological or theological rules.

It is difficult to describe "the community in Christ and in the Holy Spirit" in this context. We played with the concept of the Christian community itself as a counterculture; but we abandoned this idea because it cut us off too definitely from the communities of men of which we are also a part. Only in extreme cases may we be called to shake the dust of the city from our shoes; usually we shall have to live in a somewhat dialectical relationship, participating with a certain hesitation, identifying ourselves while keeping our critical distance. This dialectic should not hinder us, however, from being fully engaged with others in the search for justice and freedom. Our identity is in Christ and with him we identify ourselves; by him also we may be withdrawn. The criteria for so tender a relationship are taught us only when we let the Scriptures continually surprise us and keep our communion with the Lord and his people.

C. The manifestations of God are always surprising. Basically there is no realm of life and no situation where he cannot reveal himself. We believe that he is present in his whole creation. But we do not want to make this belief an operative principle for pointing out exactly where he is at work, lest we say: Here is the Messiah, or there is the Messiah, when he is not there.

Although we expect his presence with men and although we know that the Spirit translates the groaning of all mankind into prayers acceptable to God, we believe that this insight is more a reason to worship his freedom than an invitation to build our theological theories. Our preoccupation is with the revealed Christ and with the proclamation of him as he has been made known to us. Scripture tells us that Christ identifies himself with the poor and that the Spirit translates the groaning of men; this may indicate the direction in which we are invited to move but it does not give us power to pinpoint the details of his presence. The observation that Christ-like action and insights that we know from the Gospels are also present among other groups does not give us the right to claim such groups for Christ; it should lead us deeper into the process of our own conversion and bring us to worship our Lord even more humbly. He asked us to follow him, not to spy on him.

D. Traditional and charismatic groups can live together and witness together if that means that they find each other continuously under the critique and inspiration of the revealed Christ as made known to us in his word. In this conference we have once again experienced the way in which common Bible study unites us by surprising us again and again and by leading us together into a deeper understanding of God's will for all men.

Bangkok Section II:
Salvation and Social Justice (excerpt)

I. *The Mission of God*

In the power of the Spirit, Christ is sent from God the Father into this divided world "to preach the Gospel to the poor, to heal the broken-hearted, to preach deliverance to the captives and recovering of sight to the blind, to set at liberty the oppressed, and to proclaim the year of God's favour" (Luke 4:18). Through Christ men and women are liberated and empowered with all their energies and possibilities to participate in his messianic work. Through his death on the cross and his resurrection from the dead, hope of salvation becomes realistic and reality hopeful. He liberates from the prison of guilt. He takes the inevitability out of history. In him the Kingdom of God and of free people is at hand. Faith in Christ releases in man creative freedom for the salvation of the world. He who separates himself from the mission of God separates himself from salvation.

The salvation that Christ brought, and in which we participate, offers a comprehensive wholeness in this divided life. We understand salvation as newness of life—the unfolding of true humanity in the fullness of God (Col. 2:9). It is salvation of the soul and the body, of the individual and society, mankind and "the groaning creation" (Rom. 8:19). As evil works both in personal life and in exploitative social structures that humiliate humankind, so God's justice manifests itself both in the justification of the sinner and in social and political justice. As guilt is both individual and corporate so God's liberating power changes both persons and structures. We have to overcome the dichotomies in our thinking between soul and body, person and society, humankind and creation. Therefore we see the struggles for economic justice, political freedom and cultural renewal as elements in the total liberation of the world through the mission of God. This liberation is finally fulfilled when "death is swallowed up in victory" (1 Cor. 15:55). This comprehensive notion of salvation demands of the whole of the people of God a matching comprehensive approach to their participation in salvation.

II. *Salvation and Liberation of Churches and Christians*

Many Christians who for Christ's sake are involved in economic and political struggles against injustice and oppression ask themselves and the churches what it means today to be a Christian and a true church. Without the salvation of the churches from their captivity in the interests of dominating classes, races and nations, there can be no saving church. Without liberation of the churches and Christians from their complicity with structural injustice and violence, there can be no liberating church for mankind. Every church, all Christians, face the question whether they serve Christ and his saving work alone, or at the same time also the powers of inhumanity. "No man can serve two masters, God and Mammon" (Matt. 6:24). We must confess our misuse of the name of Christ by the accommodation of the churches to oppressive powers, by our self-interested apathy, lovelessness and fear. We are seeking the true community of Christ that works and suffers for his Kingdom. We seek the charismatic church that activates energies for salvation (1 Cor. 12). We seek the church that initiates actions for liberation and supports the work of other liberating groups without calculating self-interest. We seek a church that is the catalyst of God's saving work in the world, a church that is not merely the refuge of the saved but a community serving the world in the love of Christ.

III. *Salvation in Four Dimensions*

Within the comprehensive notion of salvation we see the saving work in four social dimensions:

1. Salvation works in the struggle for economic justice against the exploitation of people by people.
2. Salvation works in the struggle for human dignity against political oppression of human beings by their fellow men.
3. Salvation works in the struggle for solidarity against the alienation of person from person.
4. Salvation works in the struggle of hope against despair in personal life.

In the process of salvation, we must relate these four dimensions to each other. There is no economic justice without political freedom, no political freedom without economic justice. There is no social justice, no human dignity, no solidarity without hope, no hope without justice, dignity and solidarity. But there are historical priorities according to which salvation is anticipated in one dimension first, be it the personal, the political or the economic dimension. These points of entry differ from situation to situation in which we work and suffer. We should know that such anticipations are not the whole of salvation, and must keep in mind the other dimensions while we work. Forgetting this denies the wholeness of salvation. Nobody can do in any particular situation everything at the same time. There are various gifts and tasks, but there is one spirit and one goal. In this sense, it can be said, for example, that salvation is the peace of the people in Vietnam, independence in Angola, justice and reconciliation in Northern Ireland and release from the captivity of power in the North Atlantic community, or personal conversion in the release of a submerged society into hope or of new life styles amidst corporate self-interest and lovelessness.

IV. *Means and Criteria of Saving Work*

Speaking of salvation realistically, we cannot avoid the question of proper means. The means are different in the four dimensions referred to. We will produce no economic justice without participation in, and the use of, economic power. We will win no political freedom without participation in, and the discriminating use of, political power. We cannot overcome cultural alienation without the use of cultural influence. In this framework we discussed the physical use of liberating violence against oppressive violence. The Christian tradition is ambiguous on this question because it provides no justification of violence and no rejection of political power. Jesus' commandment to love one's enemy presupposes enmity. One should not become the enemy of one's enemy, but should liberate him from his enmity (Matt. 5:43-48). This commandment warns against the brutality of violence and reckless disregard of life. But in the cases of institutionalized violence, structural injustice and legalized immorality, love also involves the right of resistance and the duty "to repress tyranny" (Scots Confession) with responsible choice among the possibilities we have. One then may become guilty for love's sake, but can trust in the forgiveness of guilt. Realistic work for salvation proceeds through confrontation but depends, everywhere and always, on reconciliation with God.

Lausanne Congress, 1974

The International Congress on World Evangelization--a sequel to the Berlin Congress on Evangelism in 1966—met in Lausanne, Switzerland, July 16-25, 1974, with 2,700 participants from more than 150 countries, under the theme: "Let the Earth Hear His Voice," with the subtitle "Reaching the Unreached." Dr. Billy Graham was the honorary chairman of both congresses. In response to the official "consensus of the Congress" contained in the Lausanne Covenant, an *ad hoc* group of approximately 400 —largely Third World, Australian, and young evangelical participants—drew up a statement on "Theological Implications of Radical Discipleship." All the papers and responses from Lausanne are contained in the official reference volume, edited by J. D. Douglas, *Let the Earth Hear His Voice* (Minneapolis: World Wide Publications, 1975). A critique of the Lausanne Congress by Alfred Krass, a participant, was published in *Beautiful Feet*, an occasional newsletter from the Office of Evangelism, United Church Board for World Ministries (475 Riverside Drive, New York, N. Y. 10027), volume IV, no. 1, August 1974; another by Gerhard Hoffmann appeared in the *Monthly Letter About Evangelism* (August 1974) from the World Council of Churches, Geneva.

The Lausanne Covenant

Introduction

We, members of the Church of Jesus Christ, from more than 150 nations, participants in the International Congress on World Evangelization at Lausanne, praise God for his great salvation and rejoice in the fellowship he has given us with himself and with each other. We are deeply stirred by what God is doing in our day, moved to penitence by our failures and challenged by the unfinished task of evangelization. We believe the Gospel is God's Good News for the whole world, and we are determined by his grace to obey Christ's commission to proclaim it to all mankind and to make disciples of every nation. We desire therefore, to affirm our faith and our resolve and to make public our covenant.

1. The Purpose of God

We affirm our belief in the one eternal God, Creator and Lord of the world, Father, Son and Holy Spirit, who governs all things according to the purpose of his will. He has been calling out from the world a people for himself, and sending his people back into the world to be his servants and his witnesses for the extension of his kingdom, the building up of Christ's body and the glory of his name. We confess with shame that we have often denied our calling and failed in our mission by becoming conformed to the world or by withdrawing from it. Yet we rejoice that even when borne by earthen vessels the Gospel is still a precious treasure. To the task of making that treasure known in the power of the Holy Spirit we desire to dedicate ourselves anew. (Isa. 40:28; Matt. 28:19; Eph. 1:11; Acts 15:14; John 17:6, 18; Eph. 4:12; I Cor. 5:10; Rom. 12:2; II Cor. 4:7)

2. The Authority and Power of The Bible

We affirm the divine inspiration, truthfulness and authority of both Old and New Testament Scriptures in their entirety as the only written Word of God, without error in all that it affirms, and the only infallible rule of faith and practice. We also affirm the power of God's Word to accomplish his purpose of salvation. The message of the Bible is addressed to all mankind. For God's revelation in Christ and in Scripture is unchangeable. Through it the Holy Spirit still speaks today. He illumines the minds of God's people in every culture to perceive its truth freshly through their own eyes and thus discloses to the whole church ever more of the many-colored wisdom of God. (II Tim. 3:16; II Pet. 1:21; John 10:35; Isa. 55:11; I Cor. 1:21; Rom. 1:16; Matt. 5:17, 18; Jude 3; Eph. 1:17, 18; 3:10, 18)

3. *The Uniqueness and Universality of Christ*

We affirm that there is only one Savior and only one Gospel, although there is a wide diversity of evangelistic approaches. We recognize that all men have some knowledge of God through his general revelation in nature. But we deny that this can save, for men suppress the truth by their unrighteousness. We also reject as derogatory to Christ and the Gospel every kind of syncretism and dialogue that implies that Christ speaks equally through all religions and ideologies. Jesus Christ, being himself the only God-man, who gave himself as the only ransom for sinners, is the only mediator between God and man. There is no other name by which we must be saved. All men are perishing because of sin, but God loves all men, not wishing that any should perish but that all should repent. Yet those who reject Christ repudiate the joy of salvation and condemn themselves to eternal separation from God. To proclaim Jesus as "the Savior of the world" is not to affirm that all men are either automatically or ultimately saved, still less to affirm that all religions offer salvation in Christ. Rather it is to proclaim God's love for a world of sinners and to invite all men to respond to him as Savior and Lord in the wholehearted personal commitment of repentance and faith. Jesus Christ has been exalted above every other name; we long for the day when every knee shall bow to him and every tongue shall confess him Lord. (Gal. 1:6-9; Rom. 1:18-32; I Tim. 2:5, 6; Acts 4:12; John 3:16-19; II Pet. 3:9; II Thess. 1:7-9; John 4:42; Matt. 11:28; Eph. 1:20, 21; Phil. 2:9-11)

4. *The Nature of Evangelism*

To evangelize is to spread the good news that Jesus Christ died for our sins and was raised from the dead according to the

Scriptures and that as the reigning Lord he now offers the forgiveness of sins and the liberating gift of the Spirit to all who repent and believe. Our Christian presence in the world is indispensable to evangelism, and so is that kind of dialogue whose purpose is to listen sensitively in order to understand. But evangelism itself is the proclamation of the historical, biblical Christ as Savior and Lord, with a view to persuading people to come to him personally and so be reconciled to God. In issuing the Gospel invitation we have no liberty to conceal the cost of discipleship. Jesus still calls all who would follow him to deny themselves, take up their cross and identify themselves with his new community. The results of evangelism include obedience to Christ, incorporation into his church and responsible service in the world. (I Cor. 15:3, 4; Acts 2:32-39; John 20:21; I Cor. 1:23; II Cor. 4:5; 5:11, 20; Luke 14:25-33; Mark 8:34; Acts 2:40, 47; Mark 10:43-45)

5. Christian Social Responsibility

We affirm that God is both the Creator and the Judge of all men. We therefore should share his concern for justice and reconciliation throughout human society and for the liberation of men from every kind of oppression. Because mankind is made in the image of God, every person, regardless of race, religion, color, culture, class, sex or age, has an intrinsic dignity because of which he should be respected and served, not exploited. Here too we express penitence both for our neglect and for having sometimes regarded evangelism and social concern as mutually exclusive. Although reconciliation with man is not reconciliation with God, nor is social action evangelism, nor is political liberation salvation, nevertheless we affirm that evangelism and sociopolitical involvement are both part of our Christian duty. For both are necessary expressions of our doctrines of God and man, our love for our neighbor and our obedience to Jesus Christ. The message of salvation implies also a message of judgment upon every form of alienation, oppression and discrimination, and we should not be afraid to denounce evil and injustice wherever they exist. When people receive Christ they are born again into his kingdom and must seek not only to exhibit but also to spread its righteousness in the midst of an unrighteous world. The salvation we claim should be transforming us in the totality of our personal and social responsibilities. Faith without works is dead. (Acts 17:26, 31; Gen. 18:25; Isa. 1:17; Psa. 45:7; Gen. 1:26-27; Jas. 3:9; Lev. 19:18; Luke 6:27, 35; Jas. 2:14-26; John 3:3, 5; Matt. 5:20; 6:33; II Cor. 3:18; Jas. 2:20)

6. The Church and Evangelism

We affirm that Christ sends his redeemed people into the world as the Father sent him, and that this calls for a similar deep and costly penetration of the world. We need to break out of our ecclesiastical ghettos and permeate non-Christian society. In the church's mission of sacrificial service evangelism is primary. World evangelization requires the whole church to take the whole Gospel to the whole world. The church is at the very center of God's cosmic purpose and is his appointed means of spreading the Gospel. But a church that preaches the Cross must itself be marked by the Cross. It becomes a stumbling block to evangelism when it betrays the Gospel or lacks a living faith in God, a genuine love for people or scrupulous honesty in all things, including promotion and finance. The church is the community of God's people rather than an institution, and must not be identified with any particular culture, social or political system or human ideology. (John 17:18; 20:21; Matt. 28:19, 20; Acts 1:8; 20:27; Eph. 1:9, 10; 3:9-11; Gal. 6:14, 17; II Cor. 6:3, 4; II Tim. 2:19-21; Phil. 1:27)

7. Cooperation in Evangelism

We affirm that the church's visible unity in truth is God's purpose. Evangelism also summons us to unity because our oneness strengthens our witness just as our disunity undermines our gospel of reconciliation. We recognize however that organizational unity may take many forms and does not necessarily forward evangelism. Yet we who share the same biblical faith should be closely united in fellowship, work and witness. We confess that our testimony has sometimes been marred by sinful individualism and needless duplication. We pledge ourselves to seek a deeper unity in truth, worship, holiness and mission. We urge the development of regional and functional cooperation for the furtherance of the church's mission, for strategic planning, for mutual encouragement and for the sharing of resources and experience. (John 17:21, 23; Eph. 4:3, 4; John 13:35; Phil. 1:27; John 17:11-23)

8. *Churches in Evangelistic Partnership*

We rejoice that a new missionary era has dawned. The dominant role of western missions is fast disappearing. God is raising up from the younger churches a great new resource for world evangelization and is thus demonstrating that the responsibility to evangelize belongs to the whole body of Christ. All churches should therefore be asking God and themselves what they should be doing both to reach their own area and to send missionaries to other parts of the world. A re-evaluation of our missionary responsibility and role should be continuous. Thus a growing partnership of churches will develop and the universal character of Christ's Church will be more clearly exhibited. We also thank God for agencies that labor in Bible translation, theological education, the mass media, Christian literature, evangelism, missions, church renewal, and other specialized fields. They too should engage in constant self-examination to evaluate their effectiveness as part of the church's mission. (Rom. 1:8; Phil. 1:5; 4:15; Acts 13:13; I Thess. 1:6-8)

9. *The Urgency of the Evangelistic Task*

More than 2,700 million people, which is more than two-thirds of mankind, have yet to be evangelized. We are ashamed that so many have been neglected; it is a standing rebuke to us and to the whole church. There is now, however, in many parts of the world an unprecedented receptivity to the Lord Jesus

Christ. We are convinced that this is the time for churches and para-church agencies to pray earnestly for the salvation of the unreached and to launch new efforts to achieve world evangelization. A reduction of foreign missionaries and money in an evangelized country may sometimes be necessary to facilitate the national church's growth in self-reliance and to release resources for unevangelized areas. Missionaries should flow ever more freely from and to all six continents in a spirit of humble service. The goal should be, by all available means and at the earliest possible time, that every person will have the opportunity to hear, understand, and receive the Good News. We cannot hope to attain this goal without sacrifice. All of us are shocked by the poverty of millions and disturbed by the injustices that cause it. Those of us who live in affluent circumstances accept our duty to develop a simple life-style in order to contribute more generously to both relief and evangelism. (John 9:4; Matt. 9:35-38; Rom. 9:1-3; I Cor. 9:19-23; Mark 16:15; Isa. 58:6, 7; Jas. 1:27; 2:1-9; Matt. 25:31-46; Acts 2:44, 45; 4:34, 35)

10. Evangelism and Culture

The development of strategies for world evangelization calls for imaginative pioneering methods. Under God the result will be the rise of churches deeply rooted in Christ and closely related to their culture. Culture must always be tested and judged by Scripture. Because man is God's creature, some of his culture is rich in beauty and goodness. Because he has fallen, all of it is tainted with sin and some of it is demonic. The Gospel does not presuppose the superiority of any culture to another, but evaluates all cultures according to its own criteria of truth and righteousness and insists on moral absolutes in every culture. Missions have all too frequently exported with the Gospel an alien culture, and churches have sometimes been in bondage to culture rather than to the Scripture. Christ's evangelists must humbly seek to empty themselves of all but their personal authenticity in order to become the servants of others, and churches must seek to transform and enrich culture, all for the glory of God. (Mark 7:8, 9, 13; Gen. 4:21, 22; I Cor. 9:19-23; Phil. 2:5-7; II Cor. 4:5)

11. Education and Leadership

We confess that we have sometimes pursued church growth at the expense of church depth and divorced evangelism from Christian nurture. We also acknowledge that some of our missions have been too slow to equip and encourage national leaders to assume their rightful responsibilities. Yet we are committed to indigenous principles and long that every church will have national leaders who manifest a Christian style of leadership in terms not of dominion but of service. We recognize that there is a great need to improve theological education, especially for church leaders. In every nation and culture there should be an effective training program for pastors and laymen in doctrine, discipleship, evangelism, nurture and service. Such training programs should not rely on any stereotyped methodology but should be developed by creative local initiatives according to biblical standards. (Col. 1:27, 28; Acts 14:23; Tit. 1:5, 9; Mark 10:42-45; Eph. 4:11, 12)

12. Spiritual Conflict

We believe that we are engaged in constant spiritual warfare with the principalities and powers of evil, who are seeking to overthrow the church and frustrate its task of world evangelization. We know our need to equip ourselves with God's armor and to fight this battle with the spiritual weapons of truth and prayer. For we detect the activity of our enemy, not only in false ideologies outside the church, but also inside it in false gospels that twist Scripture and put man in the place of God. We need both watchfulness and discernment to safeguard the biblical Gospel. We acknowledge that we ourselves are not immune to worldliness of thought and action, that is, to a surrender to secularism. For example, although careful studies of church growth, both numerical and spiritual, are right and valuable, we have sometimes neglected them. At other times, desirous to insure a response to the Gospel, we have compromised our message, manipulated our hearers through pressure techniques, and become unduly preoccupied with statistics or even dishonest in our use of them. All this is worldly. The church must be in the world; the world must not be in the church. (Eph. 6:12; II Cor. 4:3, 4; Eph. 6:11, 13-18; II Cor. 10:3-5; I John 2:18-26, 4:1-3; Gal. 1:6-9; II Cor. 2:17, 4:2; John 17:15)

13. Freedom and Persecution

It is the God-appointed duty of every government to secure conditions of peace, justice and liberty in which the church may obey God, serve the Lord Christ and preach the Gospel without interference. We therefore pray for the leaders of the nations and call upon them to guarantee freedom of thought and conscience, and freedom to practice and propagate religion in accordance with the will of God and as set forth in The Universal Declaration of Human Rights. We also express our deep concern for all who have been unjustly imprisoned, and especially for our brethren who are suffering for their testimony to the Lord Jesus. We promise to pray and work for their freedom. At the same time we refuse to be intimidated by their fate. God helping us, we too will seek to stand against injustice and to remain faithful to the Gospel, whatever the cost. We do not forget the warnings of Jesus that persecution is inevitable. (I Tim. 1:1-4; Acts 4:19, 5:29; Col. 3:24; Heb. 13:1-3; Luke 4:18; Gal. 5:11, 6:12; Matt. 5:10-12; John 15:18-21)

14. The Power of The Holy Spirit

We believe in the power of the Holy Spirit. The Father sent his Spirit to bear witness to his Son; without his witness ours is futile. Conviction of sin, faith in Christ, new birth and Christian growth are all his work. Further, the Holy Spirit is a missionary spirit; thus evangelism should arise spontaneously from a Spirit-filled church. A church that is not a missionary church is contradicting itself and quenching the Spirit. Worldwide evangelization will become a realistic possibility only when the Spirit renews the church in truth and wisdom, faith, holiness, love and power. We, therefore, call upon all Christians to pray for such a visitation of the sovereign Spirit of God that all his fruit may appear in all his people and that all his gifts may enrich the body of Christ. Only then will the whole church become a fit instrument in his hands that the whole earth may hear his voice. (I Cor. 2:4; John 15:26, 27, 16:8-11; I Cor. 12:3; John 3:6-8; II Cor. 3:18; John 7:37-39; I Thess. 5:19; Acts 1:8; Psa. 85:4-7; 67:1-3; Gal. 5:22, 23; I Cor. 12:4-31; Rom. 12:3-8)

15. The Return of Christ

We believe that Jesus Christ will return personally and visibly in power and glory to consummate his salvation and his judgment. This promise of his coming is a further spur to our evangelism for we remember his words that the Gospel must first be preached to all nations. We believe that the interim period between Christ's ascension and return is to be filled with the mission of the people of God who have no liberty to stop before the end. We also remember his warning that false Christs and false prophets will arise as precursors of the final Antichrist. We, therefore, reject as a proud, self-confident dream the notion that man can ever build a utopia on earth. Our Christian confidence is that God will perfect his kingdom, and we look forward with eager anticipation to that day and to the new heaven and earth in which righteousness will dwell and God will reign forever. Meanwhile, we rededicate ourselves to the service of Christ and of men in joyful submission to his authority over the whole of our lives. (Mark 14:62; Heb. 9:28; Mark 13:10; Acts 1:8-11; Matt. 28:20; Mark 13:21-23; John 2:18, 4:1-3; Luke 12:32; Rev. 21:1-5; II Pet. 3:13; Matt. 28:18)

Conclusion

Therefore, in the light of this our faith and our resolve, we enter into a solemn covenant with God and with each other, to pray, to plan and to work together for the evangelization of the whole world. We call upon others to join us. May God help us by his grace and for his glory to be faithful to this our covenant! Amen, Alleluia!

A Response to Lausanne

Theological Implications
of Radical Discipleship

A number of issues have thrust themselves upon us from papers delivered in this Congress and, from the subsequent wrestling with them under the authority of God's Word, a number of us have felt the compulsion of his Spirit to share this response.

We affirm that . . .

The *evangel* is God's Good News in Jesus Christ; it is Good News of the reign he proclaimed and embodies, of God's mission of love to restore the world to wholeness through the Cross of Christ and him alone, of his victory over the demonic powers of destruction and death, of his Lordship over the entire universe; it is Good News of a new creation of a new humanity and a new birth through him by his life-giving Spirit; of the gifts of the messianic reign contained in Jesus and mediated through him by his Spirit; of the charismatic community empowered to embody his reign of shalom here and now before the whole creation and make his Good News seen and known. It is the Good News of liberation, of restoration, of wholeness and of salvation that is personal, social, global and cosmic. Jesus is Lord! Alleluia! Let the earth hear his voice!

The communication of the evangel in its fullness to every person worldwide is a mandate of the Lord Jesus to his community. There is no biblical dichotomy between the Word spoken and the Word made visible in the lives of God's people. Men will look as they listen and what they see must be at one with what they hear. The Christian community must chatter, discuss and proclaim the Gospel; it must express the Gospel in its life as the new society, in its sacrificial service of others as a genuine expression of God's love, in its prophetic exposing and opposing of all demonic forces that deny the Lordship of Christ and keep men less than fully human; in its pursuit of real justice for all men; in its responsible and caring trusteeship of God's creation and its resources.

There are times when our communication may be by attitude and action only, and times when the spoken Word will stand alone; but we must repudiate as demonic the attempt to drive a wedge between evangelism and social action.

The response demanded by the evangel is that men and women repent of their sin and every other lordship than that of Jesus Christ, and commit themselves to him to serve him in the world. All men are not already reconciled to God and simply awaiting the realization of it. Nor can biblical authority be found for the false hope of universalism; the reality of the eternal destruction of evil and all who cling to it must be solemnly affirmed, however humbly agnostic the Bible requires us to be about its nature.

Salvation is by God's grace on the sole ground of Christ's death and resurrection and is received by obedient faith. Repentance is demanded; men must experience a change of understanding, attitude and orientation; but the new birth is not merely a subjective experience of forgiveness. It is a placement within the messianic community, God's new order that exists as a sign of God's reign, to be consummated at the end of the age.

Methods in evangelization must center in Jesus Christ who took our humanity, our frailty, our death and gave himself in suffering servanthood for others. He sends his community into the world, as the Father sent him, to identify and agonize with men, to renounce status and demonic power and to give itself in selfless service of others for God. Those who proclaim the Cross must be continually marked by the Cross. With unashamed commitment to Jesus Christ we must engage in the mutual listening of dialogue, the reward of which is understanding. We need to meet men on their own ground and be particularly attentive to the powerless. We must use the language, thought-forms and imagery appropriate to differing cultures. As Christians we must live in such unity and love that men may believe. We must allow God to make visible in the new humanity the quality of life that reflects Christ and demonstrates his reign. We must respect cultural integrity while being free from all that denies or distorts the Lordship of Christ. God's Spirit overcomes all barriers of race, color and culture.

The strategy for world evangelization in our generation is with God, from whom we eagerly anticipate the renewal of his community, equipping us with love and power so that the whole Christian community may make known the whole Gospel to the whole man throughout the whole world. We believe God to be calling us into greater unity and partnership throughout the earth to fulfill the commission of our Lord Jesus Christ.

We confess that . . .

We have been failing in our obedience to the Lordship of Christ and have been refusing to submit to his Word and be led by his Spirit.

We have failed to incarnate the Gospel and to come to men as servants for Christ's sake.

Our testimony has often been marred by triumphalism and arrogance, by lack of faith in God and by diminished love for his people.

We have often been in bondage to a particular culture and sought to spread it in the name of Jesus.

We have not been aware of when we have debased and distorted the Gospel by acceptance of a contrary value system.

We have been partisan in our condemnation of totalitarianism and violence and have failed to condemn societal and institutionalized sin, especially that of racism.

We have sometimes so identified ourselves with particular political systems that the Gospel has been compromised and the prophetic voice muted.

We have frequently denied the rights and neglected the cries of the underprivileged and those struggling for freedom and justice.

We have often separated Jesus Christ the Savior from Jesus Christ the Lord.

We have sometimes distorted the biblical understanding of man as a total being and have courted an unbiblical dualism.

We have insulated new Christians from life in the world and given simplistic responses to complex problems.

We have sometimes manipulated our message, used pressure techniques and been unduly preoccupied with statistics.

We have allowed eagerness for qualitative growth to render us silent about the whole counsel of God. We have been usurping God's Holy Spirit of love and power.

We rejoice . . .

.   In our membership by his Spirit in the Body of Christ and in the joy and love he has given us in each other.

In the openness and honesty with which we have met each other and have experienced mutual acceptance and forgiveness.

In the possibilities for men to read his Word in their own languages through indigenous translations.

In the stimulation of mind and challenge to action that has come to us from his Word as we have placed the needs of our generation under its judgment and light.

In the prophetic voices of our brothers and sisters in this Congress, with whom we go forth in humility and hope.

In the certainty that the kingdoms of this world shall become the Kingdom of our God and of his Christ. He shall reign forever. Alleluia!

We resolve . . .

To submit ourselves afresh to the Word of God and to the leading of his Spirit, to pray and work together for the renewal of his community as the expression of his reign, to participate in God's mission to his world in our generation, showing forth Jesus as Lord and Savior, and calling on all men everywhere to repent, to submit to his Lordship, to know his salvation, to identify in him with the oppressed and to work for the liberation of all men and women in his name.

LET THE EARTH HEAR HIS VOICE!

The Roman Synods
of Bishops

Since the Second Vatican Council (1962-1965), Pope Paul VI has convoked four Episcopal Synods: 1967, 1969, 1971 and 1974. A synod is a representative, consultative body of the national and regional Bishops' Conferences throughout the world. Most of its members are elected by their representative hierarchies; the others are appointed by the pope. In such an international forum, more than 200 bishops share their experiences and express their "solicitude for all the local churches."

The 1971 Synod discussed "Justice in the World." In its final document, approved by Pope Paul, the synod reaffirms the Church's obligation to "give witness to justice" by the "life style found within the Church itself," and asserts that "action on behalf of justice and participation in the transformation of the world are a constitutive dimension of preaching the Gospel." The excerpt reprinted here is from the March 1972 issue of *Catholic Mind*, published in New York by America Press.

In 1974 the Bishops' Synod concentrated on "Evangelization in Today's World," the need "to bring the gospel message to all people, without exceptions based on geography, race, nationality, history or civilization" (Pope Paul's opening address). After month-long discussions the delegates found that they could not articulate easily their shared experience "without jeopardizing its [the Synod's] integrity." Their declaration contains "some fundamental convictions and a few of the more urgent guidelines" considered by the Synod. The main section of the declaration on evangelization is reprinted from *Origins* (November 7, 1974), published in Washington, D.C. by the National Catholic Documentary Service. Also reprinted from the same issue is a document prepared by a committee of Synod delegates headed by John Cardinal Krol of Philadelphia, "Human Rights and Reconciliation," which Pope Paul asked to be issued in his name "in union with the bishops assembled at the Synod."

Roman Synod of 1971
Justice in the World (excerpt)

Introduction

Gathered from the whole world, in communion with all who believe in Christ and with the entire human family, and opening our hearts to the Spirit who is making the whole of creation new, we have questioned ourselves about the mission of the People of the God to further justice in the world.

Scrutinizing the "signs of the times" and seeking to detect the meaning of emerging history, while at the same time sharing the aspirations and questionings of all those who want to build a more human world, we have listened to the Word of God that we might be converted to the fulfilling of the divine plan for the salvation of the world.

Even though it is not for us to elaborate a very profound analysis of the situation of the world we have nevertheless been able to perceive the serious injustices that are building around the world of men a network of domination, oppression and abuses that stifle freedom and that keep the greater part of humanity from sharing in the building and enjoyment of a more just and more fraternal world.

At the same time we have noted the inmost stirring moving the world in its depths. There are facts constituting a contribution to the furthering of justice. In associations of men and among peoples themselves there is arising a new awareness that shakes them out of any fatalistic resignation and that spurs them on to liberate themselves and to be responsible for their own destiny. We see movements among men that express hope for a better world and a will to change whatever has become intolerable.

Listening to the cry of those who suffer violence and are oppressed by unjust systems and structures, and hearing the appeal of a world that by its perversity contradicts the plan of its Creator, we have shared our awareness of the Church's vocation to be present in the heart of the world by proclaiming the Good

News to the poor, freedom to the oppressed and joy to the afflicted. The hopes and forces that are moving the world at its very foundations are not foreign to the dynamism of the Gospel, that, through the power of the Holy Spirit frees men from personal sin and from its consequences in social life.

The uncertaintity of history and the painful convergences in the ascending path of the human community direct us to sacred history; there God has revealed himself to us, and made known to us, as it is brought progressively to realization, his plan of liberation and salvation that is once and for all fulfilled in the Paschal mystery of Christ. Action on behalf of justice and participation in the transformation of the world fully appear to us as a constitutive dimension of the preaching of the Gospel, or, in other words, of the Church's mission for the redemption of the human race and its liberation from every oppressive situation.

* * *

The Gospel Message and the Mission of the Church

In the face of the present situation of the world, marked as it is by the grave sin of injustice, we recognize both our responsibility and our inability to overcome it by our own strength. Such a situation urges us to listen with a humble and open heart to the Word of God as he shows us new paths towards action in the cause of justice in the world.

In the Old Testament, God reveals himself to us as the liberator of the oppressed and the defender of the poor, demanding from man faith in him and justice towards man's neighbor. It is only in the observance of the duties of justice that God is truly recognized as the liberator of the oppressed.

By his action and teaching, Christ united in an indivisible way the relationship of man to God, and the relationship of man to other men. Christ lived his life in the world as a total giving of himself to God for the salvation and liberation of men. In his preaching he proclaimed the fatherhood of God towards all men and the intervention of God's justice on behalf of the needy and the oppressed (Luke 6:21-23). In this way he identified himself with his "least brethren," as he stated: "As you did it to one of the least of these my brethren, you did it to me" (Matt. 25:40).

From the beginning the Church has lived and understood the death and resurrection of Christ as a call by God to conversion in the faith of Christ and in fraternal love, perfected in mutual help even to the point of a voluntary sharing of material goods.

Faith in Christ, the Son of God and our Redeemer, and love of neighbor constitute a fundamental theme of the writers of the New Testament. According to St. Paul, the whole of the Christian life is summed up in faith effecting that love and service of neighbor that involve the fulfillment of the demands of justice. The Christian lives under the interior law of liberty, which is a permanent call to man to turn away from self-sufficiency to confidence in God and from concern for self to a sincere love of neighbor. Thus takes place his genuine liberation and the gift of himself for the freedom of others.

According to the Christian message, therefore, man's relationship to his neighbor is bound up with his relationship to God; his response to the love of God, saving us through Christ, is shown to be effective in his love and service of men. Christian love of neighbor and justice cannot be separated, for love implies an absolute demand for justice, namely a recognition of the dignity and rights of one's neighbor. Justice attains its inner fullness only in love. Because every man is truly a visible image of the invisible God and a brother of Christ, the Christian finds in every man God himself and God's absolute demands for justice and love.

The present situation of the world, seen in the light of faith, calls us back to the very essence of the Christian message, creating in us a deep awareness of its true meaning and of its urgent demands. The mission of preaching the Gospel dictates at the present time that we should dedicate ourselves to the liberation of man even in his present existence in this world. For unless the Christian message of love and justice shows its effectiveness through action in the cause of justice in the world, it will only with difficulty gain credibility with the men of our times.

The Church has received from Christ the mission of preaching the Gospel message, which contains a call to man to turn away from sin to the love of the Father, universal brotherhood and a consequent demand for justice in the world. This is the reason why the Church has the right, indeed the duty, to proclaim justice on the social, national and international level, and to denounce instances of injustice when the fundamental rights of man and his very salvation demand it. The Church indeed is not alone responsible for justice in the world; however, it has a proper and specific responsibility that is identified with its mission of giving witness to be carried out in Church institutions themselves and in the lives of Christians.

Of itself it does not belong to the Church, insofar as it is a religious and hierarchical community, to offer concrete solutions in the social, economic and political spheres for justice in the world. Its mission involves defending and promoting the dignity and fundamental rights of the person.

The members of the Church, as members of society, have the same right and duty to promote the common good as do other citizens. Christians ought to fulfill their temporal obligations with fidelity and competence. They should act as a leaven in the world and in their family, professional, social, cultural and political lives. They must accept their responsibilities in this field under the influence of the Gospel and the teaching of the Church. In this way they testify to the power of the Holy Spirit through their actions in the service of men in those things that are decisive for the existence and the future of humanity. While in such activities they generally act on their own initiative without involving the responsibility of the ecclesiastical hierarchy, in a sense they do involve the responsibility of the Church whose members they are.

The Practice of Justice

Many Christians are drawn to give authentic witness on behalf of justice by various modes of action for justice—action inspired by love in accordance with the grace they have received from God. For some of them this action finds its place in the sphere of social and political conflicts in which Christians bear witness to the Gospel by pointing out that in history there are sources of progress other than conflict, namely love and right. This priority of love draws other Christians to prefer the way of nonviolent action and work in the field of public opinion.

While the Church is bound to give witness to justice it recognizes that anyone who ventures to speak to people about justice must first be just. Hence we must undertake an examination of the modes of acting and of the possessions and life style in the Church.

* * *

Like the apostle Paul we insist, welcome or unwelcome, that the Word of God should be present in the center of human situations. Our interventions are intended to be an expression of that faith that is binding on the lives of the faithful. We all desire that these interventions should always be in conformity with circumstances of place and time. Our mission demands that we should courageously denounce injustice—with charity, prudence and firmness—in sincere dialogue with all parties concerned. We know that our denunciations can secure assent to the extent that they are an expression of our lives and are manifested in continous action.

A Word of Hope

The power of the Spirit who raised Christ from the dead is continuously at work in the world. Through the generous sons and daughters of the Church, likewise, the People of God are present in the midst of the poor and of those who suffer oppression and persecution; the Church lives in its own flesh and heart the Passion of Christ and bears witness to his resurrection.

The world has been groaning in an act of giving birth as it waits for the glory of the children of God to be revealed (Rom. 8:22). Let Christians therefore be convinced that they will yet find the fruits of their own nature and effort cleansed of all impurities in the new earth that God is now preparing for them, and in which there will be the Kingdom of justice and love, a Kingdom that will be fully perfected when the Lord will come himself.

Hope in the coming Kingdom is already beginning to take root in the hearts of men. The radical transformation of the world in the Paschal mystery of the Lord gives full meaning to the efforts of men, and in particular of the young, to lessen injustice, violence and hatred and to advance all together in justice, freedom, brotherhood and love.

At the same time as it proclaims the Gospel of the Lord, its Redeemer and Savior, the Church calls on all, especially the poor, the oppressed and the afflicted, to cooperate with God to bring about liberation from every sin and to build a world that will reach the fullness of creation only when it becomes the work of man for man.

Roman Synod of 1974
A Declaration from the Synod (excerpt)

Sustained by our faith in Christ who died and rose again to save us, and fortified in the Church by our paschal experience, we wish to confirm anew that the mandate to evangelize all people constitutes the essential mission of the Church.

Indeed the deeper and more widespread that current changes appear to us—be they in the field of religion, ideology, culture or mores, the more evident and urgent becomes the necessity to proclaim the Gospel to all nations and to every individual person.

It is evident and urgent especially for those to whom the announcement of the Good News of Christ has not yet been brought, wherever they might be on the face of the earth, so that the evangelization and the foundation of the Church might take root in all peoples and places.

Christ's love and his mandate urge all the faithful to dispense to others the gifts received freely from him. Therefore the duty to proclaim the Gospel belongs to the whole people of God, gathered by the Holy Spirit in the Church through the word of God and the eucharist.

No real Christian may absent himself from this duty that he must carry out in keeping with his state and in communion with his pastors. We hope that this Synod, together with the Supreme

Pontiff's insistent exhortation for world missionary day, will have offered to all the sons of the Church a new opportunity to renew the intimate and efficacious conviction of their rightful participation in the task of evangelization.

In a special way we address young people whom we do not consider only as a subject to be evangelized but also as particularly suited to evangelize others, especially their own age group. Furthermore we are convinced that young people to the extent that they are searching for the fundamental values of the Gospel and demanding true authenticity in conceiving and witnessing the faith, challenge us adults and compel us to renew unceasingly the new commitment to evangelize.

At the same time, we are profoundly convinced that without the grace of God, which is spread by the father in our hearts through the Holy Spirit, we would be completely incapable of carrying out this mission as it should be done (cf. Rom. 5:5). In fact this work demands incessant interior conversion on the part of individual Christians and continual renewal of our communities and institutions. In this way faith will become stronger, purer and more intimate and we will become better fit and more credible as witnesses of the faith through the coherence of our individual and social life with the Gospel we must preach.

We will acquire the ability to discover and discern the signs of the times and to recognize and respect the action of the Spirit of Christ who is always at work in the life of the Church itself and in all human history so that everyone may have the fullness of a better life.

From this one can clearly see the need for intimate union with God through assiduous prayer, meditation of the Word of God, contemplation, all strengthened and sustained by frequent participation in the sacraments. In this way the people of God may render more efficacious the testimony of a real brotherly community, diligent to respond speedily to the expectations of men of goodwill in evangelical solidarity with their more distressing problems.

In this way the Church will be a more credible witness to the joyful announcement of the savior of humankind; she will be a more suitable instrument of the Holy Spirit in the ministry to proclaim the Gospel.

Old and New Difficulties

In our discussions we did not ignore either old or new difficulties and obstacles that seem to hinder the work of evangelization. In fact some phenomena of our time have been given careful examination.

Secularization is one of them. Although it presents some positive aspects it nevertheless inclines to the ideology of secularism that completely excludes God from the horizon of human life and therefore from the profound meaning of existence.

Another is atheism in its manifold forms that is widespread in many countries. Such phenomena should be examined carefully and their causes sought more deeply so that the appeal of God —which demands greater purity in the confession and testimony of our faith—be discovered.

Another major difficulty has not escaped us, a difficulty that is used with astuteness and often with violence, that is, impeding religious liberty and the life of the Church and even reducing it to silence.

We did not forget those who are oppressed, especially all those who suffer persecution for the Gospel. Bearing in themselves the good news of the Cross they are performing excellent work of evangelization and are of great assistance to the whole Church in the fulfillment of its mission.

We are also convinced of the difficulties that arise from such a rapid and radical change in the conditions of our times, with regard to making the evangelical message more intelligible to today's people. But we also know that communication of the Gospel is a dynamic process. This communication takes place through word, work and life, each closely connected, and is determined by various almost constitutive elements of the hearers of the Word of God: that is, their needs and desires, their way of speaking, hearing, thinking, judging and entering into contact with others.

All these conditions that differ widely according to different places and times impel the particular churches towards an appropriate "translation" of the evangelical message.

According to the principle of incarnation they must devise new but faithful "ways to take root." Furthermore, the development of the means of social communication has opened new ways to evangelization in keeping with the ways today's people think and act.

At the same time we firmly believe that the Holy Spirit works unceasingly in Christ's Church through the work of those who give witness of a holy life, through the pastoral experience of those whom God called to govern the Church and of all their collaborators in the ecclesial ministries and through the fruitful collaboration between pastors and theologians.

In carrying out these things we intend to collaborate more diligently with those of our Christian brothers with whom we are not yet in the union of a perfect communion, basing ourselves on the foundation of baptism and on the patrimony we hold in common.

Thus we can henceforth render to the world a much broader common witness of Christ, while at the same time working to obtain full union in the Lord. Christ's command impels us to do so; the work of preaching and rendering witness to the Gospel demands it.

Confident in the Holy Spirit's action that overflows the bounds of the Christian community, we wish to further dialogue with other religions that are not Christian to achieve a deeper understanding of the Gospel's newness and of the fullness of revelation, and to be able to show them thereby the salvific truth of God's love that fulfills itself in Christ.

We intend furthermore to seek the collaboration of all people of good will who for reasons that are undoubtedly diverse but sincere, are in search of a deeper meaning to life or are committed to gaining more human conditions of life for others.

Liberation and Evangelization

Among the many subjects dealt with by the Synod special attention was drawn to the mutual relationship between evangelization and integral salvation or the complete liberation of peoples.

In a matter of such importance we experienced profound unity in reaffirming the intimate connection between evangelization and such liberation. Stimulating us to do this were not only the close relations with our faithful and with other people—whose life and common fate we share in—but primarily the Gospel, mercifully entrusted to us, that constitutes for all people and society the Good News of salvation.

That Good News is to be initiated and more manifest on earth from now on, although it is only beyond the confines of this present life that it can achieve its complete fulfillment.

Prompted by the love of Christ and illumined by the light of the Gospel, let us nurture the hope that the Church, in more faithfully fulfilling the work of evangelization, will announce the total salvation of man or rather his complete liberation, and from now on will start to bring this about.

The Church, as a community totally involved in evangelization, must conform to Christ, who explained his own mission in these words: "The Spirit of the Lord is upon me for he consecrated me with annointing and sent me to announce glad tidings to the poor, to give prisoners their freedom, the blind their sight, to set the oppressed free" (Lk. 4:18).

Faithful to her evangelizing mission, the Church as a truly poor, praying and fraternal community can do much to bring about the integral salvation or the full liberation of men. She can draw from the Gospel the most profound reasons and ever new incentives to promote generous dedication to the service of all men—the poor especially, the weak and the oppressed—and to eliminate the social consequences of sin that are translated into unjust social and political structures.

But the Church, supported by Christ's Gospel and fortified by his grace, can harness such dedication to the elimination of deviations, and so the Church does not remain within merely political, social and economic limits (elements that she must certainly take into account) but leads towards freedom under all its forms—liberation from sin and from individual or collective selfishness—and to full communion with God and with people who are like brothers and sisters. In this way the Church in her evangelical way promotes the true and complete liberation of all groups and peoples.

In this spirit of human and evangelical solidarity throughout these days we have wished to send the world a message on human rights and reconciliation.

By our mission we have the duty to be present among the

people of our times to bring the presence of Christ the incarnate word among them. Therefore in returning to our particular churches we, as disciples comforted by the experience of the risen Christ, will discover new opportunities to foster more effectively the evangelization of the whole world and its authentic liberation.

Certainly we are aware that we must face numerous difficulties. However we journey towards the future with great hope. This hope springs from our profound union with the crucified Christ who leads us to participate in an effective way in his resurrection.

Thus it will come about that more deeply rooted in the perennial actuality of Pentecost the Church will know new times of evangelization. While trying to be faithful to its mission in today's world the Church commits itself completely to the service of the future world. In fact, even if the destinies of this future world are unknown to us, Christ the Lord and center of human history stimulates us so that we can progress more and more. The time between Easter and the Parousia is the time of tension and aspiration towards the world that must come.

In such a period of time it is the task of the Church to prefigure and prepare the final actualization of the Kingdom of God. We know that the Lord helps his Church and continuously accompanies us on our pilgrimage. He will be with us all days, comforting us with the gifts of his grace, gradually leading us to the whole truth through the action of his Holy Spirit (cf. Jn 16:13), confirming our word with signs (cf. Mk 16:20), while we confess that Jesus Christ is the Lord to the glory of God the Father (cf. Phil. 2:11).

Human Rights and Reconciliation

Two anniversaries of special significance to the Church and the world have occurred since the Synod of 1971: the 10th anniversary of Pope John's encyclical *Pacem in Terris* (1963) and the 25th anniversary of the United Nations Declaration of Human

Rights (1948). Both documents remind us that human dignity requires the defense and promotion of human rights.

We are gathered in a Synod whose theme is evangelization, the proclamation of the Good News of Jesus. While the truths about human dignity and rights are accessible to all, it is in the Gospel that we find their fullest expression and our strongest motive for commitment to their preservation and promotion. The relationship between this commitment and the ministry of the Church has been manifested in this Synod in our sharing of pastoral experiences that reflect the transnational character of the Church, her entrance into the very consciences of people and her participation in their suffering when rights are denied or violated.

Reflecting on these experiences in light of the Gospel we address this message on human rights and reconciliation to the Church and the entire world, especially to all in positions of responsibility. It is our desire to raise our voices on behalf of the voiceless victims of injustice.

Human dignity is rooted in the image and reflection of God in each of us. It is this that makes all persons essentially equal. The integral development of persons makes more clear the Divine image in them. In our time the Church has grown more deeply aware of this truth; hence she believes firmly that the promotion of human rights is required by the Gospel and is central to her ministry.

The Church desires to be more fully converted to the Lord and to perform her ministry by manifesting respect and regard for human rights in her own life. There is renewed consciousness in the Church of the role of justice in her ministry. The progress already made encourages us to continue efforts to conform ever more fully to the will of the Lord.

From her own experience the Church knows that her ministry of fostering human rights in the world requires continued scrutiny and purification of her own life, her laws, institutions and policies. The Synod of 1971 declared that "anyone who ventures to speak to people about justice must first be just in their eyes," and failures in justice help us understand better the failings of other institutions and individuals. In the Church as in other institutions and groups purification is needed in internal practices and procedures and in relationships with social structures and systems whose violations of human rights deserve censure.

No nation today is faultless where human rights are concerned. It is not the role of the Synod to identify specific violations; this can better be done at the local level. At the same time we desire by our words and actions to encourage those who work for human rights, to call upon those in authority to promote human rights and to give hope to those who suffer violations of their rights. We call attention here to certain rights most threatened today.

"The right to life": This is basic and inalienable. It is grievously violated in our day by abortion and euthanasia, by widespread torture, by acts of violence against innocent parties and by the scourge of war. The arms race is an insanity that burdens the world and creates the conditions for even more massive destruction of life.

"The right to eat": This is directly linked to the right to life. Millions today face starvation. The nations and peoples of the world must make a concerted act of solidarity in the forthcoming United Nations Food Conference. We call upon governments to undergo a conversion in their attitude towards the victims of hunger, to respond to the imperatives of justice and reconciliation and speedily to find the means of feeding those who are without food.

"Socio-economic rights": Reconciliation is rooted in justice. Massive disparities of power and wealth in the world and often within nations are a grave obstacle to reconciliation. Concentration of economic power in the hands of a few nations and multinational groups, structural imbalances in trade relations and commodity prices, failure to balance economic growth with adequate distribution, both nationally and internationally, widespread unemployment and discriminatory employment practices, as well as patterns of global consumption of resources, all require reform if reconciliation is to be possible.

"Politico-cultural rights": Reconciliation in society and the rights of the person require that individuals have an effective role in shaping their own destinies. They have a right to participate in the political process freely and responsibly. They have a right to free acess of information, freedom of speech and press, as well as freedom of dissent. They have a right to be educated and to determine the education of their children. Individuals and groups must be secure from arrest, torture and imprisonment for political or ideological reasons, and all in society, including migrant workers, must be guaranteed juridical protection of their personal, social, cultural and political rights. We condemn the denial or abridgement of rights because of race. We advocate that nations and contesting groups seek reconciliation by halting persecution of others and by granting amnesty marked by mercy and equity to political prisoners and exiles.

"The right of religious liberty": This uniquely reflects the dignity of the person as this is known from the word of God and from reason itself. Today it is denied or restricted by diverse political systems in ways that impede worship, religious education and social ministry. We call upon all governments to acknowledge the right of religious liberty in words and to foster it in deeds, to eliminate any type of discrimination and to accord to all, regardless of their religious convictions, the full rights and opportunities of citizens.

As we observe the Holy Year of renewal and reconciliation, recalling the great year of pardon (Lv. 25) and the gift of power of reconciliation offered us by Christ (Lk. 4:18-19; Eph. 2:13-17), we reassert that the Church must strive to be a sign and source of reconciliation among all peoples. People have a right to hope; the Church today should be a sign and source of hope. Hence the Church offers pardon to all who have persecuted or defamed her and pledges openness and sympathetic understanding to all who question, challenge and confront her. We call finally upon each person to recognize the responsibility that he or she has in conscience for the rights of others. Enlightened in our understanding of evangelization and strengthened in our commitment to proclaim the Good News we affirm our determination to foster human rights and reconciliation everywhere in the Church and the world today.

The Evangelistic Witness
of Orthodoxy Today

Bucharest 1974

An Orthodox consultation on "Confessing Christ Today" was held in Bucharest, Rumania, June 4-8, 1974, as follow-up to the Bangkok Conference on "Salvation Today" and as part of the preparations for Section One on "Confessing Christ Today" at the Fifth Assembly of the World Council of Churches in Nairobi, Kenya in November 1975. The following report, one of four working documents prepared by the consultation, is reprinted from volume 18, number 4 (1974) of *St. Vladimir's Theological Quarterly*, published by St. Vladimir's Orthodox Theological Seminary in Crestwood, New York.

1. What is the evangelistic witness?

a) The evangelistic witness is not the whole mission of the Church. It has many other dimensions. Evangelistic witness is understood to be restricted to the communication of Christ to those who do not consider themselves Christian, wherever these people may be found. This includes the need of the Church to witness to some of its own nominal members.

b) The evangelistic witness is a call to salvation, which means the restoration of the relationship of God and man as understood in the Orthodox Christian teaching of *theosis*. This message has its source in the Scriptures, which witness to the redemption of mankind in Christ Jesus, yet it also includes a world-view that locates man *vis-à-vis* God and *vis-à-vis* his fellowman as individual and society, as well as his own personhood and destiny. It includes both the God-and-man (vertical) relationship and the human-being-to-fellow-human-being (horizontal) relationship.

c) By its nature, however, evangelistic witness is first of all and primarily a confrontation of man by the message, judgment, love, presence, redemption, command and transfiguring power of the energies of the one holy and undivided trinity.

d) Evangelistic witness brings to man the true response to his essential need *qua* human being. It is the bringing of the Divine response to the real need of persons as individuals and of persons in community. It is the message of human restoration and the divinization of the human. As such it speaks to the most profound human need, yet it also meets and overcomes the felt needs of human beings in more specific and concrete dimensions.

e) Because man is fallen, the evangelistic witness will also appear to him to have an element of foolishness (*moria*) and will always contain within it an element of *skandalon*, simply because the wisdom of man cannot fully comprehend the transcendent wisdom of God. Yet the evangelistic witness does more than provide a message of divine dimensions; it also conveys a way of living applicable in full within the community of believers, the Church, and in part in the world at large.

2. Why are we required to make evangelistic witness?

a) We do not have the option of keeping the Good News to ourselves. Sharing the Word and communicating the Word and confessing the Faith once given to the saints is an integral part of fulfilling the image and likeness of God and the achievement of *theosis*. Like St. Paul the believer must be able to say about all who do not know the life in Christ what he said about his fellow-countrymen: "My heart's desire and prayer to God for them is that they may be saved" (Rom. 10:1). The uncommunicated Gospel (Good News) is a patent contradiction.

b) The goal of evangelistic witness—though it may pass through many stages and pause at many intermediate places—is conversion from a life characterized by sin, separation from God, submission to evil, and the unfulfilled potential of God's image to a new life characterized by the forgiveness of sins, obedience to the commands of God, renewed fellowship with God in Trinity, growth in the restoration of the Divine image and the realization among us of the prototype of the love of Christ. More briefly and succinctly put, the final goal of evangelistic witness is conversion and baptism. Conversion is a willful turning from sin, death and evil to true life in God. Baptism is the reception of a new member into the new life of the community of God's people, the Church.

c) Though the conversion and baptism of all is the final goal of evangelistic witness, there is a need to identify many intermediate goals. The increase of love among Christians and non-Christians, entry into dialogue and brotherly conversation, the formulation of the Gospel message into the language and thought-forms of the non-Christian neighbor, the interpenetration of the structures of society, the promulgation of the will of God in reference to injustice among us and the prophetic challenge to the world's values share in the task of evangelistic witness and in part serve as a motive to speak the word of Christ to all men.

3. *In what manner do we make our evangelistic witness?*

a) It is the task of evangelistic witness to lead persons to the acknowledgement of God's saving power in their lives. "He is Lord of all and bestows his riches upon all who call upon Him." Yet "how are men to call upon Him in whom they have not believed? And how are they to believe in Him of whom they have never heard? And how are they to hear without a preacher? And how can men preach unless they are sent?" (Rom. 10:12, 14-15). After two thousand years this Pauline injunction retains its urgency and its timeliness.

b) Yet those same intervening years require of us a review of our conceptions of the methods of evangelistic witness. On the one hand it is clear that the proclamation alone is not the only way in which the evangelistic witness is made. Further, in this day and age mere preaching may no longer be the most effective way of evangelistic witness. Paul does not tell us what we are to do when the Gospel has been proclaimed and rejected, or even worse, simply ignored! Yet of one thing we are sure: We are sent by Christ to bear witness to him and his saving truth for all of mankind.

c) How is it to be done today? In the first instance this question must be directed to the attitudes and motives of "those who are sent." Those who are sent must be first conscious of their own repentance, conversion and salvation. Those who are fully aware of the new life of Grace in the community of the Holy Trinity and in the reality of the community of the Church alone are able to communicate the saving witness. This above all comes about with the knowledge that nothing we do is of effect without the energizing power of the Trinity. No matter what it is that we do in evangelistic witness we know that it is "God making his appeal through us" (II Cor. 5:20).

d) As difficult and beyond our capabilities as the work of evangelistic witness may seem, then, we undertake the task with the spirit not of fear or of inadequacy or of insufficiency— though all these in truth exist in us— but with hope that through our meager efforts it may be stored up and empowered by the gracious energies of the Triune God in whose name we undertake the task.

e) And so it is that "those who are sent" to be evangelistic witnesses do so as ones having experienced the redemption of God and who then work with the full understanding of their own insufficiency, fully expecting the grace of God to "provide the growth." Thus it is in a constant spirit of *metanoia* (repentance), with a full sense of our own limitations that we make our evangelistic witness.

f) How is this evangelistic witness to be made today objectively? The chief means of witness for the Church today is not the bold announcement of Christ as Saviour to a world that has already heard the words and still remains unresponsive. The first and chief method of evangelistic witness is the same as that of the early Church. Pagans saw the quality of life of those early believers and were so attracted by its power and beauty that they sought to find its power and its source, (e.g., Epistle of Diognetus; Libanius' praise of Chrysostom's mother).

g) The first method of evangelistic witness is the sharing of love by those who have acknowledged the love of God for them. "We love because he first loved us" (I John 4:19). It was an injunction to evangelistic witness when the apostle of Love instructed: "Beloved, let us love one another; for love is of God, and he who loves is born of God and knows God" (I John 4:7).

h) More specifically the same apostle says: "This is the love of God, that we keep His commandments . . . this is the victory that overcomes the world, our faith" (I John 5:3-4). Our obedience to his will is equally a powerful form of evangelistic witness. We have cheapened the Gospel in the past by much talking and little practice. Our obedience to God's will must now be the vehicle for our message.

i) Though the Divine liturgy is essentially and primarily the realization of the unity of the Church with Christ, and as such is in and of itself a manifestation of the reality of the Church, it may have consequences for the evangelistic witness of the Church. From all parts of the world we bring witness to the transforming and evangelizing power of the Divine liturgy.

j) Evangelistic witness wherever possible must be made to the unchurched. But this witness must be understood in the broadest manner. Certainly, it will include personal witnessing of the power of God in the individual life of the believer. The stories of the saints, the synaxaria, and the writings of the Fathers encourage the living Christian to speak of the power of the Holy Spirit in his or her own life.

k) But the Word of God cannot be contained only in the personal sphere. Evangelistic witness must also be made before the social and the political tribunal. Christians must speak the Word of God to contemporary issues of justice with all available means. Evangelistic witness will keep a vigilant eye upon all emergent social movements and concerns (women's liberation, racial consciousness, sexual freedom, demonology), to speak the word of truth. But it will seek to do its task of evangelization towards and in these phenomena not by parroting words of another age, but by reformulating the unchanging truth with an eye to its contemporization. Certainly in doing this it will also respond creatively in the patristic spirit to the ever-new and ever-changing phenomena of our times.

l) This it will do in the honored spirit of the indigenization of the Orthodox faith in reference to national cultures. Orthodoxy is proud of its foreign missionary tradition, which has not been carried out in a spirit of colonialism but rather with the intent of adapting the faith to the manners, language, traditions and life-styles of the people to whom it brings the Gospel. Wherever Orthodoxy is now active in such mission it must retain and expand that method.

m) At this time in our history, however, most Orthodox Churches find it very difficult to speak of foreign missions. It certainly is not a live option for many of the national Orthodox Churches. Their duty remains primarily within the churches and the nations in which they find themselves. Yet other Orthodox Churches are to be challenged for having both the opportunity and the resources, yet not responding to the charge "Go therefore and make disciples of all nations, baptizing them in the name of the Father and of the Son and of the Holy Spirit, teaching them to observe all that I have commanded you" (Matt. 28:19). The same may be said in reference to inter-Orthodox assistance, especially to the newer Orthodox in Africa, Alaska and the Far East.

4. For whom is the evangelistic witness?

a) The preceding section implies the answer to the title question of this section. Yet perhaps it would be good to articulate it. It would be true to say that the evangelistic witness is directed towards all of the *ktisis* that groans and travails in search of adoption and redemption (Rom. 8:22). But what specifically does this mean?

b) In the first case the Church's evangelistic witness is for the Christian who is not a Christian. There are many who have been baptized and yet have put off Christ, either deliberately or through indifference. Often such people still find it possible sociologically or culturally or ethnically to relate in some manner to the Christian community. The re-Christianization of Christians is an important task of the Church's evangelistic witness.

c) The evangelistic witness is consequently also directed to those who superficially identify Orthodox Christianity with their national culture. We cannot be content with a process of indigenization that leaves much of our national and cultural lives untouched by the spirit of the Gospel. The transfiguring power of the Holy Trinity is meant to reach into every nook and cranny of our national life. Those who live in or come from the traditional Orthodox lands are especially sensitive to this challenge of evangelistic witness.

d) The evangelistic witness will also speak to the structures of this world, its economic, political, and societal institutions. Especially necessary is the witness of social justice in the name of the poor and the oppressed. We must relearn the patristic lesson that the Church is the mouth and voice of the poor and oppressed in the presence of the powers that be. In our own way we must learn once again "how to speak to the ear of the King" on the people's behalf.

e) Finally, the evangelistic witness is directed to the new secularized man in an ever more secularized world. The forces of technology, scientific success and control over the environment have provided mankind with an enviable control over the conditions of his life. Yet that control has had many undesirable consequences. It has taught man to think of himself as fully sufficient; he now conceives of himself primarily as consumer; he is *homo economicus*; his circumscribed goals of life require no transcendent referent, no forgiveness, no restoration of relationship, no sacramental life, no *theosis*, no God. Yet exactly because he sits in that darkness, he is the object of the Church's evangelistic witness.

5. *Who performs the task of evangelistic witness?*

a) The most true and profound response to this question would be that it is God, through the power of the Holy Spirit, who does the work of evangelistic witness. We are made *diakonoi* of the Gospel "according to the gift of God's grace which was given [us] by the working of his power" (Eph. 3:7). In a further sense, it is the whole community of God that does this work. For it is "through the Church" that "the manifold wisdom of God [is] now made known to the principalities and powers" (Eph. 3:10).

b) More particularly, three groups or classes of Christians are charged, each in its own way, with the task of evangelistic witness. First are those ordained to the Lord's service. The chief evangelizer of the Church is the bishop, with his presbyterion and diaconate as well as the monastic establishment. In the history of the Church, these "professionals" of evangelical witness have carried on the work of the Church with great success. And inasmuch as they still lead the conduct of worship, preach the Word of God, visit the oppressed and suffering, speak the word of truth in the tribunals of power, proclaim the Gospel before vast audiences electronically present, communicate the Orthodox truth through the printed word, or walk the foreign mission trails, they continue to carry it. Yet we are all too conscious of our lethargy and deafness to the Divine commission. Theological schools at all levels are challenged to heal that deafness through proper and full education for evangelical witness of the candidates for holy orders. There is need to restore the claim of evangelical witness upon the priestly conscience of the servants of God.

c) The second group specifically charged with the work of evangelistic witness is the laity. We have just rediscovered the theology of the laity in the Orthodox Church. Laity are part of the "royal priesthood" of the Church. We are all—clergy and laity —called to be "a holy priesthood, to offer spiritual sacrifices acceptable to God through Christ" (I Pet. 2:5). As such, we are all "a chosen race, a royal priesthood, a holy nation, God's own people." Thus the laity shares in the whole work of the Church, including that of evangelistic witness. Part of the task of the clergy is to "raise the consciousness" of the laity regarding their roles in the fulfillment of the work of the Church. As we have noted, the primary means of evangelistic witness today is the authentic Christian life, to which every lay person is called. So also is the vital and living participation in the Divine liturgy, the personal witness of faith, the Christian involvement of the believer in the social, political, educational, cultural and intellectual life of his nation and society. Orthodoxy of doctrine, combined with evangelical behavior are the conditions of true evangelistic witness by the laity.

d) Then there are those among us called against our will to mission. Some of us become evangelistic witnesses suddenly, when the principalities and powers of the age force us into situations of martyrdom, when compromise and accommodation are not possible. Today, the ancient experience of expropriation, prison and arena is frequently repeated. When called, we must be ready for the special witness of martyrdom. Others of us are called from among the members of the Body of Christ to evangelistic witness because of the special gifts of the Holy Spirit. Throughout the ages persons have been touched by the Holy Spirit and provided with gifts of unique character. These persons may do the work of evangelistic witness. However it is incumbent upon them to do so always from within the faith and truth of the body of the Church. In turn, the Church must look upon these brethren seized of the Holy Spirit with the wisdom of Gameliel.

e) The difficult and thorny question of the renewal of foreign mission by the Church cannot be met or solved by any one of the particular Orthodox churches. We cannot deny the goal. Yet a unified and organized Orthodox approach is needed, lest we harm and do disservice to our fellow Orthodox. This certainly is an important element in our understanding of our total mission in the world today, from a pan-Orthodox perspective. Part of our mission is also to protect and preserve Orthodoxy where it is found today. An honest recognition of our limitations and existential restrictions is also required.

Letter to the
People of God

Forty thousand young people from a hundred and twenty countries gathered for a "Council of Youth" over the weekend of September 1, 1974, at Taizé, the Protestant monastic community in southeast France. Five large circus tents grouped together formed a canvas temple for worship. At the conclusion the youth addressed a statement to the Church. It is reprinted here from *Mid-Stream: An Ecumenical Journal*, volume XIV, number 1 (January, 1975), published quarterly by the Council on Christian Unity of the Christian Church (Disciples of Christ) in Indianapolis, Indiana.

Statement of the Taizé Council of Youth, September 1, 1974

We have been born into a world that for most people is not uninhabitable. A large part of mankind is exploited by a minority enjoying intolerable privileges. Many police states exist to protect the powerful. Multinational companies impose their own laws. Profit and money rule. Those in power almost never pay attention to those who are voiceless.

And the people of God? What way of liberation is it opening? We cannot avoid the question.

When the very first Christians found themselves faced with a question without a solution—when they were on the point of dividing—they decided to gather in council. We remembered them at Easter 1970 when we were seeking answers for our own age. And we opted, not for a forum of ideas, not for conferences, but for a Council of Youth; that is to say, a reality that gathers together youth from every land, committing us unambiguously on account of Christ and the Gospel.

At the heart of the Council of Youth is the Risen Christ. We celebrate him, present in the eucharist, alive in the Church, hidden in man our brother.

In the course of four-and-a-half years of preparation we have made unceasing visits to one another. We have crossed the world in every direction, even though the means at our disposal were slight. In certain localities the political circumstances have led us through grave situations.

Gradually a common awareness has emerged. It has been more particularly shaped by the voices of those among us who are living under subjection and oppression or who are reduced to silence.

And today we are sure: the Risen Christ is preparing his people to become at one and the same time a contemplative people thirsting for God; a people of justice living the struggle of men and peoples exploited; a people of communion where the nonbeliever also finds a creative place.

We are involved part and parcel with this people. That is why we are addressing this letter, so as to share the concerns that are ours and the expectations that are consuming us.

Numerous churches in the Southern Hemisphere as in the Northern, are spied on, interfered with and even persecuted. Certain of them show that without any bonds to political powers, without the means of power, without wealth, the Church can experience a new birth and can become a force of liberation for humanity and radiate God.

Another part of the people of God compromises with inequality. Individual Christians and many Church institutions have capitalized their goods, accumulating vast wealth in money, land, buildings and investments. There are lands where the churches remain connected to political or financial power and draw on their superfluous wealth to give away large sums in development aid, but still make no change in their own structures. Church institutions acquire highly efficient means of accomplishing their mission, of running their activities and bringing together their committees. But many discover that life gradually vanishes, leaving the institutions empty. The churches, losing their credibility, are more and more forsaken by the people of our time.

The Christians of the early Church shared all that they had. They gathered day by day to pray together. They lived in joy and simplicity. So they were recognized.

During the years of preparation for the Council of Youth, out of the diverse suggestions made, these are the intuitions that stand out above all the rest and to which we shall conscrate the first period of the Council of Youth:

CHURCH, WHAT DO YOU SAY OF YOUR FUTURE?

Are you going to give up the means of power, the compromises with political and financial power?

Are you going to surrender your privileges, stop capitalizing? Are you at last going to become a "universal community of sharing," a community finally reconciled, a place of communion and friendship for the whole of humanity?

In each locality and throughout the world, are you in this way going to become the seeds of a society without class and where none have privileges, without domination of one person by another, of one people by another?

CHURCH, WHAT DO YOU SAY OF YOUR FUTURE?

Are you going to become the "people of the Beatitudes," having no security other than Christ, a people poor, contemplative, creating peace, bearing joy and being a liberating festival for mankind, ready even to be persecuted for justice?

If we are actively involved in this, we know that we can demand nothing of others unless we ourselves stake everything. What do we have to fear? Christ says, "I came to kindle fire on the earth, and how I long for it to burn!" We shall dare to live the Council of Youth as an anticipation of all that we want. We shall dare to commit ourselves, together and to the point of no return, to living beyond hope, letting the spirit of the Beatitudes come springing up in the people of God, being the leaven of a society without class and where none have privileges.

We are addressing this first letter to the people of God, written from our hearts so as to share what burdens us.

MISSION TRENDS NO. 1

$2.95

Contents

ISBN: 0-8091-1843-2